Feminists Doing Development

A Practical Critique

Edited by
Marilyn Porter
& Ellen Judd

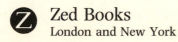

Zed Books
London and New York

Feminists Doing Development: A Practical Critique was first published in 1999 by
Zed Books Ltd, 7 Cynthia Street, London N1 9JF, UK,
and Room 400, 175 Fifth Avenue, New York, NY 10010, USA

Distributed in the USA exclusively by St Martin's Press,
Room 400, 175 Fifth Avenue, New York, NY 10010, USA

Editorial copyright © Marilyn Porter and Ellen Judd, 1999

Cover designed by Andrew Corbett.
Set in 9.6/11.6 pt Monotype Photina, by Long House, Cumbria, UK.
Printed and bound in the United Kingdom
by Biddles Ltd, Guildford and King's Lynn.

*A catalogue record for this book
is available from the British Library.*

ISBN 1 85649 693 7 (hb)
ISBN 1 85649 694 5 (pb)

Library of Congress Cataloging-in-Publication Data

Feminists doing development : a practical critique / edited by Marilyn
    Porter and Ellen Judd.
            p.   cm.
    Includes bibliographical references and index.
        ISBN 1-85649-693-7 (hb). -- 1-85649-694-5 (pb)
        1. Women in development.   2. Feminism--Developing countries.
    3. Feminists--Developing countries.   I. Marilyn Porter, 1942–
    II. Judd, Ellen R., 1950–
    HQ1240.F47 2000
    305.42--dc21   99-41268
                                                         CIP

Contents

Abbreviations & Acronyms   v
Acknowledgements   vii
Biographical Notes   viii

1   Introduction   1
     Caught in the Web? Feminists Doing Development
     MARILYN PORTER

I • The Structures That Confine Us   15

2   NGOs in a Post-Feminist Era   17
     INES SMYTH

3   Development and Women in Pakistan   29
     TAHERA AFTAB

4   Little Progress, Small Niches: the WID Mandate in   42
     Japanese Foreign Aid
     SUE ELLEN CHARLTON

5   What I Know about Gender and Development   57
     WU QING

II • Staying Feminist in Development   71

6   Research and Intervention: Insights from Feminist   73
     Health Action in Western India
     RENU KHANNA

7   The Right Connections: Partnering and Expertise   87
     in Feminist Work for Change
     BARBARA COTTRELL

 8 Women Organizing for Change: Transformational   101
    Organizing as a Strategy for Feminist Development
    COLLETTE OSEEN

 9 Taking Development in Our Hands: 112
    a Reflection on Indonesian Women's Experience
    NORI ANDRIYANI

III • Integrating the Local with the Global   127

10 Falling Between the Gaps   129
    FENELLA PORTER AND VALSA VERGHESE

11 Globalization and Development at the Bottom   142
    JOYCE GREEN AND CORA VOYAGEUR

12 Labour Rights, Networking, and Empowerment: 158
    Mobilizing Garment Workers in Bangladesh
    HABIBA ZAMAN

IV • Working with Global Structures   173

13 Women Organizing Locally and Globally: 175
    Development Strategies, Feminist Perspectives
    PEGGY ANTROBUS AND LINDA CHRISTIANSEN-RUFFMAN

14 Responding to Globalization: 190
    Can Feminists Transform Development?
    JOANNA KERR

15 The New Global Architecture: 206
    Gender and Development Practices
    ISABELLA BAKKER

16 *Afterword:* Opening Spaces for Transformative Practice 218
    ELLEN JUDD

Bibliography   227
Index   240

Abbreviations & Acronyms

ACCC	Association of Canadian Community Colleges
ACPD	Asia and Pacific Centre for Women and Development
ACWF	All China Women's Federation
ALRD	Association for Land Reform and Development (Bangladesh)
ANM	Auxiliary Nurse Midwife
APEC	Asia–Pacific Economic Cooperation forum
BINGO	Big non-governmental organization
BMC	Bombay Municipal Corporation
CAFRA	Caribbean Association for Feminist Research and Action
CAP	Community Assistance Programme (Canada)
CARICOM	Commonwealth Caribbean
CDB	Caribbean Development Bank
CIDA	Canadian International Development Agency
CMTCC	China Enterprise Management Training Centre
CRIAW	Canadian Research Institute for the Advancement of Women
DAC	Development Assistance Committee (OECD)
DAWN	Development Alternatives for Women of a New Era
DFID	Department for International Development (UK)
EIA	Environmental impact assessment
FP	Family planning
GAD	Gender and Development
GDI	Gender Development Index
GERA	Gender and Economic Reforms in Africa
HDI	Human Development Index
HPI	Human Population Index
IDRC	International Development Research Centre
INCO	International Nickel Company
IWY	International Women's Year
JICA	Japan International Cooperation Agency
JOCF	Japan Overseas Cooperation Volunteers
LIA	Labrador Inuit Association
MCEWH	Maritime Centre for Excellence on Women's Health
MDB	Multilateral development bank
MITI	Ministry of International Trade and Development (Japan)
NAC	National Action Committee on the Status of Women (Canada)
NGO	Non-governmental organization

NGWF	National Garment Workers Federation (Bangladesh)
NRM	National Resistance Movement (Uganda)
ODA	Official development assistance
OECD	Organization for Economic Cooperation and Development
OECF	Overseas Economic Cooperation Fund
PID	Pelvic inflammatory disease
SAHAJ	Society for Health Alternatives
SARTHI	Social Action for Rural and Tribal Inhabitants of India
SED	Society for Environment and Human Development (Bangladesh)
SID	Society for International Development
SSHRC	Social Sciences and Humanities Research Council (Canada)
Tk	Taka (Bangladesh currency)
UBINIG	Women and Development for Alternative Strategies (Bangladesh)
UK	United Kingdom
UN	United Nations
UNDP	United Nations Development Programme
UNFPA	United Nations Family Planning Association
UNICEF	United Nations Children's Fund
UNIFEM	United Nations Development Fund for Women
USAID	United States Agency for International Development
WAD	Women and Development
WAND	Women and Development Unit, University of West Indies
WBI	Women's Budget Initiative (South Africa)
WEDO	Women's Environment and Development Organization
WICCE	Women's International Cross-Cultural Exchange
WID	Women in Development
WIDE	Women and Development Europe
YWCA	Young Women's Christian Association

Acknowledgements

All edited collections owe numerous debts to the individuals – contributors and others – and institutions that made it happen. In this case, our greatest acknowledgement must go to the commitment and energy that brought this book together across vast geographical distances. The two editors were separated by half of Canada, and our publisher was across the Atlantic in England. Our contributors were drawn from four continents and more than a dozen countries. The book would never have passed beyond the 'good idea' stage without every participant's immediate and hard-working responses to the tidal wave of communications, demands, deadlines, revisions, changes and so on that mark the progress of a manuscript.

None of this would be possible without the energetic 'claiming' of technology, especially electronic communication technology, for progressive purposes. It may seem ironic for feminists to acknowledge the contribution of technology, but without it a book such as this would be very much more difficult to produce. Our thanks, then, to the infrastructure and to the technical support in our various institutions that have solved so many communication and data transfer problems.

We were delighted to be working with Zed Books as a publisher, and now that the process is over we would like to acknowledge especially Louise Murray, who has been the model of a supportive and constructively helpful publisher, as well as the whole production team at Zed.

Memorial University of Newfoundland provided various support mechanisms, from xeroxing to excellent library resources, and helpful, knowledgeable colleagues and friends. Outside the university Marilyn was supported and inspired by the women's community in St John's, and by her household, feline, canine and human, who offered patience, forebearance and alternative priorities. At the University of Manitoba, Lynne Dalman and Roxetta Wilde were invaluable in the accessing of papers in a wide variety of electronic formats; Paula Migliardi provided valuable assistance in locating resources in the libraries and on line. Our particular thanks go to Margaret Gulliver of Memorial University who, with enormous patience and skill, took the edited drafts and turned them into an error-free, well-formatted manuscript.

Finally, of course, we thank our contributors, whose work, experience and wisdom have created this book.

Bibliographical Notes

Tahera Aftab is Professor of History and founding Director of Women's Studies at Karachi University. She is the editor of the *Pakistan Journal of Women's Studies*, *Alam-e Niswan*, a biannual established in 1993 to disseminate and share Women's Studies research globally. From the platform of the Pakistan Association of Women's Studies, which she founded in 1992, she attempts to work closely with women outside the academy.

Nori Andriyani is on the staff of the Women's Studies Graduate Program at the University of Indonesia. She has worked on women and development issues since 1990. She is also currently working for the Canadian Cooperative Association project in Indonesia.

Peggy Antrobus is from the Caribbean. She has worked in the field of development since the 1960s. She established the Women and Development Unit (WAND) within the School of Continuing Studies of the University of the West Indies. She was a founding member of DAWN in 1986 and has since served as its Coordinator.

Isabella Bakker is an Associate Professor at York University, Toronto, Canada. She is the editor of *The Strategic Silence: Gender and Economic Policy* (Zed Books, 1994) and *Rethinking Restructuring: Gender and Change in Canada* (University of Toronto Press, 1996), and collaborated on the 1999 UNDP Human Development Report.

Sue Ellen Charlton is a Professor of Political Science at Colorado State University. Her academic interests focus on Asian politics and issues of gender and international development. Her most recent book is *Comparing Asian Politics* (Westview Press, 1997). She also has a long history of working in community organizations and local politics.

Linda Christiansen-Ruffman is Professor of Sociology, Women's Studies, International Development Studies and Atlantic Canadian Studies at Saint Mary's University, Halifax, Canada. She has been President of the Canadian Sociology and Anthropology Association and the Canadian Research Institute for the Advancement of Women (in Nova Scotia and nationally). She is the editor of *The Global Feminist Enlightenment: Women and Social Knowledge* (International Sociological Association, 1998), and is one of the founding editors of *Strategies*, a new feminist online journal.

Barbara Cottrell is a researcher, writer, adult educator and activist on women's issues. She has conducted many workshops and projects on violence against women. She is the co-author of several books, including *Workplace Learnings About Woman Abuse: A Guide for Change* (1995); *Liberty: A Manual for Group Facilitators* (1991); *and Research Partnerships: A Feminist Approach to Communities and Universities Working Together* (Canadian Research Institute for the Advancement of Women, 1996).

Joyce Green is an Associate Professor of Political Science at the University of Regina, Canada, where she teaches Canadian Politics, Women and Politics, and Aboriginal Politics using a feminist, anti-colonial, anti-racist, critical pedagogy. Her family background includes English, Kootenay, Scottish and Cree Metis; part of her intellectual work has been informed by her personal history, particularly issues that flow from politically charged hybridity.

Ellen Judd is a Professor at Anthropology at the University of Manitoba. She has done gender analysis and Women in Development (WID)/Gender and Development (GAD) work in China, as well as activist work on women's issues in Canada. She is the author of *Gender and Power in Rural North China* (Stanford University Press, 1994).

Joanna Kerr is an associate of The North–South Institute, Ottawa, Canada. She is President-elect of the Washington-based Association for Women in Development. Her publications include *Ours by Right: Women's Rights as Human Rights* (Zed Books, 1993) and *Gender and Jobs in China's New Economy* (North–South Institute, 1996).

Renu Khanna (BA, MBA) is an activist and action researcher working in the area of women's empowerment and health management. She is a founding member of SAHAJ-Baroda, an NGO established in 1984, and the Vice-president of SARTHI, a community-based NGO working in a tribal area in Gujarat. She is a Principal Investigator in the Women Centred Health Project, a joint activity of the British Medical Council (BMC), SAHAJ and the Liverpool School of Tropical Medicine.

Collette Oseen teaches in Women's Studies, Work and Community Studies at Athabasca University, as well as working as a consultant specializing in strategies for the non-hierarchical workplace. She holds a PhD in feminist organizational theory (University of Alberta), and worked in China in the 1980s, an experience that had a profound impact on her understanding of how people could work together without exploiting each other.

Fenella Porter has a Master's degree in Gender and Development, and worked for three years with Isis WICCE, based in Uganda, as a member of a small team of core staff to set up the organization in Uganda. Since returning to the UK she has worked as a researcher, editor and consultant with major UK-based international development NGOs.

Marilyn Porter was born in North Wales and educated in England and Ireland (in history and sociology). She moved to Canada in 1980 and has taught and researched in sociology and women's studies at Memorial University of Newfoundland ever since. Her work on women's economic lives in Newfoundland led her to expand her interest to areas of the economic South. For the last few years she has focused her work in Indonesia.

Ines Smyth is a Policy Adviser for Oxfam. Previously she worked as a lecturer in Development Studies at the Institute of Social Studies (The Hague), and then at the Development Studies Institute of the London School of Economics. She is most recently the author of 'Gender Analysis of Family Planning: Beyond the "Feminist versus Population Control" Debate' in *Feminist Visions of Development*, eds C. Jackson and R. Pearson (Routledge, 1999), and co-editor of *Gender Works: Oxfam's Experience in Policy and Practice* (Oxfam, 1999).

Valsa Verghese, an Indian national, is the former Executive Director of Isis WICCE, Geneva (1988–93), and was responsible for overseeing the relocation of Isis WICCE from Geneva to Kampala. She is currently working at the World YWCA Office, Geneva. She has over eighteen years' experience working on gender, development and human rights issues. She holds a Master's degree in Sociology (Bangalore University).

Cora Voyageur teaches Sociology at the University of Calgary, Canada. Sociology of Work and Native Employment were among the areas of specialization in her PhD (University of Alberta); her academic research focuses primarily on the Aboriginal experience in Canada, which includes women's issues, justice, employment, education and economic development. She has worked with many First Nation communities and organizations on community-initiated research in the Aboriginal community. She is a member of the Athabasca Chipewyan First Nation from Fort Chipewyan, Alberta.

Wu Qing is Professor of American Studies in the English Department of Beijing Foreign Studies University. She has been a Gender Equity Consultant for the Canadian International Development Agency for many years. She is a co-editor of several books, including *American Society and Culture*, vols 1 and 2.

Habiba Zaman is an Assistant Professor of Women's Studies at Simon Fraser University, Canada. She is the author of *Women and Work in a Bangladesh Village* (Narigrantha Prabartana/Feminist Bookstore, 1996) and *Patriarchy and Purdah: Structural and Systemic Violence against Women in Bangladesh* (Life and Peace Institute, Uppsala, 1998).

1 • *Introduction*
Caught in the Web?
Feminists Doing Development

Marilyn Porter

Why a Book on Feminists Doing Development?

The first feminist critiques of gender-blind development, and later of Women in Development (WID) and Gender and Development (GAD) strategies, appeared almost as soon as the original concepts did, and they have been adopted by national and international development agencies and diverse non-governmental organizations. Feminists from both the North and the South have joined in the work of making development more feminist, sometimes separately and sometimes together. But after years of effort in these directions, have women in the South (or in the economic south in the North) benefited? Have the institutions of patriarchy been weakened? Have bonds of global feminism been forged and put to practical use?

This collection presents the voices and viewpoints of feminists from both South and North who have been actively involved in the practice of development work, and who are engaged in structural and reflexive critiques of WID/GAD practices and other aspects of development projects. Our aim is to contribute to a reassessment of feminist involvement in development work, in which we can use the practical knowledge generated by feminist involvement to rethink 'development'.

Despite our efforts, we still need to critique the policies and practices of national and international development agencies who have added WID/GAD components to their development work. Feminists have long argued that it is not enough to 'add women and stir', but much mainstream development work has moved little (if any) distance from that approach. Development by and for the least privileged women in the South would imply fundamentally different strategies, not only in terms of WID/GAD, but towards the entire process of development. DAWN (Development Alternatives for Women of a New Era) pointed out as long ago as 1987 that it is from the perspective of the most oppressed – women who suffer on account of class, race and nationality – that we can most

1

clearly grasp the nature of the links in the chain of oppression and explore the kinds of actions that we must now take (Sen and Grown, 1987: 20). In this book, our approach is not to see problems in development as limited to the particular circumstances of the South, but as systemic problems in the conceptualization and practices of development in the era of globalization. To do this, we must focus upon 'studying up' in development agencies and development practices. The concretely grounded studies in the volume will examine the political, gendered, and Northern construction of development, the bureaucratic processes of policy formulation, and the control of that portion of global capital that flows through development.

The intentions behind development projects are often good, and many NGOs pursue agendas that ought to lead to improvements in women's lives. The results of so much effort expended by so many apparently sympathetic people should be beneficial for everyone. All too often they are not. Poverty, inequality and violence against women continue to mar women's lives all over the world, and economic prosperity and social justice elude all but the fortunate few. Development projects often end in frustration and recriminations. Disillusion strikes down the most ardent activist.

What has gone wrong? In this book we will address this problem in the context of the relationship between feminism and development, exploring the contradictions, ambiguities and inherent antagonisms between the two. It is our contention that it *is* possible for the world to improve, and for feminists to take an active part in that process, but only if we are clearer and more political in our understanding of the processes of development and – to anticipate a little – only if we can alter the priorities of development to better reflect the aspirations of feminism. These are bold claims and an ambitious project, so let us begin with the matter of definitions.

The Difficulties of Definition

Nearly all discussions of either feminism or development begin by pointing out the number and variety of definitions of the concepts. This problem is made worse because, as Henrietta Moore puts it, 'Feminism ... is one of those words everybody thinks they know the meaning of' (Moore, 1988: 10). Everybody also thinks that they know what 'development' means. Gilbert Rist says, 'even if everyone thinks they know what is involved, the favourable consensus surrounding the term is at the heart of a misunderstanding that paralyses debate' (Rist, 1997: 5). So, while definitions are partial and confusing, we must begin by disentangling what everyone knows from the various, and often contradictory, technical definitions of the two central concepts in this book.

In the entry on development in *The Development Dictionary* Gustavo Esteva says:

> Development occupies the centre of an incredibly powerful semantic constellation. There is nothing in modern mentality comparable to it as a force guiding thought and behaviour. At the same time, very few words are as feeble, as fragile and as incapable of giving substance and meaning to thought and behaviour as this one. In common parlance development describes a process through which the potentialities of an object or organism are released, until it reaches its natural, complete, full fledged form. (Esteva, 1992: 8)

All this applies exactly and directly to the natural world – the development of birds and bees and trees, and, indeed, to the physiological development of humans. But does it apply to societies? Development, based on this original usage, depends on two axioms. One is that the observer *knows* what will happen or what should happen. Intervention consists of encouraging or correcting a process towards the best possible fulfilment of a known and accepted outcome. The second axiom upon which the use of 'development' depends is that growth according to the pre-ordained pattern is both unproblematic and inevitably good. In fact, development seen in these terms *must* entail growth.

The transfer of the biological metaphor to the social sphere in the last quarter of the eighteenth century, documented by Esteva and others, led to the word 'development' accumulating a whole variety of connotations. This overload of meanings ended up dissolving its precise significance (Esteva, 1992: 9). Radical writers are agreed that development became a dangerous cloak for a particular ideology, especially when applied to the field of international development in the twentieth century. Put simply, the ideology assumes that the Western model of national development is the only possible one; that the world-wide expansion of the market system is the only route forward and that each society, organized into a Western-type democratic nation state, should emulate the United States and Europe as closely as possible in pursuit of economic growth.

Before we describe the ways in which the concept of international development has been refined and applied in the years since the Second World War, let us look at the macro definitions of the other principal concept in our title – feminism. The origins of the word 'feminism' are undoubtedly more recent than those of 'development', although much depends on how broadly one translates 'feminism'. Dale Spender, for example, points out that 'for centuries women have been challenging men ... and have been claiming that the world and men look very different from the perspective of women' (Spender, 1982: 15). While this is close to Spender's working definition of feminism, the word is not one that the feminist foremothers she describes would have used. Wollstonecraft's *Vindication of the Rights of Woman*, usually interpreted as the first recognizable feminist text, makes no mention of the word 'feminist', using instead the language of rights. Even when the word 'feminist' had won general acceptance after the suffragette struggle of the late nineteenth century, Simone de Beauvoir scarcely uses it in her definitive text of modern feminism, *The Second Sex*, published in 1949. Offen has pointed out that most discussions of the history of feminism that attribute the word to early expressions of ideas and actions we might now call feminism are plain anachronistic (Offen, 1988: 126). So, in a sense, the history of the word 'feminism' is the opposite of that of 'development'. The *practice* of feminism was developed and refined before the word came to be applied to it, rather than, as in the case of development, the clear meaning of the word being overtaken by subsequent changes and accretions in the meaning.

Contributors to this book come from a variety of cultural backgrounds, so we will be using a broad definition of feminism. We also recognize that some women and women activists working in the interests of women in the developing world reject the term feminism as too Northern and limited. In this introduction, and elsewhere in the book, we use the term feminism provisionally, acknowledging that it raises as many questions as answers. In our understanding of feminism – or, more accurately, feminisms – we include a diversity of concepts and practices that share a recognition of the gendered character of inequality and injustice, and that work against these to change the world in the interests of women. Solidarity and a concern with making the feminist project serve the interests of all women – including the most vulnerable and disadvantaged – is central to this concept of feminism, and to the possibility of a feminist contribution to the reconfiguration of development work. We will be assuming that everyone can define themselves as feminist as they wish, and that the forms and focus of feminism will differ according to social, political and cultural contexts, but we assume, too, that feminism contains within it an impetus to activism – that the recognition of injustice leads to action to confront it.

The symbiotic relationship between theory and practice, praxis or political action, which we take to be a hallmark of feminism, also makes it difficult to treat feminism fairly within the context of an academic discussion. It is one reason for the focus of this book on practice and practical critiques. We should note two other aspects of the definition of feminism that will affect the discussions in this book. One is that while the contributors have varied in whether or not they include men in their projects or organizations, and, indeed, whether they allow men to call

themselves feminists, we have *generally* assumed that feminism is practised by women, and certainly is defined by women's experiences. This
perspective is informed by the practical or political aspect of our definition. It leads on to the more problematic point that while we recognize
the contested nature of the category 'woman', and would certainly resist
any notion that any aspect of the condition of women was universal,
rather than being situated in the concrete, culturally and politically
specific situation, there is, nevertheless, some association between the
aims and practice of feminism and the experiences of women's lives and
struggles that provides links across the boundaries of difference. This
tension between the recognition of specificity and difference among women,
and the struggle to arrive at some kind of global understanding and
action, together with resistance to a model imposed by the North, will
underlie many of the chapters in this book.

In an article first conceived in 1976 (although not published until
1988), Karen Offen brings a historical perspective to the problem of not
only defining feminism, but defining it across national boundaries and
cultures. Her discussion remains useful. While she builds her argument
on the diversity of practices and ideas around feminism over several
centuries and in several different (European) cultures, organized around
what she calls the relational or individualist arguments, she ends up with
a set of definitions that, like ours, emphasize that it is a concept that 'can
encompass both an ideology and a movement for sociopolitical change
based on a critical analysis of male privilege and women's subordination
within any given society' (Offen, 1988: 151), and that inevitably to be a
feminist is to be at odds with male-dominated culture and society (Offen,
1988: 152). The importance of Offen's article is that it attempts to
develop a concept of feminism that will be sensitive to differences both of
situation and analysis, yet does not simply accumulate different feminisms
without any necessary political or ideological connection between them.

International Development Comes of Age

The story of international development, as a coherent practice, begins
after the Second World War. It was built, not only on the ruins of that
war, but on the rapidly crumbling edifice erected by nineteenth-century
European empire building. The extraordinary process whereby European
nation states carved up the accessible and vulnerable parts of Asia and
Africa, in most cases against the wishes of European electorates, laid
down patterns of both economic and political domination and, even more
importantly, established a concept of a the world as a single entity. Development as a separate process began, however, with a statement emanating –

not coincidentally – from the United States. President Truman's Point Four, proclaimed in 1948, began: 'Fourth, we must embark on a bold new program for making the benefits of our scientific advances and industrial progress available for the improvement and growth of underdeveloped areas.' We can see that such a statement would ensure that the features of international development were in place from the beginning – the division of the world into the developed and the underdeveloped; the dominance of the United States; the high-handed analysis of the situation in other parts of the world; the stress on economic growth and the assumption of the Western model.

The full text of Point Four also reveals the tension between two inter-pretations of development that came to underlie all subsequent aid programmes. The essential meaning of international development as the imposition of a particular ideology of the global market and economic growth, with the clear agenda of benefiting the rich economies, was obscured by a more humane rhetoric. Point Four describes the situation of the majority of humanity in heart-rending terms, and thus the missionary goal of alleviating hardship became yoked to a political and economic aid strategy that would develop the underdeveloped world so that it would no longer threaten Western prosperity.

This missionary or humanitarian interpretation of development has always been subservient to the dominant economic one, but it is here that feminists have been most active and feminist ideas have had the greatest impact. Considerable efforts have been made within development agencies to incorporate such ideas, sometimes with good grace and sometimes with great reluctance. But always the inherent tension between the needs of Western capital and the needs of the majority of people, especially in the countries of the South, bubbles below the surface. Many of the chapters in this book examine the contradictions, ambiguities and hypocrisies within development policies ostensibly aimed at helping people in the Third World.

Understanding Development: Development Studies

Meanwhile, the rapidly expanding field of Development Studies was generating its own theories and concepts. These are well documented in any Development Studies textbook, and we need not rehearse them here. They begin with modernization theory, based on Rostow's 'stages of economic growth' that all societies must pass through on their way to economic fulfilment. While Rostow buttressed his influential argument with considerable evidence, it is transparently in accord with the ideology that was taking root.

The subsequent debates and challenges to modernization theory came either from Third World writers, especially from Latin America, or from radicals in the North, who wanted to challenge the inherent exploitation involved in the emerging development model. In other words, the work of the 'dependency school' – Baran and Sweezy in the United States, Cardoso in Brazil, Borda in Colombia, Samir Amin in Africa, Gunder Frank and Galtung in Europe – was a *political* struggle supporting the interests of countries of the South (and peripheral regions of the North), as well as an intellectual struggle to break away from Rostow's model. The self-reliance models, such as the Ujamaa movement in Tanzania, are another form of challenge to a global economy dominated by the desires of the North and enforced through 'development'. For several decades, oppositional models of development were also evident in movements of national liberation and socialist construction; typically, these programmes incorporated their own distinctive elements of women's liberation. While ideas based on such movements have not influenced Northern funding priorities, these histories do directly enter the current development processes in societies in transition, and form part of the broader context of feminist understandings of development.

While the dominant understanding of development was as economic development, and as an adjunct to Western capitalism's global conquest, there was enough in the shadows of meanings around the concept to support oppositional interpretations that, in various ways and with various degrees of effectiveness, identified with the poor and oppressed and wanted to see a more equal and less exploitative world. These views, drawing on the humanitarian thread in development, and appealing to a range of altruistic and idealist intentions, raged throughout the United Nations discussions, within the development programmes of national agencies and among the proliferating NGOs that were organizing themselves around the national and international agencies. Some of these, such as Oxfam and War on Want, worked on practical alternatives to the official patterns of development, as well as stressing the humanitarian aspects in their publications and campaigns.

It is no accident that this brief and partial account of international development since the Second World War has made no mention of women, women's interests or a gender analysis. Development as unfettered economic growth would be unlikely to foreground the interests of women. There have been powerful arguments, especially from organizations such as WIDE (Women and Development Europe), that such an agenda is fundamentally and totally opposed to the interests of women. The oppositional framework, focused on inequality and material poverty and injustice, should have no reason to exclude the feminist perspective – but all too often feminist concerns are just as invisible there as in mainstream economic development. Nevertheless, there is a difference between trying to carry out a feminist agenda within an organization that accepts some of the same principles, and trying to insert feminism into a process that is fundamentally antipathetic to it.

The Feminist Agenda and the Development Process

Almost from the beginning of post-Second World War international development, feminists have been involved in trying to adapt or change development policies and programmes so as to reflect their priorities better. This effort has taken place on two main fronts. The first was to try to influence United Nations discussions and agreements. The complete absence of women and of attention to women's issues was glaring, and as women's movements around the world, but especially in the North, developed strong and articulate positions, groups of women, both inside and outside the structures, began to put pressure on the United Nations and its attendant agencies to include women.

At first, it was seen to be enough just to add some actual women to the staff, and to include some reference to typical 'women's issues' in the deliberations. This 'add women and stir' approach closely parallelled what was happening at the national level, especially during the 1960s and 1970s. The breakthrough came with the First United Nations International Conference on Women, held in Mexico in 1975, which inaugurated the Decade for Women. For the next 20 years, increasing numbers of women were able to organize around the succession of Conferences on Women in Copenhagen in 1980, Nairobi in 1985, and Beijing in 1995. While increasing numbers of qualified women became members of national delegations or played an active role within the United Nations, the most striking development was the exponential increase in women participating in NGOs and in the Forums that grew up around the formal conferences.

Opinions are mixed about the ultimate effectiveness of such United Nations deliberations and the Conventions that emerge from them, but there is no doubt about the importance of activity around the United Nations in the formation of an entire generation of feminist activists from around the world. We should not ignore the limitations of participation in United Nations events. They are confined to mostly well-heeled, well-connected, educated and articulate women. Nor can one rely too heavily on the apparent consensus reflected in various NGO statements and other documents. It is all too easy to agree in the heat and emotion of the moment – and, because they are not members of elected governments, there is no querulous electorate or Finance Minister waiting back home.

Nevertheless, the Conferences and associated activity have introduced large numbers of women from around the world to each other, to each other's concerns and ideas, and to the excitement of working with women from different backgrounds on common issues. It is certainly arguable that the consensus reached by NGO women reflects as substantial a body of opinion as that reached by the official process.

Meanwhile, feminists were also contending with development programmes and policies in their own countries and with the gendered consequences of the policies of international institutions such as the IMF. From at least the early 1970s it was clear to many feminists that feminism could not be contained in national boundaries, and this made international work a priority. What was less clear, at least initially, was that feminists would enter the development process with a clear agenda, containing elements of humanitarianism, but also with a politics that was implicitly transformational. The difficulty was that while work on the domestic front could be carried out on the proverbial shoestring, international work involved major funding of the kind that entailed reliance on large NGOs, such as Oxfam, or the national development agencies, such as the UK's Department for International Development (DFID). Direct funding of feminist projects was unusual, so that feminist involvement with development projects tended to be either as external criticisms of projects, or as employees within a development project or organization. Such a relationship was always liable to be fraught.

Dialogue did take place, however, and gradually the agencies and NGOs developed perspectives and policies on gender which gradually have come to reflect a more recognizably feminist perspective. Such policies could only draw on the oppositional interpretation of development, the humanitarian and moral impetus. Inevitably, they had to operate in a sea of ambiguity and contradiction, as the oppositional approach, whether it included women or not, was always secondary to the main economic growth imperative of national and international development policy.

Changes in the approach to women and to gender issues in development policies have been well documented elsewhere. The broad outlines are represented by the shift from Women in Development (WID) to Women and Development (WAD) to Gender and Development (GAD), but what these changes in terminology actually mean, and whether they represent a more feminist approach, is more debatable. Essentially, as it is presented by the development agencies, WID is associated with the modernization approach, whereas GAD allows a more flexible appreciation of the dimensions of power between men and women in any community.

The emphasis in WID was on including women in existing development approaches, and especially on increasing women's productive capacity. Once noticed, women's disadvantages were seen solely as a result of their exclusion from development. Critiques of WID tended to centre on its failure to take account of the differences in women's situation, especially in terms of their reproductive role and responsibilities within the household; on its tendency to assume that all women were a homogeneous group, without taking into account cross-cutting factors such as class and ethnicity; and on its exclusive focus on women, with no attention paid to gender relations and the unequal power relations between genders.

The WAD perspective takes a more critical approach, focusing on the relationship of women to development, rather than simply devising strategies to incorporate them. WAD recognized women as important economic actors, and emphasized the informal and unrecognized work that women do in the household and outside the formal economy. It is a kind of half-way house. As Eva Rathgeber puts it, 'WAD offers a more critical view of women's position than does WID but it fails to undertake a full-scale analysis of the relationship between patriarchy, differing modes of production, and women's subordination and oppression' (Rathgeber, 1990: 493).

GAD, in contrast, was seen to be based on later theories of development, ones that paid more attention to the needs of the recipients of aid, and to understanding the global economy in more politically sympathetic ways. In terms of women, it recognized women as a diverse group, and its broader scope allowed it to take account of issues such as race, class and age. It allowed consideration of both men's and women's roles and responsibilities, and emphasized the relationship between men and women in the development process. It also allowed political, social and cultural factors, as well as economic ones, to have a place within the analysis.

Within GAD, there have been increasing efforts to inscribe a more woman-centred approach on development projects. Sometimes the claims have been bold: for example, the GAD analysis addresses unequal gender power by seeking to transform unequal relations (Parker, 1995: 11). Encouraged by these kinds of statements, feminists have tried to develop more radical and far-reaching models. For example, the Women's Empowerment Framework suggests a relationship between levels of equality and increased empowerment of women.

Other schemes try to incorporate a number of ideas into an overall scheme. Buvinic (1982) and later Moser (1989) developed a five-stage description of policy approaches as they applied to women. The *welfare* approach, prevalent between 1950 and 1970, focused on improving women's primary role as mothers. The *equity* approach, which followed, was assumed to be contaminated with Western feminism, but emphasized that more was needed than simple legal equality, where women's situations were so different. The *anti-poverty* approach took a simple economic line, and attempted to address what it saw as the main problem primarily through small-scale enterprises and micro-credit schemes. The *efficiency* approach, which still prevails, fits in well with global economic policies including structural adjustment policies, and endeavours to maximize women's contribution to national productivity, regardless of the increased difficulties they face. Finally, the *empowerment* approach, which originated among Southern feminists, tries to analyse women's situation from their perspective, taking account of colonial and racist oppressions as well. The solutions posed by this approach often focus on small-scale projects, and on self-help schemes, in an attempt to circumvent the global imperative.

Naila Kabeer, in a ground-breaking article (1992), analysed the concepts being used in the proliferating gender training manuals. She identified the 'triple roles framework', which reflected Caroline Moser's experience with Third World planners, the 'gender roles framework', developed by the Harvard Institute of International Development, and used by a number of North American agencies, including the US Agency for International Development (USAID) and the Canadian International Development Agency (CIDA), and the 'social relations analysis', which was developed by Annie Whitehead at the Institute of Development Studies in Sussex. Kabeer identifies what she calls the political sub-text of traning manuals, pointing out, for example, that the Harvard framework assumes that the planner is always impartial and benign, that the focus on efficient allocation of resources favours the already powerful in a community, that it ignores political and economic differences within the community, and that it comes close to assuming that any new resource will be good for all women. There is little in this framework that would challenge existing gender roles or the allocation of power between men and women.

Feminists doing development are, indeed, caught in a web. The structural contradictions of the processes they work within, and the overwhelming power of the dominant economic institutions and mechanisms, make it seem that nothing is possible. Yet the project is too important to abandon. Feminist development has more than simply improving the material quality of life for millions of women as its object. Its transformational analysis and growing political strength mean that it can provide one of the few countervailing voices in a globalized world. We hope that the chapters in this book will show some of the ways in which feminists are wrestling with the contradictions and coming up with new solutions.

The Organisation of the Book

We have organized the book into four sections. The first is 'The Structures that Confine Us'. In it, four contributors – from UK, Pakistan, Japan and China – look at some of the structural limitations of trying to work within official frameworks. Ines Smyth offers an opportunity to reflect on the meaning of feminism in a large, mixed NGO such as Oxfam and analyses the difficulties that even the most well-meaning NGO experiences when it tries to take feminism seriously. She argues that there exists a pervasive fear of feminism in such organizations, and that this is linked both with gender stereotyping and with an understanding of development as poverty alleviation. Tahera Aftab describes the consequences of colonialism from the inside, going on to examine the role of Northern funding agencies and the Pakistan government in fostering the growth of a new elite of development specialists. Part of this discussion deals with the critical issue of tradition and religion, and the way in which the terms have been misapplied by the North, leading to a misdiagnosis of the problems that women face in a country like Pakistan. Sue Ellen Charlton, while writing as an outsider to Japan, offers a critique of the way in which the Japanese government and bureaucracy developed and implemented a WID mandate. She looks at the contribution that women's NGOs and feminists have been able to make to this process, coming to the reluctant conclusion that the nature of Japanese society ensured that they would be confined to small niches in Japan's overall development. This account makes it clear how easily the focus on women can be subverted in the pursuit of national political and economic interests. Wu Qing contributes the last chapter in this section and in it she develops her own concept of development as a feminist working in this field, pointing out ways in which the different organization of projects affects both the workers and the contribution of their projects. Her account reveals a tension between what is and what should be in projects, and how the contribution of the feminist practitioner potentially enhances the overall aims of such projects.

This leads to the second section, which is devoted to various accounts of feminists trying to change the structures and practices they find themselves in, in order to make projects more feminist – 'Staying Feminist in Development'. Renu Khanna provides detailed accounts of how a feminist approach changed two health initiatives in Western India, and the lessons to be learned from this. Barbara Cottrell, who works as a community activist in Atlantic Canada, analyses some of the pitfalls in the concept of partnership, and provides some methods for including the contribution of community women on an equal basis. Collette Oseen provides a particularly honest account of the difficulties of trying to work in a mixed project that was actually male-dominated. This experience has led her to see the *processes* of feminist organizing as crucial to the eventual success of feminist development, and to provide some models as to how this can be accomplished. Finally, Nori Andriyani contrasts the experiences of different feminist projects in Indonesia. The first was funded by Northern funders, and Andriyani analyses the ways in which the control of the funders profoundly affected the ways in which they could work. In contrast, she describes two organizations that have sprung up in response to specific needs since the collapse of the Suharto regime. These projects were independent of external funding, and consequently able to set their own political agendas and develop and adhere to their own values.

In the third section, 'Integrating the Local with the Global', the contributors describe some of their experiences of working between the local and the global levels and of trying to balance the conflicting messages and demands coming from different sources. Valsa Verghese and Fenella Porter examine the experience of one international feminist NGO that moved from Geneva to Uganda, and the puzzles and problems this created in terms of fitting into various, and conflicting, definitions of who and what they were. Next, Habiba Zaman looks at some of the contradictory effects that industrialization (as a form of development) has on women. She explores a case study of the garment workers in Bangladesh to illuminate both the benefits and drawbacks, and the ways in which women can subvert or control some aspects of their work in factories to improve their lives outside. Joyce Green and Cora Voyageur conclude this section by looking at the ways in which aboriginal communities in Canada suffer double oppressions in the process of economic restructuring and globalization. From this vantage point, they are able to offer some particularly pointed critiques of the failures of the development process in aßboriginal communities.

The final section, 'Working with Global Structures', moves the arguments to the level of global analysis and action. Peggy Antrobus and Linda Christiansen-Ruffman reflect on their experience of organizing around community issues in the North and in the South, and on the ways in which their personal collaboration developed both their analysis and their capacity to work on a global level with alliances of Northern and Southern groups around the United Nations Conferences. Joanna Kerr takes a more theoretical approach to the global forces that affect all our lives by raising, and beginning to answer, key questions going beyond what globalization means for women to whether a feminist framework could transform such an agenda, and how we might approach the task. Isabella Bakker concludes the section by taking apart what she calls 'the new global architecture', both in terms of its effects on the neoliberal gender order and in the ways in which feminist policy has tried to address it.

Behind the book's framework lie some issues that nearly all the chapters address, and some that only a few contributors touch on. Some chapters in this book examine the oppositional practices of feminists working in NGOs with feminist agendas, asking how these organizational frameworks might be more conducive to an inclusive feminist conceptualization and practice of development. Some chapters concretely address the various issues that limit feminist practices. One of the most important of these is securing access to funding, and the compromises that may be made in order to acquire adequate funding. Further problems arise with the constraints of operating within the larger environment of globalization and its model of economic growth. Feminist organizations working in the international arena are a potentially important vehicle for the creation of global links between women, but it cannot be assumed that this potential will always be realized. In particular, women from the North may carry with them conceptions of feminism and of development linked with the global metropolis, and may also carry implicitly hierarchical or ethnocentric assumptions that undermine an inclusive feminist agenda. In this book we have tried to bring together women from the South who have worked in development projects and women from the North engaged in reflexive critique of development practice in an attempt to identity ways in which feminists, North and South, can do development in genuinely and transformatively feminist ways.

PART I
The Structures That Confine Us

2 • NGOs in a Post-Feminist Era

Ines Smyth

With some exceptions, most of the literature generated by Northern development agencies on gender and on women shares one characteristic: the absence of the term feminism. Much of the writing produced by Northern NGOs, and most of the verbal exchanges which take place within them, are also notable for this absence. We write and talk about gender-sensitive policies and strategies, of gender work and gendered activities or approaches, and even of engendering or genderizing (!) this or that aspect of our work. But on feminism, feminist policies and strategies, or on feminists, there is a resounding silence.

Clearly there are differences between organizations, between the Northern organizations and their offices and staff located in developing countries and, among the latter, between countries and regions. In many countries there is considerable involvement with relevant debates and attempts to translate them into practice. But at home, Northern NGOs find engaging with feminism – its language and insights, and the practices they inspire – an alien and frightening prospect.

In this chapter I explore the proposition that as 'most development agencies shy away from the language of transformation' (Parpart and Marchand, 1995: 15), the language and substance of feminism are especially misunderstood and feared. I do not suggest that within Northern NGOs there are no individuals (usually women) who regard themselves as feminists. On the contrary, it is in recognition of their continuous struggles for greater gender equity and for women's rights that I have addressed this topic.

In support of this argument the chapter looks first at the symptoms of this fear of feminism, or in other words at the signs that indicate that certain development organizations find feminism uncomfortable and unsuited to their overall aims and manners of working. Obviously, in different organizations such symptoms vary in degree and visibility, and in the extent to which some of them are being addressed and overcome. Later, the chapter summarizes some of the main reasons behind the fear of feminism. A number of these reasons are directly related to the under-standing of development as poverty alleviation which is dominant in such organizations, while others are linked to the way in which certain strains in feminism (and in gender and development) thinking have been mis-interpreted and even coopted. A final section contains a more optimistic view than the rest of the chapter may otherwise suggest. While the comments apply broadly to British NGOs working in development, many of the examples used are drawn from Oxfam GB. This is for two reasons: one is that this is the organization I know best, as a member of its staff; and the other is that Oxfam is one of the largest and oldest NGOs in the UK, with programmes spanning development, advocacy and humanitarian activities, and one of the most overtly and concretely committed to gender equity. To date, Oxfam remains one of a handful of NGOs that have adopted an explicit policy on gender.

Fear of Feminism: the Symptoms

Feminism has many variants, at least in part because it is rooted in women's own experiences and lives. While keeping this in mind, feminism can be broadly defined, and the definition chosen helps locate the author – or the speaker – in the complex spectrum of possible positions she or he may adopt (Thompson, 1992). For present purposes, I define feminism as being rooted in the recognition of women's oppression at all levels (Moore, 1988). More crucially I define it, with Wieringa, as 'not a one-dimensional social critique, but a multi-layered, transformational, political practice and ethics' (Wieringa, 1995: 3). It is from this notion of feminism as political practice, as well as from the language of transforma-tion (see Parpart above) that most development organizations shy away.

The language

A feminist vocabulary appears on the whole to be absent from the language and concerns that are prioritized by Northern organizations. Reports, correspondence, grey material and publications are, with few exceptions, silent on the subject. Though without scientific proof, I would claim that corridor, telephone and electronic conversations, meetings and correspondence are equally devoid of an explicit feminist language, while they are at relative ease with terms such as gender, gender policies and strategies, and even with the verb 'engendering'.

There are exceptions to this rule. Ironically the exceptions are some-times the publications produced by the NGOs themselves. Oxfam, for example, has an extensive list of books on gender-related subjects, many of which challenge the extreme caution on feminism which is expressed elsewhere in the organization. It also attempts, with varying degrees of success, to instil an awareness of gender issues into all other material officially published. The specialist journal it produces, *Gender and Development*, is often the vehicle through which the experiences of practitioners may be analysed using an explicit feminist perspective and related terminology.

Material prepared and used in developing countries much more often addresses, and explicitly issues from, a feminist perspective. This material often concerns organizations that are referred to as 'feminist' rather than 'women's' organizations. A study of documents produced by Oxfam also revealed that in different geographical regions the engagement with feminist ideas is extremely varied in degree. The reason why the work in Latin/Central America and the Caribbean appears fully conversant with and active in feminist debates may be not only the vigour of the feminist tradition in the area but, equally, a history of programme staff (mostly female) who have responded sympathetically and creatively to the opportunities the context has offered. In other regions and countries, for example in India and Lebanon, there are signs that there is an equally challenging dialogue with local feminist organizations and forums.

Furthermore, it is undeniable that individual members of staff in many countries are part of feminist networks and organizations in their own right. Individual feminists working within many development organizations face stark choices. They can take an overt feminist stance (for example by using feminist language and by favouring links with feminist organizations). By doing so they may experience open derision and antagonism from colleagues and senior managers; they may be charged with using strategies which are alien to the Southern communities they work with; and, in a particularly painful twist, they may be accused of 'imposing feminism' as a form of Western imperialism. They may, on the other hand, become closet feminists, conforming to the approaches dominant within their organizations while continuing, as far as possible, to seek spaces to prioritize women's rights. For some, such strategies amount to cooption and instrumentalism, while for others they represent a skilful manipulation of bureaucracies (Miller and Razavi, 1998).

Another characteristic is that at certain times opportunities arise for feminism to be discussed openly within such organizations. The activities which preceded and followed the Beijing Conference involved considerable exchanges between Northern development organizations (as well as Northern feminists) with feminist and women's organizations world-wide. The discussions around the themes of the Platform of Action were often couched in explicit feminist terms. However, these various forms of engagement were rarely noted at the headquarters of the organizations; the ideas have remained the purview of small circles of people (often the gender specialists and other sympathetic people), but have rarely become common currency for the organization as a whole in an explicit and long-term manner. The consequence has been that individual feminists have often found themselves silenced, and have had to adopt working strategies which they experience as a compromise.

By contrast, and as mentioned earlier, Northern NGOs are fully conversant with the terminology of 'gender'. The significance of this will be discussed below. Here it is sufficient to say that perhaps one of the most worrying aspects of the ease with which gender terminology is used, is its lack of clarity and precision. Not only is the term gender often equated with women, but it is also used as a short-hand for anything which may be remotely related to either women or men or the relations between the two: from gender analysis as a methodological approach, through gender training as a practice, to gender equity as a goal. This contributes to creating considerable confusion and mystification which, in their turn, generate fear.

Avoidance of the household

Another sign that many Northern organizations are uncomfortable with feminism and its language is their reluctance to enter the domain of the household, both in theory and in practice. It is generally agreed that feminists have made the personal political, and extended to the private the boundaries of what constitutes social reality and policies (Clough, 1994). It is also acknowledged that even after the importance of this sphere of social life has been formally accepted (UNDP, 1995a), most Northern NGOs have been unable or unwilling to enter it.

As White (1997) points out, a so-called 'women's programme' extends the working time of those involved. In addition, more progressive initiatives – often defined as having the strategic interests of women at heart – introduce them to unconventional productive or other fields. But the relevant organizations do little to encourage men to relieve wives, sisters or daughters of this increased burden by sharing responsibility for housework or other typically female tasks. In doing so, development agencies show their reluctance to challenge established norms and practices dominant within the household, especially when such practices put into discussion male roles and their privileges.

This argument can be taken further: not only are many Northern NGOs reluctant to confront unequal relations within household and family groups, but they also tend to operate within conventional – and eurocentric – parameters which reaffirm certain relations as universal and valid. This is in contrast to what are normally singled out as the comparative advantages of development NGOs: their concern for social justice, their understanding of and respect for diversity between and within cultures, their ability to hear and speak to the poorest and most marginalized members of communities, their adoption of ways of working which ensure their participation (Bobbington and Thiele, 1993).

For example, in most humanitarian interventions relatively little change is being made to the practice of distributing resources (food, blankets, tools, other goods and opportunities) through the head of the household, who is usually male and always adult. The immediate consequences, such as the failure of such resources to reach the most needy, or the frequency with which they are diverted to other uses (conflict, economic gain) instead of ensuring the survival and welfare of affected populations, are documented and recognized. The long-term impact of reinforcing oppressive and discriminatory family and household norms rarely seems to be a concern for the aid agencies involved.

This reluctance to 'enter the household' as symptomatic of a fear of feminism is particularly interesting in the light of the importance that the household has for feminist analyses. It is within the household that many strands of feminism find the roots and causes of women's subordination, though with considerable differences in terms of the way in which household relations have been constructed and understood. As Pearson and Jackson state:

> The development of the domestic labour debate helped pave the way for the creative fusion of feminist and socialist analysis, and the subsequent irreverent deconstruction of theory of intra-household relations and budgeting, from both sides of the political spectrum (1998: 3)

Violence and masculinity

Another illustration of their unease with feminism is the unwillingness of many organizations to include violence against women, and especially domestic violence, among the problems they address. Statistics and qualitative information related to the universality, incidence and severity of this violence (UN, 1989; Caputi and Russell, 1992) cannot fail to point to the scale of its consequences in terms of the distress and suffering to women world-wide. Research is increasingly showing both the analytical links between development and violence against women, and the variety of its practical manifestations (Davies, 1994). All the same, many Northern NGOs do not seem to acknowledge violence against women as a 'development issue'. Some Northern NGOs do support activities in this field. For example, Oxfam gives financial assistance to organizations that work with both survivors and perpetrators of domestic violence, or which address legal and other welfare aspects of the problem. In South Africa Oxfam is working with the KwaZulu-Natal Programme for the Survivors of Violence, which intends to confront openly male violence in communities as well as supporting individual women who have been affected. In

Indonesia, the agency is creating links with the women's organizations active in the aftermath of the violence and sexual assault suffered by women of Chinese descent during the riots of May 1998.

Despite this, the work Northern development organizations carry out in relation to domestic violence and violence against women more generally is not the outcome of a systematic analysis of its causes and consequences in relation to development, nor of an organizational strategy which gives priority and direction to this work or which tries to measure its impact. Despite the emphasis on gender as inclusive of both women and men, a consideration for men is fairly new in development circles, and it is broader than, though related to, the concern with male violence mentioned above. In the British context, the issue of men, and more frequently that of masculinity, is attracting considerable attention both in academic and in social policy circles. Papers delivered at a recent conference covered the spectrum of opinions: from the unconditional welcome of considerations of men in all disciplinary contexts, to the warning that especially for the practice of social policy and of development the concern for men and masculinity could represent one more, newer, way of relegating women's rights again to a lower level of priority (for some of these issues see White, 1998 and Sweetman, 1998).

A focus on men appears to be particularly attractive to European social policy debates, especially in the context of the concept of 'social exclusion'. As already stated by several commentators (Jackson, 1998; Porter, 1988) such analyses prioritize areas of social exclusion from formal production and from official political involvement – that is, from conventionally male arenas. Thus notions of social exclusion tend to be predictably gender-biased, in that they represent a concern for the effects of current economic trends on men's employment, and on their alienation from their roles as providers and as active citizens.

The attempts being made to transfer the concept to development thinking and to the reality of developing countries (IDS Bulletin, 1998) remain theoretical in nature, but the interest displayed by Northern NGOs and other development agencies may be a sign that a focus on men, masculinity and male exclusion is being welcomed by male development practitioners as a promising antidote to the frightening prospects offered by feminism.

Fear of Feminism: the Causes

In the section above, some of the signs of the suspicion in which Northern NGOs hold feminism were described. The main example used was that of Oxfam. In other organizations fear of feminism may manifest itself in entirely different ways. A common manner is through avoidance, silences and muted resistance, all of which are difficult to document. In the sections below, some of the reasons for the fear are examined. They have different origins, some being related to the nature of NGOs and their selected fields of intervention, while others are linked to tendencies and trends within feminism itself.

Poverty, politics and feminism

NGOs – their characteristics, their functions and the changes they are experiencing – have become a subject of academic study in their own right. It is often remarked that in the Northern context, including in Britain, NGOs have evolved from having a responsibility for service provision to being members of civil society, nurturing and strengthening the growth of democracy in developing countries (Korten, 1990). It should be mentioned here that despite the popularity of the notion of civil society as the arena for the emergence of new social movements (Watts, 1995), feminists have been reluctant to engage with it, mainly because it fails to tackle 'issues of the allocation of institutional power, resources and, more specifically, gender-specific access and influence' (Lang, 1997: 103).

Nonetheless, giving NGOs a central role within civil society dovetails with recent changes at the level of official donors where, at least for Britain, an ethical approach which includes the safeguard of human rights has been acknowledged as a legitimate aim for development aid (DFID, 1997). This would indicate that NGOs are taking more overtly political roles. Nonetheless, Northern NGOs find it difficult to accommodate feminism as one of their explicit values. The reason is that feminism is indeed a political project and the charity laws of the country prevent NGOs from engaging in political activities, as does their reliance on public financial support. This is despite the shift mentioned above and despite the frequent reminders that this is unavoidable:

> NGOs should be under no illusion about the political nature of their work; they are trying to engineer certain social changes in certain areas for certain target groups. This is a political act .... (Jorgensen, 1996: 39). The focus on poverty and its alleviation is also a constraint. Most Northern NGOs, have embraced an understanding of poverty which goes well beyond lack of the material means of survival or absence of wealth. Poverty has come to include all forms of material and non-material deprivation and social marginalisation. For example, for Oxfam there are four key aspects to poverty: not having enough to live on, not having enough to build from, being excluded from wealth and being excluded from the power to change things for the better (Oxfam, 1998: 26).

However, this has not gone far enough to justify embracing feminism as a political project. As Jackson states:

> gender justice is not a poverty issue and cannot be approached with poverty reduction policies, and it is important to assert the distinction

between gender and poverty in the face of the tendency in development organizations to collapse all forms of disadvantage into poverty. (Jackson, 1998: 59)

Pop feminism

As we have seen, development agencies such as Oxfam find it expedient to address themselves to matters of gender, while remaining silent on those of feminism. This reluctance in development agencies to use feminist terms and ideas is, at least in part, due to their unconscious acceptance of what Eisenstein (1997) calls 'pop feminism'.

In most Western countries many of the concerns that twenty years ago preoccupied a large but still relatively limited number of women (most of whom would have been active in the women's movement), are now common currency. Issues of equal opportunities at work, of responses to violence against women, of sexual harassment, have become mainstream concerns (Mann, 1997). However, according to Eisenstein (1997), the popularization of these concerns occurs hand in hand with an extreme simplification and misrepresentation of feminism itself. Thus Western feminism is popularized both in the West and globally in a rendition which erases its diversity and its complexities. Ironically, pop feminism both sanitizes its radical roots and demonizes them by offering to global audiences versions of feminism which emphasize alternatively individualism, female supremacism, 'victimhood' and an over-preoccupation with sexual matters. This is not to say that variants of Western feminism do not suffer from these flaws, nor to deny the validity of the attacks against its hegemonic stance. It is simply to say that development organizations appear, in their reluctance to engage with feminism, to have 'bought in' this popularized version of it. Perhaps the most detrimental aspect of this perception is that it ignores the very essence of feminism, its roots in women's experiences within specific contexts:

> Feminism itself refers to political movements that emerge in specific historical conjunctures, and we may expect various forms of feminisms to bear the mark of their political, cultural and historical context. (Gal, 1997)

The bureaucratization of feminism

The early 'women and development' and 'gender and development' frameworks focused on gender inequalities in countries of the developing world (or the South), and on the links between macro policies and trends and their impact on gender relations and women's welfare in rural and urban communities. More recently, new impetus has been brought to the field with the attempts at recognizing and influencing the gendered nature of social institutions at all levels. The usefulness of this approach is undisputed, not least because it has applied a feminist critique of bureaucracies to development organizations, including NGOs themselves (Goetz, 1995).

This has come at a time when international and national development agencies have attempted to mainstream gender, in other words to ensure that a consideration for gender issues is built into all the aspects and stages of development work. A widespread view is that mainstreaming represents the bureaucratization of further concern:

> The variety of ways in which gender has come to be institutionalized and operationalized in the development arena presents a contradictory and ironic picture. There is a disjuncture between the feminist intent behind the term and the ways in which it is employed to minimize the political and contested character of relations between men and women. (Baden and Goetz, 1998: 25)

The disjuncture is also a parallel between the need to mainstream in development policy circles, on one hand, and, on the other, the burgeoning critique in academic and activist circles of development bureaucracies and their role in perpetuating gender-based hierarchies. To a great extent the latter has spurred the former, and provided the conceptual means of carrying out organizational assessment for the purpose of 'mainstreaming'. At the same time, the former – the development agencies attempting to 'mainstream' – have appropriated the feminist critiques and adapted, coopted and depoliticized them for their own ends.

The process of cooption is not new, nor limited to this field. For example, the post-Cairo era has been characterized by the appropriation by 'the population establishment' of feminist terms and concerns. The superficial and instrumental nature of this adoption is evident, yet it raises questions with regard to the most appropriate strategies feminists and health advocates can adopt in pursuit of reproductive rights (Smyth, 1998). What is striking in the field of 'mainstreaming' is that what is being appropriated are the very processes and institutions feminist critiques of bureaucracy and administration were intended to attack.

Gender, culture and differences

While feminism is silenced, in most Northern NGOs we are more (though not entirely) comfortable with gender and, more recently, diversity issues. The discourse of gender and development has undergone, in this decade, a shift from the previous Women and Development approach. This is the case even for the large, influential UN bodies, among which 'many agencies changed the nomenclature of their programs from WID to GAD' (Jahan, 1995: 10). Whether the change was exclusively in the nomenclature and not in the practice is the topic of an ongoing debate, as are the commentaries which critically evaluate whether GAD does or does not represent a radical alternative to WID (Hirschmann, 1995).

For example, at Oxfam headquarters the demise of WID has also been accepted, together with a shift to a GAD approach (see, for example, Cleves, 1993). This goes hand in hand with acknowledging the weaknesses and limitations of 'women's projects' (Wallace and March, 1991). Many in this and other organizations agree with this position and thus insist that social change must involve both men and women. But while for many this reflects a genuine desire to confront gender inequalities at all levels, for others it is a regressive step, which allows them to avoid a commitment to struggle against the subordination of women and for their rights, since those are conflated with women's issues and 'women's projects', and are thus to be rejected – a neat manoeuvre which uses progressive reasoning to introduce an anti-feminist stance.

There is another mechanism which keeps feminism at a distance. One of the most frequently voiced concerns in relation to gender among development practitioners, including those working in Oxfam, is that it imposes priorities and world views which are at odds with local values and priorities. While among field staff this is a genuine concern, not to be dismissed lightly, it could be said that implicit in the absence of a feminist language in the organization as a whole there is a sense that this would be much more unacceptable than gender in terms of ethics, and more dangerous in terms of strategies.

One cannot fail to note a discrepancy here. Development organizations such as Oxfam express reluctance to impose what are considered Northern cultural values on gender; at the same time, they appear fairly unconcerned about exporting Northern views and practices on how best to grow crops, dispense credit, manage an organization or communicate with people. As Mehta puts it, 'Why is it that challenging gender inequalities is seen as tampering with traditions or culture, and thus taboo, while challenging inequalities in terms of wealth and class is not?' (1991: 286). Despite the paradox, the fear of imposing Western and inappropriate gender views and practices continues to be felt keenly in many development NGOs.

This dilemma is not unique to development practitioners. In fact, it represents perhaps the most salient current feminist debate. One of the best known formulations is by Chandra Mohanty (1988). According to Mohanty, Western feminism depicts women in developing countries as all and always poor, oppressed and passive. In so doing Western feminists perpetuate negative stereotypes. They are thus part of the oppressive systems they denounce, and undermine the possibility of alliances between feminists from different backgrounds and with different identities.

Under direct fire from the same analyses are the 'gender experts', who are seen to participate in the wholesale denigration of indigenous knowledge – for example in their acceptance of planning frameworks as technical models universally applicable and superior to any other form of thinking and problem solving (Marchand and Parpart, 1995b).

The theoretical underpinning of these ethical and professional dilemmas lies in the poststructuralist understanding that identity is not fixed but contingent and fragmented. As a consequence the entire edifice of feminism, built on the experience of women and their subordination, collapses in the absence of women as the subject of both (Charles, 1998). There are plenty of valid feminist responses, mostly with the intent to 'recognize and value difference but at the same time not to abandon the feminist project of women's liberation' (Charles, 1998: 10). The point here, however, is that these debates have offered the more sophisticated in development organization excellent scope to justify their anti-feminism via the totally acceptable route of anti-imperialism and sophisticated post-modernism. The hegemony of Northern feminism and its consequences are perhaps the greatest personal and professional challenge to those who work in the field of gender and development in the North. For some the solution to the problem lies in the recognition that women's groups and movements in the South have their own voices through which they are able to 'resist and delegitimize dominant discourses' (Marchand, 1995: 71). This could be said to resonate with what feminists from the South have been advocating: alliances of women's movements which span existing differences of geographical location and of power (Sen and Grown, 1987).

For others, feminists can seek a solution by engaging in various forms of micro-politics. This means being active in struggles which are 'embedded in the daily lives of individuals' to redefine the practices and discourses of the institutions they inhabit. This new form of feminist activism is advocated because it can involve individuals in all aspects of their identity – gender, class, race and so on – without prioritizing one over any other. Though couched in a different language, this is the position of those who are attempting to bring gender 'home' to development institutions by relying on the commitment and abilities of certain 'change agents'. Micro-politics are said, though tentatively, to be valid cross-culturally, and to begin to offer the possibility of avoiding feminist postcolonial domination. Presumably micro-politics are not proposed as an alternative to collective action by women (Parpart, 1995: 19), which many believe to be one of the fundamentals of feminism despite its conceptual and practical difficulties.

Conclusions

To summarize: Northern development organizations find it safer not to engage with the language and practices of feminism. There are several possible explanations for this foreclosure. One is that such organizations adopt a narrow vision of 'poverty' as the exclusive focus of their activities. Others are that development NGOs are reacting to mass-marketed pop feminism; that this is the effect of the process of bureaucratization induced by 'mainstreaming'; and, finally, that certain tendencies within feminism itself – for example, those derived from a postmodernist perspective – are being used perversely to deny the validity of feminism.

The reaction is to remain safely in what is believed to be the less contentious gender and development discourse. This chapter agrees with the many analyses which decry the de-politicizing effect of the use of the term gender. But I am not proposing that development organizations such as Oxfam should become 'feminist organizations', in the sense that their sole goal should be that of struggling for women's collective action against patriarchal structures and norms. In addition, I do not deny that a gender discourse can be radical and transformational. On the contrary, I agree with the position that gender and development is about strategies that aim to redress gender-based inequalities and hierarchies of power (Macdonald, 1994). My argument is also based on the understanding that the languages of gender and of feminism are complementary, rather than antagonistic or synonymous.

Women's organizations in the countries of the South come in many shapes and sizes. It is possible to generalize, however, and say that, even when their membership includes academic and middle-class women, they can more legitimately speak for the women whom Northern organizations wish to support and empower. Such organizations, regardless of their relative position in relation to Western feminism, by definition, develop and verbalize (to varying degrees) powerful critiques of local culture. Thus, in both ethical and strategic senses, they offer organizations such as Oxfam the route out of the gender and culture impasse.

At the same time, this chapter maintains that the lack of explicit engagement with feminist terms and ideas in such organizations prevents them from participating fully and explicitly in the debates about hegemonic Western feminism, and in the search for alternatives. A possible outcome of this could be that Northern development agencies may, by default, help to promote the hegemony of Western feminism.

At the more practical level, this attitude may be preventing them from giving sufficient support, space and opportunities to individuals and groups within their own staff who are dedicated to feminism in whatever way. Similarly, it may be preventing these agencies from working together with the feminist organizations which are born out of analyses of local circumstances in the South. Such groups may see feminism as something imported from the West, and for that reason consider it irrelevant, while at the same time struggling to define the terms of their own feminism. These are also the very organizations which would offer a way out of the 'gender and culture' dilemma in which so many development organizations seem to be stuck.

3 • Development and Women in Pakistan

Tahera Aftab

Let it be understood that we can no longer afford to keep our women in the background; they must be made to take part in all things natural to their instincts; and, above all, they must be prepared to stand on equal intellectual footing with their European sisters. (Mrs Ali Akbar's address at a public mixed meeting at the Stree Bodhi Jubilee, Bombay, 1908)

In this chapter I do not claim to present an exhaustive critique of feminist theories or development strategies. Instead, I limit myself to my own experiences, shared with my colleagues and co-workers within and outside academia. I shall draw upon my own continuing involvement in research and activism with women's advocacy groups and with women at the grassroots level. However, I also intend to raise questions about the concepts, meaning, goals, agencies, and entire infrastructure of development, both locally and globally. Some of these questions emerged in classroom discussions in the Women's Studies programme at Karachi University. Others reflect queries from women who can be described as 'grassroots women' (in development jargon). I want to begin by acknowledging my gratitude to both my students in Women's Studies and women outside academia, especially to those who, by sharing their everyday lived experiences with me, helped me to arrive at a true understanding of development. This chapter, therefore, addresses three interlinked questions: How is development being defined for non-Western women? How is the development process being formed by local agencies? Is the existing gap between the developed and the underdeveloped diminishing or increasing? In short, what is meant by development at all? What does development mean to feminists, to donor agencies, to the governments of Pakistan, to the project writers, to the field workers, and to the majority of women and men who are its objects?

Beginning with Women

From the vantage point of my teaching, research and intervention, I

29

learned the advantage of dovetailing my own lived experiences of three generations of women with those of my students, who were mostly in their twenties. This mix of the past indefinite with the present continuous, which I call the 'Women's Studies brew', was then available to be shared with women living in Karachi's peripheral rural slums and inner city hovels. Thus, this chapter begins from the experience of women and is a more contextualized analysis of 'feminism' or of 'development strategies'. It seeks to resonate the voice of women themselves.

Inspired by Maria Mies's argument that feminist research must motivate some kind of change in the lives of women through activism and consciousness raising (Mies, 1983: 142), and choosing methods that 'give research subjects more power' (Cancian, 1992: 627) I decided to crawl out of my fantasy world of academia. Stepping out of the sheltered cocoon of theories into the sunlit world of stark realities was nothing short of a second birth.

Less than four kilometres from my workplace and my home at Karachi University are several clusters of rural settlements. These peripheral villages are mostly populated by Baluchi people. Some of the men from these settlements are employees of Karachi University and work as *naib qasids* (office attendants), *malis* (gardeners), and *chowkidars* (watchmen), jobs ranked low in the hierarchy of the campus. Traditionally sons of retired employees replace their fathers, creating an interesting bond between the campus and these men that spans more than thirty years. The full-time office attendant and the part-time gardener employed by the Women's Studies Centre come from this area. We decided to visit their homes.

On this first visit my ethical dilemma was, and remains, an utter embarrassment mixed with a deep sense of remorse at our continuing control over knowledge as a tool for perpetuating social control and economic exploitation. The homes we visited in this area are mostly one- or two-room houses with tin roofs and mud walls. Some are made of brick with main entry doors. None have running water, which is fetched from a nearby water pump that has no faucet and is fixed at a level lower than the ground. Thus the water pump is submerged in a puddle of murky water mixed with earth and airborne matter. As the waterport is shallow and small, the work of filling the water jars is done by small children, mostly by little girls. Water is carried by women and girls. The fuelwood used for cooking consists mostly of tree twigs collected by young girls. Children, from toddlers to early teens, play around, swarming like honey bees over a neighbourhood in which no functioning school is visible.

Each house has goats and poultry. The courtyard of beaten earth serves several purposes – open-air kitchen, laundry, playground, poultry pen, and goat shed. Some houses occupied by families with more income are furnished and have electric fans, TVs and radio sets. At our first visit we were treated with reservation. Baluchis have age-old customs of hospitality and our hosts were eager not to show any lack of respect for strangers.

Next it was our turn to invite them to the Woman's Studies Centre. There was some initial reluctance to accept our invitation and visit us because the university campus was the workplace of the men of this community. It was a place where the male authority of these families was centred; it was at the same time the place where these men experienced subordination in their everyday life experience within the power hierarchy of the campus. We realized that their reluctance in 'allowing the women' to come to us was not because they wanted to control women's mobility; it was based more on their fear of losing their authority in the eyes of their women if they witnessed the reality of the low status of their husbands and fathers. Recognizing that a hierarchy of power structure exists in all situations, we invited both men and women. This marked the beginning of our long friendship with our future partners in exploring the practicality of Women's Studies, and, indeed, of all knowledge.

Once the ice melted and a relationship based on mutual trust began, we started talking about several things, things that these women would never have dreamt of discussing with strangers. We talked about women's needs, about our concerns for our children and our families. We moved from issues relating to water supply, school for children, health care, drug abuse, and transportation to matters such as the marriages of our daughters, menstruation, menopause, birth spacing, and even abortion and miscarriage. We developed an agenda of mutual concerns.

Since our first visit in March 1992 much has happened to advance the development issue in this community. The experience gained in our work together with these women remains as the inspirational source for this chapter and for my other work. I want to recognize that whatever small improvements have come to Pakistan women have come through the daily struggles of individual rural and urban women themselves. Women in Pakistan are conscious of their strategic needs; but they prioritize their practical gender needs. This often creates a conflict situation, as donor agencies – whom I would prefer to identify as 'development controlling agencies' – display preconceived notions of priorities of the development agenda that reflect their dominant metro-politan theories (Ford-Smith, 1989). This domination must come to an end (Pheterson, 1990). The Karachi University campus and the Baluchi settlements can provide us with two illustrations of development and underdevelopment. Later I shall be looking at various aspects of these two terms. But I will begin by looking at the general scene in Pakistan as an 'underdeveloped country'.

The Context of 'Development'

Pakistan emerged as a new country out of colonial hegemony in India in 1947 with a fragmented economy, a chaotic system of civil administration and an elusive system of security and development. In the early decades of its existence the indicators of development were virtually unknown. The agenda for the future was envisioned through an urban-elite/feudal kaleidoscope. More shocking and harmful was the alliance between two opposite, conflicting agents of power – the urban elite and the feudal landholder – each centred around its own *axis mundi*, each encapsulated in its own orbit. While policy planners and development strategists were able to achieve little, the public preacher filled in the space. It was assumed and mandated from the pulpit that *taqva* (piety) is a panacea for all existing inequalities. This exhortation mirrored the refusal to accept the reality of the challenges, proposing instead that the masses would silently endure their life in the pit of poverty and deprivation.

No other event in the last several hundred years has so dramatically altered the life of Pakistan women as the construction of Pakistan and its appearance on the world map as a politically independent state in 1947. The concept of men as providers and protectors of women changed forever, first during the traumatic period of partition of the Indian subcontinent and then, 24 years later, during the catastrophe of the fall of Dacca when, after a bloodbath, Bangladesh emerged as a new country. Pakistan women had never been mere silent witnesses of events. As front-line marchers during the closing days of colonial hegemony, Muslim women brought to Pakistan the nascent world of their dreams, a zeal of partnership. The post-1947 male Pakistan decided differently. Immediate defence priorities suddenly devalued women's role and at the same time added more meaning and significance to muscle power. Another factor in the new Pakistan state also affected women. British usurpation of Indian territory in the late eighteenth and early nineteenth century had done more harm to protected and princely states than to the 'annexed areas'. Major parts of Pakistan were located within these princely states. In their quest to strengthen their hold in the region, the colonialists had formed alliances with the local feudals, thereby consolidating their control over weaker sections, including women. The new government of Pakistan saw advantages in continuing and maintaining the colonial *status quo* of power. While one can offer pragmatic defences for this decision, it has resulted in a state that is inherently 'anti-women'.

Today Pakistan's population is estimated at about 124.45 million (January 1994), of whom 85.25 million live in rural areas and 39.20 million in urban areas. The current growth rate of around 3 per cent is significantly higher than that of other South Asian countries. Based on the Pakistan Demographic Survey of 1991, the crude birth rate is estimated at 39.5 per thousand live births and the crude death rate at 9.8 per thousand. The infant mortality rate is put at 102.4 per thousand. During the Third Five Year Plan (1965–70) a vigorous attempt was made to implement the government's population policy in order to achieve the development objectives of improvement in living standards for the people of Pakistan. Therefore, an ambitious Family Planning scheme was launched on 1 July 1965 by a semi-autonomous body, the Pakistan Family Planning Council. In mid-1966, the population of West Pakistan was estimated at 54 million.

These grim statistics stand as evidence of chaotic mismanagement of the development programme at all levels. In a recent statement Nafis Sadik, talking of future strategies for Pakistan, said:

> The strategy must include sustainable political commitment, mobilizing support of all civil society including Parliamentarians and community leaders, in implementing an effective national program that recognizes the linkages between gender, population, and development.

This statement can also be read as a critique of what has happened so far in Pakistan. In reality, the exploitation of human resources seen by Pakistan has created health hazards, environmental degradation, gender-based discrimination and fast-increasing violence against women and girls. Long-standing ethnic, linguistic and sectarian conflicts have created a phantom leadership in the country. The 1950s and the 1960s were crucial for Pakistan as the country had to galvanize all its resources for the rehabilitation of its people and the protection of its boundaries. It was precisely during these decades that the international development planners started advocating definitions of development and underdevelopment. Instead of censuring the colonial hegemonists who had fleeced and plundered colonial nations for centuries, these planners devised a new definition of 'development' to which the nations would have to conform. They marketed these definitions and demands with even greater zeal than was ever done in the past by the missionaries with their definitions of 'civilized' and 'non-civilized'. Now 'growth in the capital stock was seen as the means of achieving development, and the growth rate of *per capita* GDP became the sole measure of development.... Income at the national level ... became a measure of individual well being' (UNDP, 1990: 104).

Development and Women: The Discourse in Pakistan

Development, in socio-historical contexts, is a complex process (Young, 1993: 136) involving the interplay of many factors. The policies of national governments are directed towards it, and at the same time it represents the fundamental rights of all citizens. Development is uniquely related to people, and cuts across time factors. All true development is intertwined with the past, the present and the future of a group of people. Thus development is contextualized and is spatial.

But what is development? Who decides the boundaries between development and underdevelopment? Who empowers 'them' to decide this? Will this race for attaining development come to an end? How? When? How can it be achieved? Development for what? The list of questions was never-ending as we in Women's Studies became overwhelmed by bulky UN-generated reports, by the seminal studies of development wizards, and by the sprawling helplessness in the lives of the old and the young in the squatter settlements outside our gates. Young quotes a definition given by the South Commission: 'Our vision is for the South to achieve a people-centered development: a form of development that is self-reliant, equitable, participatory and sustainable. We envisage a process of development achieved through the active participation of the people, in their own interests as they see them, relying primarily on their own resources, and carried out under their own control' (Young, 1993: 15). Postcolonial nations as survivors of colonial marauding and systematic pillage are wary of the 'visions' of others for them; they want to have their own visions and to make their own dreams come true. Maria Mies thus warns that 'it is important to recognize that questions of conceptualization are questions of power, that is, they are political questions. In this sense, the clarification of conceptual position is part of the political struggle of feminism' (Mies, 1989: 36).

The growing debate over the changing conceptualization of development and its relationship to market-oriented economies and technology has resulted in the fragmenting of human societies in terms of First, Second, Third and now Fourth worlds. Much has been written about the misconceptions on which this categorization is based. But lying behind these debates is a suspicion about the very capacity for development in societies like India, Pakistan and other South Asian regions. It is distressing that this labelling of nations as 'underdeveloped', and other examples of male-based terminology, should also be used, or implied, in feminist discourse. To us, women from the so-called Third World countries, it is another form of the continuation of the colonial hegemonic psyche; the only difference being that instead of 'heathen debased women' we are now 'Third World women', lacking in knowledge and technology, while our benefactors are no longer 'heathen women's friends' but development planners, feminists (with no prefixes or suffixes), WID, WAD, GAD experts and international consultants – expensive imported items.

What gnaws us more than the continuity of hegemony under varied forms is the exuberant voluntary collaboration of women of the 'Third World' in perpetuating this exploitation. This collaboration has resulted in a plethora of tales of misery and distress to which 'Third World women' are mercilessly subjected in the name of religion and tradition by their callous men. 'Tradition', in this discourse, emerges as a monolithic, unchangeable entity. This chapter cannot enter into a study of the nature, formation and growth of traditions. It is relevant here to note, however, that all traditions, religious and social, represent a society's effort to make adjustments to a given situation and that traditions are thus, by definition, movable, changeable, and – contrary to the general assumption – not static. Traditions grow in response to or as a result of certain historical forces that remain operative as creative, negative or passive forces. Traditions are not formed in a vacuum. They are created by human agency; they survive because of patronage and they become strong when they are validated by an authority.

Let me give one example that directly affects Pakistan women. In the nineteenth century the British colonialists needed collaborators in the North West Frontier provinces and the Punjab (areas that now constitute major parts of Pakistan) in order to use their territory as a buffer zone between their illegal land holding in India and Russian territorial extension. Thus the British imperialists cemented their alliances with local chieftains by validating oral patriarchal traditions which they codified as 'tribal laws'. These tribal laws are in total contradiction to Quranic laws. In Pakistan today two opposite sets of laws operate: the Constitution of Pakistan, upholding gender equality, and the tribal law that rejects women as independent human beings.

In Pakistan, and other societies where religion and religious ideology continue to be stimulants for public and private activity, there is a murky interpretation – touted by some sociologists, anthropologists, and develop-ment planners – of all traditions as religious traditions. It is time to halt the colonial hegemonic practice of confusing religion and religious traditions with folklore; or feudal customs and colonial interventions with a judiciary and courts of law. There is, indeed, a huge body of thought and philosophy within Islam that offers alternatives to the Western model of social, economic and political development. But this is not 'tradition'. I cannot stress too much that a true and sustainable development is possible only when the development process acknowledges and respects, rather than belittling and rejecting, the religion and faith of its own society. In my view, shifting the blame for gender disparity and crimes against women to socio-religious traditions is tantamount to shielding the colonial hegemonists and blaming the victims themselves. This theory also diverts attention from the continuous poor planning and governance of the current ruling juntas. The targeting of religion and religious traditions as anti-women has resulted in an overall boom of '*parda* literature' focusing on the effects of *parda* and segregation of women as determinants in impeding progressive social and economic change in women's lives. Observance of *parda* is not the issue for the development of more than fifty per cent of women in Pakistan. This is evidenced by the numbers of wage-earning women – women working in the homes of 'elite' women as domestic helps, or in the stone quarries and brick kilns, or repairing the road pavements; or as beggar women, street girls and women of the 'red-light areas'. None of these women conceal themselves behind a veil. Shockingly, some of these women working either as domestic 'servants' or as roadside labourers are not workers by choice but 'bonded labourers'. This is an illustration of what I perceive to be gaining ground in Pakistan's urban centres: a long-term alliance between feudalism and capitalism, protecting itself well into the next millennium.

The agenda for women and development is therefore mostly based on the presumed wrongs done to women in Pakistan by 'tradition', and not on the actual causes. The most obvious result is that the masses in the country will continue to live in 'absolute poverty', to borrow a term from Robert McNamara. Women's groups have not yet organized strategically against feudalism – and its by-products, such as feudalistic 'democracy', feudalistic distribution of resources, and feudalistic access to opportunities and facilities. Without eradicating feudalism, talk of women's upward mobility is both misleading and meaningless.

How Does 'Development' Happen?

The second UN Development Decade (1970–9) saw increased integration of women's issues into development planning. Esther Boserup's monumental work *Women's Role in Economic Development*, published in 1970, brought the truth to the forefront that no development is complete without the 'full integration of women in the total development effort', as it is only through this integration that 'the whole society of men, women and children' will benefit (Boserup, 1975: 8).

In the 1970s the idea also developed of creating special cells or units within the government machineries with responsibility for women and development. In Third World countries, where gender and women's issues were yet to emerge as policy concerns, women's bureaux were the sites for experimentation with this new mechanism. These bureaux were expected to 'include women in high-level decision making committees and [ensure that] more women [were] recruited at all levels of national ministries, agencies and project staff' (Nelson, 1981: 49).

By the time Boserup's ground-breaking study became known in

Pakistan, the country was already clenched in the claws of its longest military dictatorship. Nothing has harmed the cause of women and development more than the ambiguity that emerged during the 11-year period of martial law. One example illustrates this sufficiently. In 1979 the dictator, Zia-ul-Huq, and his cronies issued a series of martial law ordinances instituting *Hudood* (penalties prescribed by Muslim jurists for theft, adultery, fornication and consumption of alcohol). In the same year the Women's Division in the Cabinet Secretariat was created at Islamabad. This odd combination shaped the early years of women's agitational activities in Pakistan's major cities. As middle-class, urban-based women were faced with greater opposition, they increasingly focused on an exclusive agenda of issues mainly relevant to urban women. I do not intend to trivialize or minimize the activism of these women or the gains they achieved, but their initiative was neither broad-based nor representative of all Pakistan women. I want to emphasize, however, that women's activism has yet to reach a mature stage of operation, even today.

The Women's Division was established to identify and highlight problems faced by women; to undertake research; and to establish links with women at the grassroots level. It was expected to act as a catalyst for women's development. As the four provinces of the country were the implementing authorities, Women's Project Cells were created at the provincial level to help and monitor the implementation of various schemes and projects. Although some piecemeal research was done under its aegis, and some individual women emerged as 'success stories', the Women's Division mostly functioned as an idle symbol of government's 'concern' for women's 'development'.

It must be noted that the period of the establishment of the Women's Division was notorious for its anti-women legislation and frenzied bashing of women's actions and voices by the state-owned media. During this decade women who remained marooned on this isolated island of the Women's Division later on emerged as leading names in women and development. With the emergence of a woman prime minister, the Women's Division, by now a fully fledged ministry, entered into a new era of self-glorification. In line with the populist rhetoric of the government, the Women's Development Ministry also declared high goals for its work: to formulate public policies and make laws to meet specific needs of women, ensuring equality of opportunity in education and employment and fuller participation in all spheres of national life.

Contrary to Nelson's expectations (cited above), the Women's Development Ministry and its Women's Project Cells emerged as havens of male hegemony, creating and sustaining new forms of female subjection. The rapid succession of governments in Pakistan failed to find women suitable for appointment to the various offices within the Women's Development

Ministry. Thus the male-centric controlling hand, dictating masculine theories of research and learning, remains the major scourge of the women's agenda in Pakistan. In fact the Women's Development Ministry, from its inception, was more a symbol of government's compliance with the international agenda than an instrument for change. Indeed the model in Pakistan is almost the same as Gordon has described for the functioning of women's bureaux elsewhere in similar situations (Gordon, 1984).

Over the past several decades there has been a surge of activities concerning women and development in Pakistan. The country has attracted the attention and interest of international donor agencies, including those of the UN. With local partnership, a laudable breakthrough was achieved in the area of opinion building and putting pressure on the government. This partnership has caused some money to flow into the hands of the local NGOs as well as to the government of Pakistan. Little has been used effectively and more has been wasted. The pitiable state of women, reported year after year in donor agency annual reports, bears witness to this. Why is this so? One tends to see truth in Wilber and Jameson's assessment of the net result of such activities: 'International Conferences have been held, billions have been spent on foreign aid, and thousands of experts now earn their living from development' (Wilber and Jameson, 1988: 3).

During the last two decades there has been a marked proliferation of NGOs focusing on development-related issues, the provision of social services, and human rights protection. This process is advanced further when donor governments and other funding bodies embrace local NGOs as 'partners in action'. In Pakistan demographic changes, urbanization, an increase in labour force participation, a rise in age at first marriage, and bad governments with a faulty understanding of international pressures contributed to this trend, but the precipitating factor was the availability in Pakistan of women between their mid-twenties and mid-thirties, either with a post-graduate degree from a university in the West or with strong links to a Western country.

Development as it is conceptualized and practised, mainly by the NGOs, is a concept framed by parameters that are not indigenous in design or purpose. In fact the very language or development jargon in circulation within NGO circles – 'NGO', 'development', 'project writing', 'field work', 'data collection', 'questionnaire', 'funding', 'report writing' – is based entirely on English words. Equivalent terms in the local languages either are non-existent or are not used. This use of a foreign language creates alienation; one interlocutor automatically becomes powerless while the other becomes powerful; one lives in a pit, the other has all that is fresh and fragrant. This imbalance between the NGO 'experts' and ordinary women is the first sign of how ineffective development strategies are that are initiated by international bodies and practised by their local collaborators.

It is saddening to attend seminars and workshops organized by local NGOs in collaboration with 'donors' and 'funding agencies' in the conference halls of five-star hotels. Introducing themselves in these seminars, young women and girls from rural areas or urban slums say, *'Mein ngo hun'* (I am an NGO), or in response to 'What do you do?', give the answer *'Mein ngo chalati hun'* (I run an NGO). Some of these women are hastily collected for the seminar and some are brought in by an enterprising woman or a man who either has received 'funds' through 'connections' or is on the look-out for funds. So while funds are expanded and executive summaries of completed projects are bound in volumes, the life of the masses in the squalor remains unaltered. Development theorists and economic experts acknowledge this dilemma: as Mahbub ul Huq reports: 'in country after country, the masses are complaining that development has not taken touched their lives' (quoted in Griffin, 1989: 166). Geeta Chowdhry goes further, believing that 'the main purpose of these projects is to promote capitalism; the development and assistance of Third World women is incidental' (Chowdhry, 1995: 35).

The women's movement in Pakistan, both historically and in its current form, is class-bound. Its front-line marchers are urban-based, educated women having family ties with 'elite men'; its agenda caters mostly to the needs of the same class and reflects their aspirations. The rest of the women, living in rural or in urban slums, are often unaware of the development debates and strategies. Feudalism and patriarchy, two sides of the same coin, control the life of men and women of this class to such an extent that it becomes mere existence. Pakistan women, like women in all such situations, confront a doubly oppressive, subordinate position.

This subordination has gained legitimacy through the unleashed pronouncements of pseudo-religious public preachers. The public prominence of this feudal, pseudo-religious junta has a corollary: Pakistan, like some other South Asian countries, has a prolonged record of abuse of public mandate, civil strife, embezzlement of public funds, abrogation of fundamental human rights, and plundering of public resources by persons fraudulently elected to public offices. This disarray within the government has resulted in major dislocations in the development processes, with far-reaching negative implications for women's issues. At the same time it is equally true that harm is caused by rampant bureaucratic corruption and the inhumanity of military regimes supported by fraudulent politicians and pseudo-theologians. This half-century's exploitative power games have undermined the democratization of institutions. At the same time, they have turned women's issues, which are national issues of development, into peripheral, trivial issues.

What are these issues? Are women treated as slaves in Pakistan? Has anything been done to release them from bondage? There are hosts of similar queries about women – some true, some mythical, and some imaginary. In this chapter, my analysis of the causal factors of women's dependency and subordination in societies such as Pakistan moves beyond the frivolities of *parda* polemics. My concern is more to explore the meaning of development as it affects the lives of women.

Going Back to the Women

At this point another significant question arises. Is feminism an artifact of library-based scholarship? Is it an expression of anger? Is it an expression of agitation and rejection? In short, is there, and can there be a feminism beyond and without theories? Do theories of feminism(s) form the core of feminism itself? Can Maryam, 38-year-old mother of three daughters and four sons, living in an extended family of 15 members in a squatter settlement with no running water and no cooking fuel, be a feminist? She is a fighter, she fights for her family and for herself. She has a deep faith in her own capabilities. She manages to bargain for her identity. Feminists in the North have no knowledge of her strategies; indeed they do not know of her existence as a woman conscious of her needs and of her abilities to seek the satisfaction of these. Nor does Maryam. She lives and acts the way it is possible for her, without being bothered to know the nuances of feminist ideologies and theories. In our Women's Studies Centre, we try to make her voice heard and not be lost in the jabber of feminist debates over labels.

One of our successful strategies to address these and other such questions was the introduction of Women's Studies at Karachi University in 1989–90. Women's Studies in Pakistan has an interesting history of its own. A five-year project entitled 'Women's Studies Centres' at the universities was prepared by the Women's Division. The main objective of the project was to introduce and promote the discipline of Women's Studies in Pakistan. A document detailing guidelines for setting up these centres was prepared by the Women's Division. It said that Women's Studies 'which has been well established in the West' aims at (1) building up a body of knowledge based on lost or undiscovered lives of women; (2) studying the roots and structures of inequality that lead to invisibility and exclusion of women from the concepts and methodologies of intellectual inquiry; (3) creating strategies for empowering women in their struggle against inequality and oppression and for effective participation in all areas of society and development; and (4) developing or creating alternative concepts, approaches and strategies for development.

As Director of the Centre of Excellence for Women's Studies, my first concern was to develop a model of Women's Studies suited to our needs in Pakistan. Later, this was discussed at a workshop held in partnership with UNICEF at Karachi University in 1991. The workshop's main focus was: what is the potential for Women's Studies in Pakistan and what specific issues and questions need to be raised and addressed to develop a Pakistan perspective of Women's Studies? The main conclusion was that if Women's Studies at Karachi University is to move beyond merely being an academic discipline and exercise for researchers and students, then clear and strong links must be forged from the beginning between the Women's Studies Centre and women's activism. Another very significant learning experience during the sessions was a vigorous analysis of development and its relevance to women in Pakistan. Mere inclusion of women as a special category in development projects, as subjects of study and research, was no guarantee of women's development. While there was unanimity of opinion that research on women's issues is lagging far behind in Pakistan and that women's experiences need to be explored, another significant question was also raised: is Women's Studies going to document the obvious? We talk about the forms of oppression but we are evasive about the forces behind them. Are we afraid of these forces? How long will we remain in hiding and seek shelter?

By adopting a more contextual position, we were able to establish the need to develop a feminist perspective with reference to Islam. This, the argument stressed, would counteract the tactics of pseudo-religious practices that suppress and coerce women in patriarchal subordination. In this discussion, we could not ignore the ambivalence regarding Islam and the way it is preached in Pakistan. Therefore we decided on a more pragmatic study, and less emotional defence, of religion.

The issue of development, which is the theme of this chapter, and which was the expected aim of Women's Studies, was the issue that generated the most intense debate. The delegates, representing almost all shades of opinion amongst women in Pakistan, were wary of the term 'development'. The consensus was that development will occur for women when they themselves are mobilized in the change effort. Change is built up from the bottom and not imposed from above. Further, economic development and the development of social infrastructures of health, education, housing and other social services are necessary but not sufficient conditions for development. Social resources need to be vested in the people. Hence by social change we mean fundamental change in group relationships, the development of autonomy and self-reliance, and the promotion of rights and justice for all. Development will remain ineffective and remote as long as women's needs are not reflected in the development agenda. This can be achieved by establishing an ongoing dialogue amongst women at all levels.

4 • Little Progress, Small Niches:
The WID Mandate in Japanese Foreign Aid

Sue Ellen Charlton

Since the early 1990s, when it replaced the United States, Japan has been the world's largest bilateral aid donor in terms of volume. By 1995 Japanese official development assistance (ODA) constituted almost a quarter of all disbursements by the Development Assistance Committee (DAC) of the Organization for Economic Cooperation and Development (OECD), the international organization that groups the wealthiest aid donors in the world.[1] Despite domestic economic problems in the late 1990s that prompted reductions in development assistance, Japan still remained the largest donor by volume, disbursing roughly twice the total ODA of the United States.

Japanese foreign aid, including its mandate to address gender concerns, is characterized by several unique features. Seen through a comparative perspective, however, the Japanese approach to integrating gender into ODA shares the strengths and the weaknesses found in many bilateral aid programmes. International thinking on the nature of development *has* evolved in the past quarter-century, from basic human needs and participatory approaches to the 'WID regime' and Gender and Development (GAD), and feminists have been central to the reconceptualization of development processes. Although fewer in number than in many countries, Japanese feminists – including scholars, practitioners and politicians – have drawn on the international debate to nudge the Japanese government in the direction first of drafting, and then of implementing, a WID mandate.

This chapter is the story of how Japanese feminists did make a difference in Japanese ODA in the late 1980s and early 1990s, and also why their progress has largely been confined to the small niches of Japan's overall development policy. There are four themes in this story. First, Japanese ODA – like all national ODA policies – reflects primarily the concerns and priorities of the donor country. For Japan this means that its foreign aid must be understood in the context of its strategic and economic role in international relations since the Second World War.

42

Second, Japanese aid (again, like that of other countries) is grounded in policy-making views of what development means and how it happens. The Japanese government has been slower than most to view gender as central to the conceptualization of development problems or processes.

This slowness in turn points to a third theme, the central role of the Japanese bureaucracy in aid policy making, and the resistance of this bureaucracy to gender concerns in general, and feminist voices specifically. The fourth theme – the confluence of circumstances leading to a women-in-development (WID) mandate in Japan's ODA – can only be understood in the context of the other three themes of post-war globalization and Japanese foreign policy, development conceptions and priorities, and bureaucratic decision making. This chapter first explains this context, then describes in more detail how the WID mandate emerged.

Japanese ODA in the Context of Globalization

Japan's development assistance programme emerged in *ad hoc* fashion in the wake of the country's unique history. Central to this history was Japan's role in the Second World War, the impact of the American bombings of Hiroshima and Nagasaki, and the subsequent US occupation from 1945 to 1952. As a consequence of these events, the Japanese government sought over the decades to define a foreign policy that met several criteria. First, policies had to be compatible with Japan's status as a junior partner in the mutual security alliance with the United States, particularly during the 1950s and 1960s. Later, as Japan matured into a wealthy industrial country, its policies were crafted to respond to Western pressure for sharing the burden of maintaining international peace and security (as defined by the dominant Western powers), while also pursuing its own interests. Third, Japan's foreign policy had to take into account constitutional constraints, strong pacifist sentiments among many Japanese, and the suspicions of its Asian neighbours, all of which argued for a non-military definition of major-power status. Economic development assistance met these criteria. Put differently, ODA had everything to do with Japan's search for a new international role after the Second World War, but very little to do with what poor people, especially women, saw as their real needs for grassroots development. Hence the term 'yen diplomacy' has been used to describe Japanese development assistance.

Yen Diplomacy and Japanese Aid

Japan's emphasis on foreign aid and 'development cooperation' reflects the search for a non-military, collaborative international role that is compatible with the country's economic stature and maximizes national influence. Defining this role was a process that took nearly three decades.[2] Characteristic of this process of definition was the largely reactive nature of Japanese policy, a point that becomes important in understanding when and how the WID mandate was ultimately adopted. On one hand, ODA policy has reacted to international priorities that have been articulated by the United States, the Development Assistance Committee of the OECD, and other multilateral organizations; on the other hand, ODA reflects domestic definitions of what will serve both economic and political goals. In balancing international and domestic pressures, of course, Japan is typical of every aid donor; the difference is the degree to which governments take the initiative in crafting aid policies – and Japan, particularly on gender issues, has been a follower.

A closer look at the qualitative and quantitative features of Japanese ODA suggests that underlying the global political context of yen diplomacy are key assumptions about the nature of economic development and how aid recipients should go about developing themselves. Behind these assumptions, critics argue, is economic self-interest and an ODA policy that privileges Japanese businesses and contributes to a late-twentieth-century Asian sphere of influence for Japan. The various dimensions of this argument cannot all be examined here, but certain elements of it bear mentioning because of their significance for the feminist criticism that Japanese economic assistance, *by its very structure*, has been hostile to women's needs and goals in development.

All countries include a variety of disbursements under the formal heading of ODA, including technical cooperation, food aid, emergency relief, debt relief, contributions to multilateral organizations, loans, and the administrative costs of handling all of these. Further, especially in an era of economic globalization, ODA is only one part of a country's economic relations with another country; private investment and the activities of private (or non-governmental) voluntary organizations are also part of the broader picture. By the mid-1990s Japanese bilateral grants and grant-like contributions (such as technical cooperation) were about US$6.3 billion and development loans about US$4.1 billion, or a ratio of 60:40. This ratio represents a gradual shift away from loans to grants and technical assistance, although the proportion of loans is still high (OCED/DAC, *1997 Report*). Given the context of bilateral aid throughout the world, ten billion dollars constitutes a potentially powerful tool for influencing the course of development, however the sums are distributed. Therefore, it is important to ask where and how Japanese aid has been spent.

Table 4.1 Major Recipients of Japanese Aid (% of total ODA)

1970–1		1980–1		1994–5	
Indonesia	22.9	Indonesia	11.2	China	9.8
Korea	19.8	Korea	6.9	Indonesia	8.3
India	10.2	Thailand	5.9	India	5.4
Pakistan	7.9	Bangladesh	5.0	Philippines	5.1
Philippines	4.4	Philippines	4.7	Thailand	4.5
Myanmar	3.5	Myanmar	4.1	Pakistan	2.4

Source: Adapted from *Development Cooperation, 1996 Report: Efforts and Policies of the Members of the Development Assistance Committee,* (Paris: Organisation for Economic Cooperation and Development, 1997), pp. A75–6.

Traditionally, the major recipients of Japanese aid have been in East and Southeast Asia. Although the recipients have changed and the total proportion of bilateral aid going to Asia has dropped in the past quarter-century, this regional pattern persists, as Table 4.1 indicates. Using Indonesia as an example, we can see the typical pattern of Japanese aid distribution and what the implications are of the regional focus on Asia. By the early 1990s, Japan's aid to Indonesia was approximately US$1.8 billion, roughly 55 per cent of which consisted of project loans for infrastructure development. Approximately US$110 million went for technical assistance and basic human needs, areas generally identified as more hospitable to grassroots development and women's priorities. Much of the remaining aid went to alleviate balance-of-payments problems. During this same period, Indonesia was the second-largest recipient in the world of Japanese direct foreign investment (the United States was the largest), and Japan was Indonesia's largest trading partner for both exports and imports (Kingston, 1993). Japanese economic interests have been complemented by geopolitical concerns: Indonesia borders on both the Straits of Malacca and Lombok, a shipping lifeline to Middle Eastern oil. Thus – at least until the economic collapse of Indonesia in 1998 – it was clear that 'promoting Indonesia's economic development [is] a means to strengthen Indonesian and regional political stability and to foster friendly relations between Japan and the region' (Kingston, 1993: 43). The Japanese presence in Indonesia also reflects the ambivalent legacy of Japan's occupation of the country from 1942 to 1945.

Another trend in Japanese ODA has been an increase in the proportion of aid that goes to multilateral organizations. From the mid-1980s to the mid-1990s Japanese grants and capital subscriptions to multilateral organizations increased almost ten-fold (OECD/DAC, *1996 Report*). Much of this money was earmarked for debt relief by multilateral development banks (MDBs) such as the World Bank and the Asian Development Bank. Heightened Japanese presence in these banks has been accompanied by more influence for Japan's ideas regarding the relevance of its own growth experience for the situation in developing countries. By the late 1980s Japanese representatives to the MDBs were articulating a preference for an 'Asian development model'. Central to this model is the assumption that government leadership in forging private–public sector cooperation (in contrast to the US emphasis on private initiatives) is a more successful approach to economic development. Thus, both in favouring Asian countries in its ODA policies and in touting an Asian development model based on its own experience, as well as that of countries such as Taiwan, Singapore and South Korea, Japan's ODA policy has been Asia-centric (Yasutomo, 1995; Rix, 1993).

Critics of the Japanese development model point to the negative consequences of rapid economic growth for average citizens, including environmental pollution, government–industry collusion and corruption, over-construction of megalopolises and the concomitant destruction of small towns and villages, as well as the desecration of nature. More specific criticisms target the linkage between the private interests that benefit from this growth strategy, such as the construction industry, and Japanese aid programmes. Although the Japanese government has pursued a policy of untying ODA since the 1980s, evidence indicates that Japanese firms still benefit heavily from aid programmes. Formal tying, or requirements that procurements of goods and services be limited to Japan or other specified countries, affect only about a third of bilateral ODA, but the web of relationships among Japan's engineering and construction firms and the government aid policy system means that Japanese companies are often the first beneficiaries of the country's economic assistance (Orr and Koppel, 1993; Rix, 1993; Ensign, 1992).

Taken together, what does the historical pattern of Japanese ODA imply for a feminist critique of the globalization of development and Japan's policy in particular? First, the long-term emphasis on project loans in contrast to other forms of aid has been justified historically by the government's assumption that the recipe for the country's spectacular economic growth after the Second World War can be followed by other countries. Second, this economic growth can best be achieved by investing in large-scale, capital-intensive projects, particularly those that contribute to building a country's infrastructure. Both philosophically and administratively, this approach makes it difficult to incorporate gender concerns into thinking and planning for development. Third, infrastructure loans have also served the interests of the industries closest to the government, such as construction. Finally, the historical concentration of much Japanese ODA in Asia reflects national self-interest more than the most pressing needs of poverty in the world. Asia, particularly Southeast Asia, has come to represent an economic sphere of interest for

Japan, both in terms of primary resource extraction and in terms of creating an export market for Japanese manufactured goods.

Aid, Gender and the Japanese Bureaucracy

Given the broad context of Japanese aid as just described, it is easy to understand why Japan was not in the forefront of those donors taking initiatives to make their aid policies more sensitive to gender concerns. More to the point is the question of why and how a mandate to address issues of women and development emerged at all. To answer this question, the discussion turns to the domestic ODA policy-setting process in Japan, paying particular attention to the role of the bureaucracy.

The aid bureaucracy

Bureaucracies play an important role in the formulation of aid policies in many countries, although in most industrial democracies other political actors (such as legislatures or cabinet officials) are generally more significant in setting the broad priorities for development assistance. Japan, which is well known for the prominent role of the national bureaucracy in policy formulation in general, presents a different picture. For more than a century, responsibility for initiating and directing Japan's economic development strategies has been lodged with the central bureaucracy, which historically enjoys a great deal of discretion both in the initiation and drafting of all important legislation and also in helping to pass bills in the legislature, in addition to the more typical activities of implementation.

Policy making on Japanese ODA is characterized both by this bureaucratic discretion and also by decentralization among the national ministries. The ODA budget is not a unified budget but an aggregate of items in the separate budget accounts of as many as eighteen ministries (Oda, 1992). Hence aid is exceedingly difficult to scrutinize, either for legislators or even for cabinet ministers. Although a question raised in parliamentary debate or in a legislative committee periodically influences ODA policy, and cabinet ministers (or the Prime Minister) may endeavour to initiate policies, most of the responsibility for defining priorities rests with the bureaucracy.

Bureaucratic decentralization means more than a budget difficult to oversee; it also contributes to bureaucratic leverage and inter-ministry competition because allocations for ODA, like other allocations, reflect the ebb and flow of power and status of particular government organizations (Orr, 1990; Rix, 1993). Because of its power in determining aid levels and allocations, the Ministry of Finance is especially important in the aid bureaucracy. The Ministry of International Trade and Development (MITI), a prime mover in Japan's foreign economic policy since the 1950s, influences much of the qualitative structure of aid. Generally, MITI has favoured aid that enhances Japan's overall commercial and financial standing in the global economic system. The Ministry of Foreign Affairs plays an overview role in the aid process and is primarily responsible for both bilateral and multilateral diplomatic relations.

Gender and bureaucracy

Where do women fit in this bureaucratic maze? Feminists have for some time maintained that bureaucracies are not gender-neutral. Kathleen Staudt, for example, argues that in fact bureaucracies are 'gendered': their origins, structures and norms reflect the fundamental gender constructs of the society in which they operate (Staudt, 1990; 1985). Where gender roles are clearly differentiated in society, the reproduction of these roles in government institutions means that we cannot assume that bureaucracies are gender-neutral. Although there have been dramatic changes over the past half-century in Japanese economic, political and social organizations, all of these are still, to a large degree, segregated by gender. The Japanese bureaucracy is a clear example of this pattern. Several distinctive attributes of this bureaucracy explain why it is male-dominated in both its personnel and its culture, and hence unlikely to be sympathetic to policy initiatives that benefit women.

With few exceptions, Japanese who aspire to a high-level bureaucratic career must graduate from an elite state university, such as the University of Tokyo or Kyoto. Access to elite higher education has traditionally depended on passing a competitive examination which requires, in turn, an elite secondary education. Women's access to secondary and post-secondary education was guaranteed as a result of post-Second World War Occupation reforms, but patterns of enrolment in colleges and universities continue to be skewed by gender. Enrolment in junior colleges, where the curriculum emphasizes home economics, humanities and education is feminized, whereas enrolment in universities is predominantly male. For a woman to have progressed in her career to a level of significant influence in a national ministry by the 1980s, she would have had to have been a student in a top-rated university by the 1960s. During this period, the proportion of female students enrolled at Tokyo and Kyoto universities averaged less than four per cent (Anderson, 1975: 376).

This elitism produces another characteristic of the Japanese bureaucracy, its overwhelming maleness both in staffing patterns and in office culture. Although an increasing number of female university graduates were recruited by the 1980s and 1990s, fewer than five per cent of

Japan's high-level bureaucrats – those who passed the A-level exam for the top tier of the civil service – were women in the late 1980s, the period when the ground was being laid for the development of a WID policy in Japan's aid programmes (Koh, 1989).

The male-dominated office culture has resulted not just from the overwhelming numbers of men, but also from bureaucratic norms that emphasize group cohesion and stability and penalize those who deviate from the dominant values and patterns of interaction (Jun and Muto, 1995; Miyamoto, 1994). Mirroring broader social patterns of interaction, the emphasis on the group reflects both vertical relationships of mutual obligation and support and horizontal relationships that mix values of obligation, harmony and cooperation with intense competition and peer-group pressure. Vertical relationships are, of course, intrinsic to bureaucracy, which by nature is hierarchical. They are also characteristic of Confucian relationships imported from China and systematized under Japanese rule from the seventeenth to the twentieth centuries. Confucian-based relationships, in turn, privilege status, education, seniority and, of course, (male) gender.

The vertical relationships that privilege men with elite university education and the horizontal relationships that pressure group members to identify first and foremost with their office-mates combine to create a male bureaucratic culture. Even high-level female bureaucrats typically find that male superiors expect them to serve tea or clean up the office (Koh, 1989). But most women are non-career and work at the bottom of the hierarchy. They are not socialized into the professional administrative culture, but they have the 'privilege' of going home at quitting time, unlike their male counterparts. The result is 'that after five o'clock the offices turn into a male-only quasi-homosexual society' (Miyamoto, 1994: 48).

In a now classic description of gender-based conflict in a bureaucratic setting, Susan Pharr described the revolt of female civil servants working for the city of Kyoto in the 1960s. A group of female civil servants, with support from several younger men, refused to serve tea to the other men in the office. The protest was designed to draw attention to working conditions that the women wanted to change, such as expectations that they clean the men's desks and ashtrays. These objective conditions, Pharr argues, defined the subordinate status long assigned to women in the broader society and carried over to the modern workplace. The symbolic importance of serving tea in Japanese culture epitomizes a traditional gender ideology based on the asymmetry of the sexes.

> By pouring tea for men, women express their deference and inferiority to them. At the same time, the symbolic act of serving tea is linked to woman's role as nurturer, a gender-based function that appears in most of women's social roles. In this sense, the tea-serving ritual accentuates the

differences in behavioural expectations for the two sexes while ceremonially acknowledging and approving their traditional functional justification. (Pharr, 1990: 67)

With this background, the discussion turns to the late 1980s and the circumstances that led to a WID policy in Japanese development assistance. ODA policies reflect bureaucratic initiatives, yet nowhere in the Japanese bureaucracy was there either a philosophy or a group of women well-placed to play a leading role in setting policies that would reorient Japanese aid, however modestly, in the direction of more responsiveness to gender issues. To what can one attribute the shift?

The Emergence of a WID Mandate in Japanese ODA

The period of the late 1980s to the early 1990s saw a convergence of events that created an opportunity for the adoption of policies designed to address women's concerns and needs in Japanese economic assistance. Underlying these events was the international climate of the 1980s, a decade in which women's issues in several arenas were given high international visibility. Considering Japan's sensitivity to international trends and pressures in the foreign policies of its Western, industrialized partners, the importance of this international climate should not be ignored.

The most notable trend for women during this period was the emergence of an international women's movement. As early as the late 1960s and early 1970s, women's groups in a number of countries pushed for the designation of an International Women's Year and Decade by the United Nations. These efforts led to the declaration of 1975 as International Women's Year and the sequence of UN world conferences on women in 1975 (Mexico City), 1980 (Copenhagen), and, at the end of the Decade, 1985 (Nairobi).

Paralleling and often overlapping the women's movements was the growing pressure to integrate women into economic development projects and, simultaneously, the demand by many development practitioners and scholars to redefine the meaning of development itself. The use of foreign aid funds to improve women's access to training and education was first proposed by the Swedish parliament in 1963 and, by 1968, Sweden had suggested to the UN a long-range programme for the advancement of women (Murphy, 1995). In the United States, an amendment to the 1973 Foreign Assistance Act required the US Agency for International Development (USAID) to promote programmes integrating women into the development process of countries receiving US development assistance. Very quickly, other OECD/DAC members (except Japan), as well as multilateral lending and development agencies, adopted similar mandates to address women's roles in development.

These mandates dovetailed with the growing concern during the same period that many of the early expectations about the benefits of development had been unfulfilled. One of the issues that received attention was the growing conflict between the prevailing economic development models that privileged capital-intensive investment, rapid industrialization and export-oriented agriculture, and the growing numbers of very poor people, often rural and female, in many countries that had been targeted for development. Increased poverty and uncertainty about the effectiveness of conventional development strategies constituted an 'exogenous shock', calling for international attention to the role of women in development processes (Kardem, 1991).

In Japan, the Ministry of Foreign Affairs established a task force on WID in 1989, but there is no evidence that it generated any proposals for a WID policy. As noted earlier, there were (and are) few women at managerial levels in any of the national ministries directly involved in foreign aid policy. Overall, in fact, the number of women working directly in the field of development assistance was small: the first WID specialist was hired by the Overseas Economic Cooperation Fund (OECF), which manages bilateral loans, in 1987; two were employed by the Japan International Cooperation Agency (JICA), which manages grants and technical assistance, in 1989 (Fusae Ichikawa, 1990). The largest numbers were and are in the Japan Overseas Cooperation Volunteers (JOCF), a government-sponsored technical cooperation programme staffed by young Japanese. Although there were some 900 female volunteers by 1990, they did not constitute an organized voice articulating a gender-sensitive development policy (Oda, 1992).

Moreover, although a small, autonomous Japanese feminist movement had emerged in the 1970s, it was neither organized nor powerful enough to serve as an effective pressure group, even had development aid matters been of special interest. Japan has a relatively long history of women's groups, but typically they have been created or coopted by the state as part of a broad strategy of social management. This pattern characterized women's organizations established after the Second World War, such as the national Housewives Association, as well as those predating the war (Garon, 1997). These groups emphasized women's domestic roles as mothers and wives; their activities were consistent with government priorities and rarely concerned international issues.

The most likely group to address gender issues in any dimension of Japanese foreign policy was the International Women's Year (IWY) Liaison Group, which represented some fifty women's organizations and was formed to monitor the implementation of IWY resolutions by the Japanese government. At a 1985 conference marking the end of the

International Women's Decade, representatives of the participating organizations passed a resolution calling on the government to increase assistance to women in developing countries, but not until *after* the formal adoption of the government's WID policy did members of the Liaison Group meet directly with high-level foreign ministry officials in the 1990s to press their positions on ODA.

Thus Japan is a case in which one needs to look not just outside the government but outside the country to determine the source of the pressures leading to the articulation of gender issues in development assistance. A primary impetus for formulating a WID agenda was the Development Assistance Committee of the OECD.[3] The OECD/DAC adopted WID Guiding Principles in 1983, stating that 'DAC Members are prepared to make explicit their policies on women in development as well as to elaborate and implement appropriate procedures or specific and reviewable plans of action.' The Principles called on DAC members to furnish information on action taken on WID matters in the yearly memorandum on ODA that they present for DAC review (OECD/DAC, *1984 Report*).

In 1989, Japan was elected a member of the Bureau of the Expert Group on Women in Development of the DAC. Also in 1989, the Expert Group adopted a revised version of WID Guiding Principles, urging members to operationalize WID in their development assistance. Then, in the autumn of 1989, an opposition Dietwoman in the upper house of the legislature, the House of Councillors, asked during a floor debate what progress had been made in implementing the DAC mandate. Her question was a political red flag in a year that was notable for the attention garnered by women and women's issues in Japan. For the development of the WID mandate, this domestic political climate within which the legislator asked her question was significant.

During the 1970s and 1980s the Japanese government, despite its inaction on women and development issues, had taken several steps to bring Japan into line with policies recommended by international organizations, especially those connected with the 1975 and 1985 UN conferences on women. For example, an Office for Women's Affairs was created under the Prime Minister's Office; reform of the civil code was undertaken to improve women's legal status; the Diet ratified the Convention on the Elimination of All Forms of Discrimination against Women and also passed an Equal Employment Opportunity bill. Although these did not revolutionize the structures of gender discrimination, they did indicate an evolving national mood.

This evolution was symbolized in the 1989 election for the upper house of the legislature, the House of Councillors. In this election, 22 women (the largest number in history) were elected, for a total of 13 per cent in the House. (Women constituted less than two per cent of the lower House of Representatives, which had been elected earlier.) Although development assistance was not an issue in the election, gender was. The Socialist Party, which made a good showing, was headed by Takako Doi, the first woman to lead any Japanese political party; both by example and by words, she urged more women to become involved in politics. Her campaign was fuelled by the prime minister's involvement in a sex scandal and by the ruling party's imposition of a consumption tax that was especially unpopular with women.

This election turned out to be an anomaly, as the Socialist Party subsequently crumbled and the electoral gains made by women levelled out. The 1989 election nonetheless was a benchmark in the slow increase of women's presence in a variety of prominent public offices, such as mayor, prefectural vice-governor and high court justice, as well as local and regional elected assemblies. Despite the modest numbers, and the recognition that many of the women in public office may be at best conservative feminists, the significance of the trend should not be discounted: it was an elected legislator who, by the pressure generated through her public question, served as a catalyst for the government's action on WID.

The first step the government took was to establish an *ad hoc* Study Group on Development Assistance for Women in Development under the auspices of the President of JICA in 1990. Advisory councils, study groups and research committees attached to government agencies are an important part of Japan's bureaucratic decision-making system. At any given time there may be 200 of these groups, whose memberships typically combine representatives from public and private organizations. Following this pattern, the eight-member Group included four academics and a representative from OECF, and was chaired by Japan's first female ambassador (then retired). The Group, assisted by a JICA task force, met seven times (including a public meeting for comment) and carried out site visits to JICA projects in Asia, Africa and Oceania. In February 1991 the Study Group issued the first comprehensive report in Japan on WID, along with its policy recommendations. Stating that Japan 'has been undeniably slow to come to grips with the issue in comparison to governments of other industrialized countries', the Study Group called on the Japanese government to identify basic policies and strategies for WID and to specify which areas would be given priority. The Group suggested that emphasis be placed on promoting women's economic participation, education, health, and roles in environmental management and protection (JICA, 1991).

Although the purpose and duration of the Study Group were restricted, it played an important role in legitimizing the government's commitment to a WID policy, and its discussions and recommendations constituted a turning point in the development of a Japanese WID agenda. Based on the

Group's recommendations, JICA established the Environment, WID and Other Global Issues Division, and the OECF issued guidelines on WID in 1991. In 1992, the government's ODA Charter committed Japan to pay attention to the integration of women as participants and beneficiaries of development. In 1993, the OECF established a section in charge of WID, and JICA put into operation a set of guidelines for integrating WID considerations into JICA projects. Since 1994, a budget for the dispatch of WID experts at the project planning stages has been approved annually.

Assessing Japan's WID Mandate

It is too soon to judge the long-term implications of a policy in effect for less than a decade, although there is abundant evidence, both anecdotal and statistical, that generally women's lives in the countries receiving Japanese ODA have not been revolutionized any more than they have been in countries receiving aid from donors with much longer histories of WID policies and guidelines. The non-transformative nature of WID mandates, including Japan's, reflects a combination of factors: the 'add women and stir' approach that characterizes the mandates; implementation problems; the underlying conceptualization of what development means and how best to achieve it; gender values among both donors and recipients that resist fundamental reallocation of money or power to the benefit of women (coupled with some recognition that reconceptualizing development would do just this); a global political economy that privileges economic transactions dominated by large 'players' over small ones, whether rural farms or urban businesses; and the ultimate reality that development assistance reflects the *national* priorities, however indirectly, of the donor. These interests may be overtly strategic, or they may be more subtly and indirectly commercial. Japanese ODA offers illustrations of both motivations, as suggested earlier.

This discouraging assessment must be tempered by two important points. One is the simple recognition that history shows few instances anywhere of progressive measures helping women or other disadvantaged groups in a short period of time. But change obviously does happen, and the Japanese case illustrates the importance of even small numbers of women in a position to influence policy as well as the more diffuse significance of the growth of feminist movements in the 1970s and 1980s. The ideal may be a convergence of grassroots, transnational feminist pressure with well-placed, domestic progressive elites (both male and female).

The second point, therefore, is to ask what practical signs there are that the Japanese WID mandate (and by extension other such mandates) has the power to bring progressive change to the development process. This chapter closes with some observations about this potential.

Little Progress, Small Niches

As noted at the outset of this chapter, the adoption of a WID mandate in Japanese foreign aid is part of an international trend to make both bilateral and multilateral development assistance more gender-sensitive. The ultimate success of this effort, however, depends on fundamental changes in the complexion of aid bureaucracies, as well as in the way in which development is conceptualized. Changes in both areas are occurring in Japan, but only incrementally. After several years of WID policies, for example, one evaluation pointed to the implications for women of assumptions that still dominated Japanese approaches to ODA in the 1990s: (1) the emphasis on growth-oriented development has not altered the theory that the trickle-down effect automatically benefits the poor; (2) analysis of gender roles, including the intra-household distribution of resources, has not been part of the initial conceptualizing and planning processes; and (3) development management of projects emphasizes economic efficiency and cost effectiveness and still operates on the premise that it is primarily men who engage in productive activities (Aoki, 1996). As a consequence of these embedded assumptions, WID projects have tended to emphasize fields such as nutrition and health, despite some important exceptions.

Moreover, one cannot assume that there will be no reversal of the commitment to WID that does exist in Japan's bureaucracy. Shifts in problem definition are notorious in foreign aid, and changing bureaucratic personnel and culture is a slow process. In 1997, for example, the president of JICA was considering abolishing the Environment, WID and Other Global Issues Division.[4] The plan was forestalled by a small network of women with connections to the president. Through this network, the need for the Division and the importance of the WID mandate was explained, and the organizational change was shelved.

The emergence of an 'old-girl network' can be traced to the Study Group on Development Assistance for Women in Development discussed above. Elite networking is a relatively new phenomenon, but one that holds out promise for gradually modifying Japan's bureaucratic culture at the top, while the slow influx of female recruits helps transform the middle administrative ranks. At the same time, the absence of a strong feminist movement outside the government – one well placed and committed to maintaining pressure on politicians and bureaucrats dealing with issues of development – is less promising. As other studies have suggested, long-term, fundamental policy changes are most likely to occur in capitalist democracies when changes in state bureaucracies and the conventional political arena (including political parties) are pushed, monitored and reinforced by autonomous feminist movements (Waylen, 1996). In the absence of this combination, one must conclude that WID is a small niche in Japanese ODA, and its long-term impact is likely to be marginal, particularly in view of the domestic and international contexts within which that ODA is organized and distributed.

Notes

1. The DAC promotes and coordinates its members' ODA. On the volume of Japanese ODA, see the OECD/DAC annual reports, for example: *Development Co-operation: Efforts and Policies of the Members of the Development Assistance Committee; 1997 Report* (Paris: OECD, 1998). [Hereafter cited as OECD/DAC, *Report.*]
2. There is a substantial literature that explains the history and rationale of Japanese ODA. See, for example, Islam, 1991; Koppel and Orr, 1993; Orr, 1990; Rix, 1980 and 1993; and Yasutomo, 1986 and 1995. None of these addresses any gender issues in aid policy making or implementing.
3. This is my conclusion based on interviews in Japan in 1991 and 1993. See also Oda, 1992: 87–9; and Kurata, 1996: 18–19.
4. As reported to me by a technical expert working for JICA, the plan was forstalled when she contacted a prominent academic in the women's movement who then contacted a well-known (female) intellectual, a friend of JICA's president. Through this network, the need for the Division was explained.

5 • What I Know about Gender and Development

Wu Qing

Development

From my perspective, development means self-improvement, bringing one's talents or a creation into reality, causing one's personality to unfold or evolve gradually or become more mature regardless of gender, race or class. We are all human beings before we are women or men. Therefore, men and women should be treated equally – not just in theory, but in practice. Development also means growth, expansion, making something stronger, more effective or more available to everybody. It also means to build up something that does not exist. Finally it means bringing the potential of each person into full play. This will not only benefit an individual, but the whole society and the whole world as well.

I used to think that development always meant expansion, progress, improvement and growth. Yet after being a consultant on Women in Development (WID) for the Canadian International Development Agency (CIDA) for many years, and through personal experience and reading the literature on development, I came to know that development does *not* always mean progress, improvement and growth, or at least not the kind of progress and growth thought about by people who have a gender equity perspective. When the needs, demands and interests of half of the world's population are neglected, ignored and forgotten, when development policies are made without hearing the voices of women and when women are not included as agents and partners participating in the whole process of development, how can those development policies be complete? We know that the World Bank issues its *Social Indicators of Development* annually. But it does not include the work women do at home, and the farm work women do in the fields, in *per capita* growth. In contrast, the growth rate definitely includes the gains of a new factory when it goes into production. More often than not, the majority of the new recruits in the factory are men as they are better educated with more marketable skills and fewer or no family responsibilities. The main reason is that there is gender discrimination. Besides, the traditional idea that 'women's place is in the home', while men's domain is the public world, still prevails not just in China but in many parts of the world, and in many international institutions. Although women made up 44.96 per cent of the labour force in 1990 in China (Zhang Ping, 1995: 1), they were underrepresented politically and socially. Most of them are doing work that is the extension of housework. They are teachers in day care centres, kindergartens, grade schools and high schools; medical workers in clinics in villages and townships; nurses in hospitals; clerical workers in governmental institutions. They are street cleaners, saleswomen, waitresses, cooks, seamstresses and so on. They are in dead-end jobs, with low pay and little prospect of promotion or advancement.

Background

China had a planned economy from 1949 to 1978, in which all economic activities were strictly controlled by the central government. It was not until the policy of reform and opening up started at the end of 1978 that the Communist Party of China shifted its emphasis from class struggle to economic development, and its development policies and practices became more integrated with Western and international approaches to development.

Since 1979, China has introduced several economic reforms aimed at increasing the speed of development and changing the structure of the economy. In 1982, the most important one was that collective land was redistributed according to a new Household Responsibility System, with each household allocated a certain amount. The ultimate ownership remains the same – the state owns the land – but its immediate use and management is in the hands of households. Thus a new set of agricultural production relations has been established. Through the household contract system, the household now has decision-making power in production and land management. With the expansion of rural markets (commodity production replacing domestic sidelines) and the diversification of the economy, agricultural output has increased substantially.

Under the policies for increasing rural labour productivity, a small proportion of the rural population engages in food production, using more efficient methods. At the same time, opportunities for alternative forms of employment have greatly expanded. As a result, the social relations of labour are being reorganized. At present, 50–80 per cent of rural farm work is done by women. Rural women are comparatively disadvantaged in this context in that the economic reform favours those with higher educational or technical levels, who are more adaptable to social changes, and who are in areas where there are more resources; rural women generally have lower educational levels and are often less mobile than men, especially after marriage.

In urban areas, factories and enterprises now have more autonomy in production, management and recruitment. From 1949 to 1978, the government guaranteed jobs for urban people in China, in a system known as the 'Iron Rice Bowl' or guaranteed income based on universal job assignment. With the competitive labour market emerging, however, women are at a disadvantage. Under the Responsibility System being applied in the cities, employers are concerned about losses incurred by women's requirements for maternity leave and absences related to child care and care for the old. These benefits are mandated by law, but must be paid for by individual enterprises. Many factories are cutting back on non-productive expenditures, such as day-care centres, kindergartens and child-care facilities. The replacement of regular workers by contract workers permits all workers, and especially female workers, to be fired or not hired. In addition, now workers are paid according to quantity and quality of work, and often women (with a less favourable educational and technical background) lack the competitive market skills to benefit from this wage structure.

Since the founding of the Communist Party of China in 1921 the interests of women and the interests of the revolution have been presented as congruent. The idea is and always has been that whatever is good for China is good for the Chinese people – both men and women. If men can benefit from a policy or a project, women will definitely and automatically benefit from it. In addition, there were some literacy projects for women in rural areas and minority areas in the late 1940s and early 1950s. In the early 1950s, the central government encouraged the masses of rural women to participate in agricultural production. Within three years over 60 per cent of women aged from 16 to 61 were mobilized to work in the fields (Liu, 1953: 14). But the work they did required very little skill. In some areas training workshops for women were offered. They were taught how to transplant rice seedlings, how to use a plough and so on. As in the past, the division of labour between men and women was quite clear. Men worked in the fields and women ran the home, took care of the young and the old, and went in for sideline production (such as raising chickens, pigs and rabbits). Between 1949 and 1952, about 3.9 million women participated in all kinds of water conservation projects (General Office of the Central Committee of the Communist Party, 1956: 67). To help make their lives easier, many day care centres were set up in some parts of the country (Liu, 1953: 17). In 1958 alone, 5.4 million women in rural areas helped with the building of a network of waterways. As a result, 34,700 ditches, ponds and reservoirs were built (*Women of China*, first issue, 1959). The name of each project began with the symbolic date 8 March to remind people that they were built by women. In the late 1950s, when people were called upon to build furnaces and smelt iron, many women's teams were formed. Members of teams worked together and lived together. They tried to compete with the men to see who could contribute more to the nation. These were projects run by women, not for the benefit of women but for the benefit of all people, men and women. They were *not* WID projects, let alone gender projects.

Even when women and men were doing the same kind of work, requiring the same performance and achieving the same economic results, women always earned less than men. The idea was that men and women are different not only in physical strength but also in education, intelligence and wisdom. It was not until the late 1980s and early 1990s, when some international organizations started to set up their offices in China and to support economic development projects in rural China involving women, that the Chinese government commissioned research and feasibility studies to find out about women's needs. But any work which is related to women in China is normally done by the All China Women's Federation (ACWF). The mandate of the ACWF is to improve the situation of women within the general guidelines set by the Communist Party. Yet it is given few technical and financial resources with which to do its work. Very often it has to raise its own funding to start projects for women. Since 1989 the ACWF has started a campaign – 'The Two Studies and Two Competitions' – among rural women throughout China. The 'Two Studies' are to learn how to read and write, and to learn at least two technical skills to get rid of poverty. The 'Two Competitions' are to see who achieves more and who makes greater contributions to the community and society. The ACWF runs literacy classes, provides scientific and technical training programmes for women, and has also initiated a special educational scholarship for girls, the Spring Bud Programme. The goal of the programme is to try to offer as many scholarships as possible to girls in areas of economic scarcity, as girls are often denied the opportunity to go to school (if their families can only afford to send one child to school, it is usually a boy). But I think all of these programmes and projects lack the gender dimension. It is vital to have a systematic and long-term strategy to lobby and sensitize the decision makers at each level of the government to gender issues, to organize follow-up activities and make sure that there is a mechanism as well as a strategy in place to ensure the improvement of the socio-political and economic situation of women. The other group of people needing to be sensitized is in the media sector. WID and GAD workshops should be provided for them as they reach millions upon millions of people every day.

My Involvement

My involvement with CIDA's development strategy in China started in May 1989, when CIDA was reviewing its experience with regard to WID in the China programme: its aim was to improve effectiveness and efficiency, and develop a more coherent WID strategy. As part of its deconcentration strategy, it also planned to involve local experts more in the development, monitoring and evaluation of its programmes. When the WID Representative at the Canadian Embassy in China heard that a group of Chinese women professors at Beijing Foreign Studies University had developed a professional interest in the role and status of women in China, I was approached and asked whether a WID coordinating group could be formed to assist with project monitoring, project identification missions, feasibility studies, evaluations, research and networking. A group of four was formed and I was elected group leader. We were to work for CIDA on a project basis, while continuing our teaching work.

The Gender Approach

I was lucky enough to get involved first in reviewing CIDA's WID strategy for China, which offered a gender perspective on the role of women. It also stimulated me to compare what I knew about the situation of women in China with what I had read about women in the US and Canada. This project gradually helped to raise my gender awareness and enabled me to have a better and deeper understanding of women's issues in China.

The objective of CIDA's strategy is to better the condition of Chinese women and provide an equitable role for their participation in the development process. The future of China cannot be separated from its development efforts. In recognition of that fundamental notion, and as CIDA's goal is to achieve sustainable development, the development strategy for the China programme places strategic importance on the idea that women must preserve – and enhance – their place in the productive economy so that they will have the power to go forward into an equitable future. This idea coincides with the view in China that the right of women to full equality is largely a matter of women's economic independence. Women's equality is not only a legal matter; it also entails a comprehensive attainment of equality in all respects, and most particularly in access to work and to education.

The second project I was involved in was to develop an inventory of women specialists in China with expertise on WID issues. This project enabled me to renew ties with those who had established contact with me in (and since) 1985. This project has grown into an NGO which is now called the Chinese Women's Health Network, with me as the president. Some members of the group have translated *The New Our Bodies, Ourselves* (Phillips and Rakusen, 1989) and it was released in May, 1998. The group plans to put out two more books for Chinese readers: one for women and the other for men.

The work of a WID consultant for CIDA provides me with opportunities to visit project sites in different parts of China where I meet women from different ethnic groups. China, so large in size and population, is equally diverse in culture, history, social values, economy, religion, ethnicity, income, stages in development, and even in issues. I feel there is a continuing need to learn more about issues and problems and to think of ways to solve them. Generalization is dangerous. Wherever I go, I always try to find out facts from the local people: officials, high and low; ordinary people, women and men, old and young. I ask questions, observe activities and listen to people before I arrive at conclusions.

Local Projects

My first project was to analyse and evaluate how women had benefited from the existing CIDA project at the Harbin Cattle Breeding Station in Heilongjiang, and to present recommendations. The women considered in my study were not only those involved in the project itself but also women peasants who raised cows that used imported Canadian semen. The WID component was not part of the feasibility studies, nor part of the project design. It was, in fact, added to the evaluation at the end of the first phase of the project. I was to find out how women had benefited from the project, without any WID input, in the first five years. The aim was to provide women with more opportunities to be agents as well as beneficiaries in the project. When I found that there were very few women at top management level, I was told that that was the 'tradition'. People, including some women, were shocked when I said that women's voices should be heard and that representation of women was vital to making the programme a success. From this first site visit I learned several things.

First I learned that gender awareness never comes naturally. It will take years to change people's attitude and ideas. But I think the most important thing, before a project is started, is to find those men and women who are gender-sensitive and to get them involved from the very beginning. If not, the staff have to go through gender-sensitivity training workshops to acquire the perspective needed if the project is to include and benefit every single person. These gender-sensitive people will then conduct a thorough and down-to-earth study on the problems and issues of local people. A gender breakdown of facts and figures will show the strong gender bias in the area. The analyses of the situation have to be accurate and to the point. The findings are to be shared with the women and men in the location at gender workshops for decision makers as well as for local women activists. These workshops are vital, especially for women on the staff as they will start to think with a gender perspective and gradually to look at problems and issues from a new angle – discovering in the process some of the answers to their frustrations in their work, for they themselves face covert discrimination every day. Through these gender-sensitivity workshops they get to know that with long-term effort, and if they are in close touch with women and know the needs and demands of their sisters, and work with them and for them, they can help change the socio-political and economic status of women in general. Some of them feel that all of a sudden their horizon is broadened and that gradually their confidence begins to grow.

The second thing I learned is that to help people – both men and women – understand what WID is and why it is important, it is necessary to work out a strategy to publicize this idea. One should concentrate first on women at mid-management level, because usually there are very few women at the top levels. When we do gender awareness training it is women with whom we first form alliances. When they realize what WID means and the importance of it, it is much easier to find out how to sensitize the men at the top, as the women will suggest who to approach first and how to go about it best. Once that is achieved, it is much easier to work among people in the targeted institution.

Donor countries very often think about their own impact and interests first, and the interests of the recipient countries second. For example, if the second phase of the project had been launched as planned, the Harbin Cattle Breeding Station would have received the necessary WID training during the second five-year programme, which would have enabled the Station to be truly self-reliant technically and economically. The Station would have played a more important role in the production of quality milk, raising better cattle and providing better support to peasants in the area when they did extension projects. But when inquiries were made to find out whether there would be a second phase, the answer was no: the Canadian government had already had enough impact in Harbin, with two streets and several shops bearing the names of some famous Canadians.

My second project was to carry out a WID evaluation mission in Huining, Gansu Province, investigating WID issues and making recommendations. I think that the Huining mission has been of great benefit to my awareness. It made me more sensitive, observant and careful in finding out facts that are closely related to people's livelihoods and their human rights, especially women's right and issues. For example, the mission group visited several carpet factories employing 2,000 girls aged between sixteen and the mid-twenties in Huining county.

These women had received the benefit of several years of semi-independent living, during which they became more self-reliant and confident, and acquired new values and new ideas. But, on marriage, this investment seemed to be wasted since they were unable to continue their carpet work in their villages unless they had enough funding to start their own cottage industry. Besides, they had no resources available to them with which they could capitalize on their new confidence, and no other marketable skills with which to earn an income.

After living away from home in a small town or township, their expectations for themselves personally, especially for potential marriage partners and for their living standards, were raised. On marriage these aspirations might remain unfulfilled, since they generally would move back to villages and probably into semi-arranged marriages.

In one carpet factory there were altogether 287 people but only 12 men. The men held all the management and technical positions: manager, deputy manager, heads of all the workshops, technicians on each shift. There was only one woman representative, and her sole job was to issue toilet paper, sanitary napkins and gloves. When I went around to see the facilities used by the workers, I counted the latrines and found that there were ten. Interestingly enough, this time there was 'equal' distribution: five for men and five for women, or 2.4 men sharing one 'male' latrine while 55 women shared the 'female' equivalent. But women have periods, which last three to five days, or a week or two, and sometimes even longer. What a contrast! What equality! This really shocked me. Women were definitely underrepresented politically, technically and socially: small wonder, the arrangement of the latrines.

Since then, whenever I visit a school, a factory, a hospital or a public building, I always check the facilities – dormitories, canteens, latrines, public baths, day care centres, libraries, roads, and so on. But on top of that, I always try to get gender disaggregated data. Very often there are none – but asking for them, I think, is in itself the first lesson of gender analysis. The figures given often show how women are underrepresented in the institution. People, both women and men, are shocked by the numbers as they seldom think about them in terms of gender.

I always enjoy working with my Canadian counterparts, women with a gender-inclusive perspective. I don't feel the cultural differences. After exchanging and sharing some information about women's status in China or Canada, we at once form an alliance. There are more similarities than differences between women in China and Canada in terms of women's political, social and economic status, their demands and needs, and the problems and issues they are facing, as they are all second-class citizens in everyday life. I also feel that they are in many ways my friends as well as my mentors, as their experiences, their perspectives, their devotion and their initiatives have helped me gradually to broaden my outlook and improve my work. Without their support and help, I would not have accomplished what I have done. Once this understanding and friendship are established, we set about working for a common goal, trying to work out a long-term and sustainable strategy, organizing gender equity working groups at project sites, designing gender equity working plans with both men and women, getting enough funding to support the gender side of the project, and making sure that there is a permanent WID specialist on the project. This is not easy as we have to learn to sensitize the men and women involved, lobby the decision makers (mostly men), and work with men from both countries. This feminist approach and sisterhood are vital to the success of these projects.

Differences between WID and GAD

My understanding of WID and GAD deepens every time I do a project. It is always a learning experience for me. I have gradually got to know that WID is limited to improving the conditions of women in the projects financially supported by CIDA, which are often short-term. Only a few targeted women can benefit, and those who benefit from the project are excluded from the development process. In my view, the development *process* is more important than the benefits women get. They learn to play the role of an equal partner and become more self-reliant and independent in the process. If women are not included at the very beginning and if they are not trained, the strong traditions will reassert themselves when the proactive project is over and there is no more money to support it. WID is a women's project to increase their productivity, their income, their ability to look after the household: sometimes, in one word, to increase the load of the already heavily burdened women.

WID is an approach that views women as the problem, the focus, and tries to integrate them into the existing development process. This integration itself will help the projects to develop more efficiently and effectively, because women's initiatives will be brought into fuller play. But men, the usual decision makers, often think that women, whether their efforts are brought into play or not, will surely and automatically benefit from a project, if men will. Sometimes I feel that even those men (both Chinese and Canadian) who are involved in CIDA's China programme often look at gender specialists with a frown, meaning: Why are you here? This is a project which requires high technology. What can you do here? Sometimes, some Canadian specialists don't even bother to look at you straight in the face, when they talk to you. That is why in my WID Third Mission Report (October 1994) for the Gansu Forest Tree Nursery Project, I wrote the following:

> CIDA's goal to enhance the role and participation of women as agents and beneficiaries of its cooperation programs in forestry is very, very difficult to reach in the Gansu Forest Tree Nursery Project. WID is very often thought of as a burden, something that is an addition or that can be done without, not just by the Executing Agency or the Chinese side, but sometimes by CIDA as well. From my recent findings, I feel definitely that WID is not an integral part of the project nor an essential part of different group missions. ... The Assessment and Recommendation Report of March 1994 has 25 pages. Regrettably, there is not a single line on WID in the targeted mission report. (Wu, 1994: 3–4)

GAD aims to improve women's position. It is long-term, requiring strategic thinking and down-to-earth analysis. I think it is the only approach to development so far that is healthy and brings human potential into full play – for both women and men. The most important thing is to change the unequal relations that have existed between men and women for thousands of years, and that have prevented equitable development and women's full participation. Only when women and men are equal partners and equal decision makers can development become sustainable, people-centred and people-friendly. During the GAD process women are empowered and the unequal relations between the two sexes are transformed. To reach the goal, strategies should be worked out to address the practical needs of both women and men.

Improvement and Creativity

I would like to state some of my principles here.

First, we are human beings; we are not animals. Therefore, we can think for ourselves. We go to school to learn to think rationally, to collect facts thoroughly and analyse them carefully, to identity issues and problems, and to try to find solutions. Being human beings, we should be creative, resourceful and not afraid of making mistakes and facing crises. The phrase 'crisis' in Chinese is *weiji*, which is formed of the first character of each of two words, 'danger' and 'opportunity'. They are the two sides of a coin. It means that when we face crises, there are also opportunities. It means that we can take advantage of a bad situation and make it turn around to serve our own purposes. Everything has two sides. It really depends upon how we look at crises, how much confidence we have in ourselves and how well we can cope with them. Since we are social beings, we do not just live for ourselves. We should do our bit to help make the world a better place to live.

We are human beings first, women second. We should not be constrained by stereotyped gender roles, which expect women to be beautiful, gentle, dependent, kind and supportive; good wives, loving mothers, and fine homemakers, even though they also have jobs. The husband is the breadwinner and decision maker at home. But I think the relationship between a husband and a wife should be like that of *yin* and *yang*. According to the Chinese, when *yin* and *yang* are balanced, a person is healthy physically. If not, a person falls ill. If in a family or a society, men and women can share power and treat each other equally, then society will be harmonious and stable. There will be lasting peace the world over.

Being a WID consultant, I know that the length of time of a project is limited and that my chances of visiting a project site depend on how serious the executing agency is about WID, because it involves a budget earmarked for it. I know that if the concepts of WID and GAD are to stay and not leave when I leave, a WID group has to be formed locally to act as a watchdog to help supervise WID work, to sensitize people to women's issues and to continue when the project is over. The concepts should not just stay in the minds of people involved in the project, but they should be part of the community. In this way the general status of women in China can be changed gradually. Whenever I am at a project site, I always try to talk to as many people or groups of people as possible about sex and gender, WID and GAD, self-reliance and participation, so as to raise their gender awareness, sense of citizenship and responsibility, sense of law and supervision, and so on. I think people with this kind of awareness form the basis on which a sustainable development project is built. If invited, I go to talk to women working in local government, the Women's Federation, and so on. I also try to bring women from as many related institutions as possible together, like women from the local Party Committee, the government, the Women's Federation, the Trade Union, and the Youth League, to form a network so that they can make use of the existing resources and reach out to untapped sources. There is the saying, 'Two heads are better than one'. For example, I talked to over 100 women from different sectors of Longnan Prefecture twice to sensitize them to women's issues and to build up their confidence. When I was walking down the street, I was often stopped by women who would come up and tell me how much they had changed after they heard my lectures.

As my trips are usually short, I have to be able to talk quickly to as many women as possible and identify those who already have some gender awareness so that I can work out a strategy with them. Then I also have to make the time to talk in depth with women, very often individually, like peeling onions, one layer after another, to get to the core. Once they trust me and agree with what I say and how I look at things, we become good friends. They start to tell me everything about themselves, even their private affairs, as they want to get advice from me. Personally I feel that, being a woman while doing projects, I work with my heart and passion, and try to reach out to as many women as possible. I am not working for a specific project, but for the community in general. That is why I also try to reach out to as many institutions as possible to tell people about CIDA's WID policy.

For example, in 1990, when the planning of Phase III of China Enterprise Management Training Centre (CMTCC) at Chengdu was under way, I was asked by the executing agency, the Association of Canadian Community Colleges (ACCC), to do a WID study and make recommendations. I found that most women have been socialized and institutionalized to believe that they are inferior to men, that they should depend on their men, and that they should be satisfied to play their traditional gender role both at home and outside the home. When they face discrimination, they do not know that it is sex discrimination against women in general. Very often they think it is an individual case. They do not have a strong sense of group identity. Many people, including women themselves, are still emphasizing the biological difference between men and women. Many women think that they are inferior to men in many ways. They are not good at numbers. They lack logical thinking and originality. They are afraid to make decisions. I know it takes time for people to change their attitudes as well as their ways of thinking. Yet, with some help, it is not too difficult for women to gain confidence through practical training. Several gender workshops were held in Chengdu to raise the awareness of women. Then a WID group was set up with a lot of support from the new Canadian project officer. She came to the meetings, talked about Canadian women and their gradual changes, and provided economic help to reach out to more women involved in the extension programmes. This group is still functioning, getting funding from the Global Fund for Women to sensitize women of different ethnic groups in poverty-stricken areas and also to teach them technical skills so as to bring in more income.

To sum up, to improve the present development strategy, the first thing we need is consciousness raising. If people, the decision makers, do not have gender awareness, women will always be treated as second-class citizens. Therefore, there will be double standards, there will be separate projects. But we know that *separate can never be equal*. It is vital to sensitize people in the media sector, who have great influence over the general public. It is vital to sensitize women to help them gain self-esteem and confidence, so that they will try to better themselves economically, socially and politically. Then they will definitely become first active participants, then agents and partners of projects.

The second thing is to develop policies that are woman-friendly, making sure that there should be a gradual increase of women in the decision-making process. At the same time, there should be workshops to train women and to help them raise their skills in management at each level. Gender-sensitivity workshops should be offered to men on project staff. It is vital to convince them that to include a gender perspective in doing and planning every project and programme in future should be the norm in China.

To truly realize this goal, a third condition is important – a budget to support it. There has to be enough funding to make sure that there are GAD specialists available to endorse and supervise proactive, long-term gender strategies and programmes.

PART II
Staying Feminist in Development

6 • Research and Intervention: Insights from Feminist Health Action in Western India[1]

Renu Khanna

When I first started working on women's issues, especially women's health issues, nearly ten years ago, I was often perplexed by the insistence of my feminist friends on discussing issues of sexuality. It was almost as if, in order to prove one's radicalism as a feminist, one constantly had to discuss ways of expressing sexuality, sexual preferences, masturbation, orgasm and the like.

A part of me conceded that sexuality was an important aspect of the human experience, and that women had been socialized over generations to stifle and deny their sexuality. Yet I felt that there were many more urgent and pressing issues that women, especially in developing countries, needed to discuss and organize themselves around. The issues of livelihood, education, child care, housing, and so on were much more basic to decent and dignified living, in my opinion, than sexuality. It was only when I started grappling with the struggles of service provision for woman-centred health that I began to see the direct relationship of issues of sexuality to women's gynaecological morbidity and other aspects of their emotional and physical health.

In 1988, when we started the Women's Health Programme at SARTHI,[2] our aim was to take care of the common gynaecological problems of local women. From 1990, over a period of three years, we trained a few local women to work as 'barefoot gynaecologists'. They gradually began identifying and diagnosing women's complaints and treating them with locally available, and validated, herbal remedies. During the first two years' work with the ten barefoot gynaecologists, we found that the majority of the complaints that they had treated were 'white discharge', that is, excessive vaginal discharge. We also discovered that, in many of the cases, white discharge was the result of an infection that could have been transmitted by the partner. During history taking, the barefoot gynaecologists found that the husbands also had symptoms indicative of an infection and that, when they treated both the woman and her partner, the woman's symptoms gradually disappeared. We realized that women's health had to do with men too. Any programme that was aimed at reducing morbidity in women had to address itself to men and to issues of sexuality and sexual relationships.

Our understanding, through SARTHI's work, was muted but it was brought into a sharper focus through discussions with a gynaecologist friend.[3] She narrated several incidents that revealed the central place of sexuality in a women's health programme. In her gynaecological practice, she encountered women who had absolutely no power to say 'no' to their partners. Women were literally objects to be (ab)used to satisfy their partners' sexual appetites. There were other women, on the other hand, who had no avenues to express their own sexual desires, or to fulfil their desires in a safe way. We have learnt since, both from our experience and the contemporary discourse on sexuality within the context of reproductive health and HIV/AIDS, that the concept of sexuality is directly related to gender identities and how masculinity and femininity are constructed in specific cultural contexts. While the two examples cited above are extreme examples, women do behave in complex ways to negotiate sexual relationships and to subvert gender power relations. So whether we are talking about a rural situation or an urban situation, about chronic infections or acute infections, about preventive care or curative care, about a village level health care provider or a fully fledged medical professional, we have to give sexuality and sexual issues an important place in women's health.

Apart from these direct ways in which women's health and sexuality are related, discussions of sexuality assume an importance within the context of empowerment and its effect on women's health. Women's status is influenced by public norms and values which influence the expected and acceptable behaviour, and roles and relationships of women. Each woman internalizes these public images and forms her own self-image from them. The self-image of the rural women involved in the SARTHI project was mostly one of extreme shyness, obedience to men and elders, with little confidence in their own ability to direct their own situation, so a key aspect of our work was to help women improve their self-perception and increase their self-confidence and sense of control. In our experience, reclaiming our relationship to our body by reflecting on and sharing our bodies' histories in self-help groups, and understanding its structure and its processes, is one of the important paths to an enhanced sense of control. To look at the history of one's body, one necessarily has to examine it also as a medium through which one expresses one's sexuality. In this sense, too, the concept of sexuality and discussion of it as a part of the discourse on women's health becomes important.

Thus in my own understanding it became increasingly clear that strategies and programmes for women's health would remain incomplete if concepts and methods of dealing with sexuality were not incorporated in them.

Case Study 1: The Bombay Study of Pelvic Inflammatory Disease

In 1992, the Health Department of the Bombay Municipal Corporation (BMC) and the Liverpool School of Tropical Medicine initiated a research study on Pelvic Inflammatory Disease (PID) in slum women. The data gathering on the social and behavioural factors for this study was carried out by auxiliary nurse midwives (ANMs), who were already employed by the BMC, and not by professional researchers. The idea was to build capacity within the BMC structure, not only to carry out this kind of research in future, but also to help in the implementation of an action programme which would follow the research. The action research process also provided valuable insights into some factors which would be necessary for the implementation of woman-centred health programmes through the BMC.

Thirty ANMs were prepared through regular and ongoing training to communicate with women on their reproductive and sexual health problems and to do research (that is, to conduct interviews and focus group discussions) with women on reproductive and sexual health. Over a period of about 30 months, the ANMs were taken through a training process to build their perspective towards women's health and to improve their skills of communicating with women on most personal issues, like sexuality. Perspective building was done because it was felt that health care providers need to have a broader perspective of women's health than they usually get through their formal training. While treating women, health care providers need to be conscious of the fact that the health status of women is a result of an interplay of cultural, social, economic and political factors. They also need to be aware that women's bodies are arenas on which power inequalities of gender, caste and class are enacted.

While all health care providers need to have this kind of a world view of women's health, we believe that women health care providers, especially the so-called para-professionals, have a crucial role in addressing women's health needs. As para-professionals, they are more accessible for ordinary women. In many health programmes the female para-professional, or the ANM, is the first point of contact with the health care delivery system for community women.[4]

The Role of the ANM

The role of the ANM in India was created after Independence when the government of India realized that a special functionary was needed, especially in the rural areas, to provide primary health services to a large number of people. The ANMs were earlier trained over a two-year period. The emphasis at that time was on midwifery and maternal and child health (MCH). In 1975 the government decided that the job of the ANMs needed to be expanded to include other areas besides MCH. This was done to equip ANMs for the Multipurpose Health Worker Programme. Although their job functions were expanded beyond MCH and FP (Family Planning), the training period was reduced from 24 to 18 months.

The ANM is expected to perform several functions, yet in practice her role is limited to motivation and handling family planning 'cases' and conducting the MCH programme. She has been reduced to the position of an agent of the population control establishment in India. She is given targets for the number of sterilizations or spacing methods that she has to fulfil in a year. Thus, like the 'beneficiary' woman, the ANM too has been made into an instrument of the family planning/population control establishment.

However, the ANM or the female health worker (FHW) is first and foremost a woman. As a woman she, too, has had a set of experiences within her family and the society, or with respect to the health care system, that impact on her health. She, too, has been a health care seeker and has confronted the patriarchal system as a woman patient. Her role as a health worker for women has to be built upon these sets of experiences, which are common to all women despite their class and caste differences in some form or the other. If the ANM identifies herself as belonging to the 'class' of women, she will be far more effective than if she considers herself as an entity 'other' than the 'beneficiary' woman out there. She will be effective in that she will have an intimate understanding of the struggles of the 'patient' as a woman and will be able to respond sensitively to her needs. This is radically different from identifying herself as a part of the health system, as the 'nurse' who has to teach all those dumb women about how many children they should have.

Thus, it is not only the set of tasks that the ANM performs that have to be changed. There also has to be a change in the perspective and understanding of how she performs her role. The ANM (and the health care system) has to understand that, as a front-line worker, she is in the best position to respond to women's needs and problems with empathy. The sensitivity and empathy will grow out of reflection, articulation and analysis of her own experiences as a woman.

But the most critical point that needs to emphasized here is that we believe that women health workers, to be able to discharge their responsibilities towards women's health, can do so most effectively if they go through a process which makes them aware of themselves as *women*, constantly confronting patriarchal forces. However, changing the role of the ANM for women-centred health care is not just a matter of changing her job description. It calls for a host of other changes: in perspective or world view; in training content and processes; in structures and systems.

Through the critical module of training for ANMs in the PID Project, we sought to bring about:

1 an increase in awareness of how various cultural, social factors affect women's health status;
2 greater sensitivity and ability to analyse the situation of individual women;
3 change in attitudes leading to more empathic behaviour towards women.

The training included examining how sexuality and sexual issues are related to women's health; how to communicate about sexuality and sexual practices and how to conduct structured and semi-structured interviews about sexual and gynaecological problems and experiences.

An important aspect of the training was the emphasis on sharing and reflecting on general perceptions of sexuality. The ANMs reflected on their own experiences of their illnesses and their encounters with the health care system. They spoke about experiences of when they first became aware of their femininity and their sexuality. The training then went on to more cognitive or theoretical content. After a general overview of how social, cultural, economic and political factors affect women's health, the training programme examined the role of sexuality and sexual issues. In addition to understanding this role, health workers also need to develop skills in communicating about matters related to sexuality and sexual practices.

Since sexuality is the most private aspect of ourselves, we decided to approach this theme very gently. Sessions on sexuality were built into the entire training (30 months) and ranged from discussions on things that happen to other people to reflection on and sharing of our personal experiences. We believe that unless we, as trainers or health workers, have started on a process of coming to terms with, and understanding, our own sexuality, we will not be able to communicate sensitively and effectively with the women with whom we are working. As an example of the participatory exploration methods that we use and the meaning we give to explicit terms, one of the early sessions on sexuality was on language related to sex. The objectives of the session were to help the participants recognize their own reactions and feelings towards language related to sex and to realize the importance of being able to talk to women about sex in their own language.

The facilitator stuck five sheets of newsprint on different walls of the room. Each sheet had one of the following words as a title: man, woman, penis, vagina, sex. Then the facilitator announced that participants had to move around to each sheet and write as many alternative words (to the title) as possible. Some participants had a lot of fun writing 'dirty' words, others felt shy, some others actually exhibited anger and hostility, a few took refuge in scientific terminology.

When the facilitator announced that she was going to read out the words, two or three participants reacted very strongly and said that they objected to her reading them aloud. The facilitator asked them why did they not want to hear these words and the reasons were:

- we feel *sharam* (ashamed, embarrassed) to hear these words;
- we do not use these words;
- these words are dirty;
- we are not used to hearing these words;
- they are used only by slum or lower-class people;
- our culture and upbringing does not teach or allow us to use those words;
- cultured, educated people do not use these words;
- unmarried girls cannot use the words.

The response of the participants brought out perceptions about sexuality. For example, some shared that they did not feel ashamed but enjoyed the exercise as they had never done this before. These words may sound dirty but they convey the same meaning, and the health workers hear these words every day, as they are commonly used by ordinary people. Some others said that our attitudes come from our culture, or sometimes are learnt from the surrounding environment. One of them added that even educated, college-going boys and girls use these words every day.

Another session was on our first experience of awareness of our own bodies. The objectives of this session were to help the participants to begin to understand their feelings related to their bodies. The participants were asked to get into small groups of three. Each person had to tell the others in her group about when she first became aware of her own body or what was her first experience of being a girl.

In addition to the experience of the first menstruation, this exercise brought out the first experience of development of breasts or noticing of pubic hair. This sharing also led to surfacing of experiences of childhood sexual abuse. The facilitator had to ensure that there was sufficient time to allow this, when it began to happen. She was also able to evoke a feeling of trust and support within the group, and was able to create a safe and loving space for healing to take place.

These were a few of the sessions on sexuality that were conducted with the ANMs in the Bombay project. The point that needs to be emphasized is that we started with a research agenda, namely, a study of the clinical, social, and behavioural aspects influencing PID. In order to train the field investigators to elicit good quality data on sensitive issues like sexuality, we had to build in intervention, in the form of ongoing training, into the research process. Thus research and intervention went side by side, leading to development as we understand it: personal transformation at one level and transformation in social relations at another level, so that there is greater gender equity and gender justice.

Case Study 2: SARTHI

In the early years, SARTHI's work could be categorized as pure service delivery, in which SARTHI functioned as an implementing agency and the villagers were the 'beneficiary community'. Later on, sometime around 1988–9, the organization and empowerment of the village communities to become partners in the process of service delivery became an important characteristic of SARTHI's work. This meant that there was a lot more dialogue and discussion with the village people, and the formation of village-level groups, separate for men and women, to help plan and implement development programmes.

Evolution of the women's health programme

By 1987, the local women, who were now enthused, thanks to an improved cookstove (*chulha*) programme, started suggesting that SARTHI launch a health programme for them.

The organization felt quite unequipped to respond to the health needs of the women. Attempts to recruit medical professionals were unsuccessful. SARTHI was too remote and lacked the infrastructure which could attract and retain doctors. After a year of uncertainty, self-doubts and questioning, and encouraged by the counsel of friends, SARTHI decided to start a 'limited' women's health programme.

It was decided to train a carefully selected group of traditional *dais* and other interested local women to carry out a Maternal and Child Health Programme.[5] At that stage, the programme was restricted to MCH because that is what we felt comfortable with. There were enough training resources, in terms of both the literature available and the trainers willing to help us. Thus over the next 18 months SARTHI gradually developed a community-based MCH programme.

In the second phase, SARTHI carried out action research with the traditional healers and herbalists on the local plant-based medicines traditionally used by the women for their health problems. Simultaneously, with the help of Shodhini[6] resource persons, eight *arogya sakhis* (barefoot gynaecologists-cum-counsellors) were trained in the period 1990–1. The *arogya sakhis* were closely guided in their practice and the use of local medicines by the resource persons. The preparation of *arogya sakhis* was a participatory action research process. The group of eleven women consisted of eight local inhabitants, two programme planners/coordinators, and one (sometimes two) outside resource persons working together as equal members of a self-help group. The research question, how to treat common problems of women, was jointly defined. The data were generated jointly: we each used our own bodies, relating them to our life experiences. We talked about our current illnesses and sources of stress that could be resulting in these illnesses. The analysis was done collectively as was the planning for follow-up action.[7]

The group met each month for a three-day residential retreat, over a period of 18 months. The early meetings were devoted to discussing the stories of our bodies: our experiences of adolescence, the onset of menstruation, pregnancy and childbirths, major illnesses. We also talked of our interactions with the formal health care delivery system and became acutely aware of how powerless and humiliated we had been made to feel at the hands of this system.

By revealing our histories, with their painful events as well as their joys, we gradually built a closeness and trust amongst ourselves to begin the self-examination process. This was most frightening. We were deeply conditioned to feel acutely shy and embarrassed to reveal ourselves to others or even to look at our own external genitalia. We were revulsed by the idea of seeing the insides of our bodies, seeing where the 'dirty' and 'polluting' flow comes from each month. As we resisted the self-examination, we began discussing our feelings, giving words to the fear, embarrassment and shame, tracing their roots and arriving at an understanding of how strongly patriarchal forces controlled us. At a certain point we decided that we had discussed enough; there was nothing more to be expressed until we actually went through the experience of self-examination. The resource person was the first one. We learnt about the structure of the woman's body on her live body. We saw what the cervix looked like, we learnt about the secretions of the vagina. Some of us were still afraid of what evil might befall us, one said that she felt 'like vomiting'. But the curiosity and desire to learn in all of us had awakened. This is what kept us going throughout. In addition, quite early on, the self-help group became a place where each of us shared our physical complaints and received the appropriate treatment (herbal, nutritional, exercise and other kinds) which we then practised through the month. We reported on the results at the subsequent meeting. Initially we were quite amazed at the 'success' of the remedies. Shantaben reported how the tiny boils on her labia had disappeared with the treatment of crystal sugar and fennel seeds, and we could see that there were none of the boils that were present the previous month. Waliben said that her vaginal discharge had reduced considerably with the garlic treatment. These reports filled the group with elation.

Sharing of personal problems, conflicts and traumas in a supportive atmosphere brought about a release at one level. If any of the group members could help, plans were made for these actions. The little self-help group became the members' own little space to withdraw into each month. In this space, they learnt about themselves, about women's health and about how to work in the community. Through the discussions and collective analysis, they could develop their own perspective on the situation of women in their own society and how this affects their health and lives in general. By examining, diagnosing and treating each other in the self-help group for about six months, the women built up enough confidence to begin to practise as health workers in the villages.

As health workers, they took complete histories of the women who approached them with their symptoms. They persuaded the women to undergo an examination, including a bi-manual and *per speculum* examination when necessary. Based on the history and the examination, they prescribed the tested herbal remedies that they had learnt about and had experiences with in their self-help group.

Issues and Discussion

The lessons and issues emerging from case studies, described above, have to be examined within the context of development paradigms and feminist health action. In this section, we explore what 'development' means to feminists, the implications of feminist notions of development for health action, and the role of research, research models and paradigms suited for feminist health action.

Development

We define the term development as the process by which poorer nations of the world increase productivity and their provision of basic services, frequently utilizing financial aid, commodities and transfer of technology provided by already developed countries and/or international assistance organizations. Most development programmes continue to overlook women's involvement and contribution to the economy. Development is not merely a matter of economics. It also has political overtones: Who owns the resources? Who has access to and control over them? Whose contribution to society and economy is more valued and why? These are some questions related to concepts of equity and social justice that should be raised in all developmental efforts. Such a redefinition of development creates a vision of a world where

> inequality based on class, gender and race is absent from every country, and from the relationships among countries. Where basic needs become basic rights and where poverty and all forms of violence is eliminated. Each person will have the opportunity to develop her or his own full potential and creativity, and women's values of nurturance and solidarity will characterise human relationships.... (Sen and Grown, 1987)

Feminists with such alternative notions of development are not willing to wait for the tangible fruits of development (such as increased income, and goods and services in the hands of women) as end products. As we see it, development should incorporate strategies and processes which empower women, challenge existing gender roles and the sexual division of labour and rewards, and continually transform gender and power relations. Participation of women as equal partners and decision makers in developmental efforts is a core value for feminists doing development.

Feminist health action

Health action is also a political issue as far as feminists are concerned. The state, preoccupied with population control, controls women's bodies and targets poor women's bodies as receptacles for contraceptives. Health businesses promote the commodification of health and control women's bodies with health and cosmetic technologies. These technologies are aimed at upholding societal images of women as beauty symbols. The family and community members exert control over women's bodies by deciding when and how many children they should have. Thus feminist health action is aimed at asserting the control of their bodies by women themselves. It entails informing women about their bodies and rights related to their bodies. It also entails organizing them for collective action to claim their health rights.

Feminist health action is about egalitarian relationships between health care providers and their clients and between health researchers and the subjects of their studies. Participatory action and two-way communication are central to both research and development from the feminist perspective.

Methodological issues in research

How can we do research on women in ways that help them gain control over their bodies? Does doing research on women necessarily imply treating them like objects, subjecting them to an outsider's scientific dispassionate scrutiny, probing persistently into the dark recesses of their consciousness and then walking out of their lives when the data have been collected? A commitment to women's empowerment means that we do research 'with' women rather than 'on' women. This kind of a research model, called participatory action research, is one in which, at all stages, the control remains in the hands of the community, with the community assuming the role of both researched and researcher. The participatory research model is the least invasive, especially when the research questions are related to sexuality, gender and health.

Participatory action research in its pure form, however, is an ideal research model. It is not possible to formulate *all* research questions using the paradigm of participatory action research, in which total control rests in the hands of the community. The idealized model of participatory action research requires ideal self-actualized human beings in an ideal, egalitarian society. Reality, as we all know, is laced with imperfections and deviations from the ideal. So whenever we embark on research, we have to honestly try to minimize differences between the roles and power of the researcher and the researched. We need to ensure that there is reciprocity and mutuality, and that the research process itself results in the empowerment and transformation of all involved (Gluck, 1991).

The model of action research – without participation – appears to be the next best option. In this the research agenda may be set outside of the researched community but there is an attempt to raise the awareness of the researched and the researchers. Along with the research process, an educational process is attempted. Through the educational process, the 'researched' as well as all those associated with the research process – that is, the 'researchers' – reflect on what happens, on what they find through their research and what it means. The endeavour is to make the research process non-exploitative, at least, and empowering, at best.[8] 'Action research has the potential to reposition the researcher/subject power relationship in many ways. It creates a social space and a dynamic of reciprocity that give participants the power to make meaningful contributions to their own community' (Benmayor, 1991).

But educational processes by themselves are not enough. Much of the education provided by educational institutions the world over is offered through patriarchal institutions. Feminist principles and method-ologies need to be woven in to make the educational processes truly empowering.

Research and intervention – a thin line?

In research models of this kind – that is, participatory and action research – the division between research and intervention tends to be an artificial one. SARTHI's Women's Health Programme was an 'intervention' programme in response to women's articulated needs. The village women wanted services for safe deliveries and later for treatment of common gynaecological problems. The process by which this programme developed over a period of five years could be called participatory action research.

The Bombay PID Project, on the other hand, started as a 'research' project. Because of our commitment to empowerment of women, the project had educational and consciousness-raising inputs. Thus at every stage we can say that there was an intervention, in the form of training to build the perspective and skills of the research team. The data from the research was analysed collectively and frequently, and this became the basis of the next stage of data collection.

In both these experiences, the research phase and the intervention phase were not discrete and easily separable phases. Patai appears to feel the same: 'Responding to an apparent sense of inadequacy of conventional research practices, feminist scholars ... have attempted to focus on the research process as an occasion for intervention and advocacy' (Patai, 1991: 139).

The processes that were common in the Bombay PID and SARTHI projects were periodic workshops, characterized by reflection and analysis of the participants' own experiences. An additional component was the sharing of information and concepts from other sources, and skill-building sessions which helped the participants in their health work. Another hallmark of these processes was a genuine attempt to make them democratic and participatory. We were also conscious that in both the SARTHI and Bombay projects we were feminist groups first – that is, we looked at the world through women's eyes and validated women's experiences and affirmed women's realities.

Transformation

Another lesson that we learned from both these experiences is that before effective research and interventions on issues related to sexuality, gender and sexual health can take place, the researchers need to examine, and change, their own attitudes and behaviours in relation to sexual and gender-related issues. We think that personal transformation is a prerequisite for good research and effective intervention. Our training as health professionals does not equip us to deal satisfactorily with issues of the sexual health of our clients. Information and conceptual knowledge related to sexuality and its connection with health are not enough. We need also to learn how to relate easily to different individuals about sexuality. This demands that we become aware of our notions of sexuality, our prejudices and inhibitions.

In an evaluation done 20 months after the process was initiated in the Bombay Project, some of the ANMs had the following to say:

Earlier I used to consider the woman guilty but I never saw the reason behind whatever bad work she was doing. For example, if an unmarried girl was pregnant or a widow had relations ... I used to type each person ... but each person is different.

Previously when I was working in the [field] area or in the hospital, I looked at a patient merely as a patient and gave treatment. But now when we take a woman's interview, then I feel, I too am a woman and the person in front of me is also a woman. Whatever questions we ask her are applicable to us.

Before working on this project, I used to feel shy if anyone asked me about sex or if, in the health post, the friends discussed about it. But now, since I'm working on this project, I don't feel anything. On the contrary, while taking in-depth interviews, if I have to ask about sexual relations and if the woman feels shy, I ask her myself, 'Why do you feel shy? Tell me....'

Conclusion

This chapter examines the role of research in feminist health action. It elaborates on the processes necessary to translate research findings into meaningful interventions in the field of sexuality, gender and women's health. On the basis of experience in two field situations we may conclude, first, that where empowerment of women and helping them gain control over their bodies is an aim, the research model itself needs to be a focus of attention. Participatory and action research models are better suited to facilitating empowerment as well as yielding the kind of good quality data that we need. Research methodologies which draw on feminist principles such as 'the personal is political' and woman-centredness are also to be preferred while doing research with women on sexuality, gender and health.

Second, in research and development models which are participatory and action-oriented, the division between research and intervention tends to be an artificial one. Intervention in terms of ongoing training is part of the research and development process. The training is experimental and built on personal reflection and collective analysis. It aims to widen the perspectives of all those involved in the research and development processes, as well as to build their communication and analysis skills.

Third, personal transformation is a prerequisite of good research and effective intervention. Before effective research and interventions related to sexuality, gender and sexual health can take place, the researcher and the one who carries out the intervention need to examine, and change, their own attitudes and behaviours in relation to sexual and gender-related issues.

Notes

1. An earlier version of this chapter was first presented at a conference on 'Reconceiving Sexuality: International Perspectives on Gender, Sexuality and Sexual Health' in Rio de Janeiro on 14–17 April 1996.

   I acknowledge all our colleagues and friends, working with whom we have learnt about the linkages between sexuality and women's health. Specific mention must be made of the Shodhini group, including Rina Nissim, Dr Janet Price, Nirmalben (Coordinator, Women's Programme, SARTHI), Swati Pongurlekar and Korrie de Koning (PID Project, Bombay). Thanks are also due to Chinu Srinivasan for acting as a sounding board and helping clarify many issues in the process of writing and to Dr Bert Pelto for providing feedback on the earlier version of this chapter. Korrie de Koning has been a great team-mate and has contributed significantly in improving this version.

2. Social Action for Rural and Tribal Inhabitants of India (SARTHI) is a registered society working for integrated rural development in the Santrampur Taluka of Panchmahals District in the state of Gujarat. The voluntary agency, founded in 1980, works in approximately 150 villages of this predominantly tribal *talu ka*. Much of the population consists of marginal farmers who are dependent on rainfed agriculture and who also have to migrate seasonally. The range of programmes include: installation of handpumps for drinking water, agricultural improvement, wastelands development, education through eight non-formal schools, rural industries for income generation, development of alternative energy sources, women's development and awareness generation.

3. Personal communication with Dr Veena Mulgaonkar.

4. For related discussion see Khanna, Pongurlekar and De Koning, 1996.

5. For a detailed report of the health programme, see: Khanna, 1992.

6. Shodhini is a network of women in India who have been working for alternatives in women's health based on the self-help methodology and plant-based medicines. For more details see *Touch-me, Touch-me-not: Women, Healing and Plants* (New Delhi: Kali for Women, 1997).

7. For some issues in participatory action research, see the author's 'Participatory Action Research in Women's Health' in Korrie de Koning and Marion Martin (eds), *Participatory Research in Health: Issues and Experiences* (London and New York: Zed Books, 1996).

8. For more discussion on these issues, see Khanna, 1997.

7 • The Right Connections: Partnering and Expertise in Feminist Work for Change

Barbara Cottrell

I recently attended a meeting of the Women Down Prospect, a group I will describe later. One of the women said:

> The school has opened up a lot and is much more willing to be a community resource, and the government is too. We all feel more connected to people like the city councillor and the fire department, the dentist, all the people who are around in the community. They all commented on how nice it is to see what's happening in Terence Bay and Lower Prospect. They see that a group of women have put together these newsletters. It alters their view; they see our community differently and have a much more positive sense of it. They see us as a community that produces positive things.

This woman's words brought it together for me: feminist community development work is about who we work (or partner) with and how we do this partnering. Over the last decade I have been involved in many feminist participatory action research projects, and have come to believe that if feminist research is research for change, it must be grounded in women's experience and women's lives. It is not just research, but also community development. I've been involved in projects as paid and unpaid coordinator and project manager, as an independent research consultant and as a participant, and as a member of the steering committee or board member of a number of organizations which conduct feminist research. In this chapter I will discuss my work with two of these organizations: the Canadian Research Institute for the Advancement of Women (CRIAW), a national organization committed to research which promotes social justice and equality for women, and a regional Canadian women's health research centre, the Maritime Centre for Excellence on Women's Health (MCEWH).

The common thread that runs through my work is the process of women working together to create, expand and sustain a fairer, better world for us all. Lately we've called this working together 'partnering', and I'm one of the many women who have explored the way the term has been used and misused and misunderstood, and how these misunderstandings and misuses can harm or even destroy relationships, especially those between feminist activists and government bodies. One of the forms of partnering that I've looked at particularly closely is the relationship between community- and university-based women. As one of a team of women who conducted the CRIAW study and wrote *Research Partnerships: a Feminist Approach to Communities and Universities Working Together* (Cottrell *et al.*, 1996) I examined projects which were attempting to contribute to change towards equality for women, identifying some of the characteristics of and barriers to successful partnerships.

In Canada, because much of our feminist work is conducted with government funding, we sometimes feel we must allow government to dictate how we do our work, including the issue of partnership. This creates problems because feminists and federal government bureaucrats differ in their definitions of the research process, a point I have come to see as central in the debate between feminists and government. I can best explain these views by beginning with an example from my own experience as a feminist researcher.

Whose Agenda?

The opportunity was exciting, the setting was magical. By a tree-surrounded lake on a gorgeous, warm summer evening, I was one of the twelve members of the MCEWH Steering Committee with the gift of a two-day working retreat, away from phones, families and other interruptions. Feminist research is a continuous learning process and in the Committee we consciously work at identifying who we are and where we are located – as individuals in general and as members of this group in particular – so Board and Staff had come together for longer than the usual rushed two-hour once-a-month meeting to build trust and mutual respect and to discuss our work for the Centre. First, Terri Sabattis, a Maliseet[1] friend of the Centre, called on the four directions to bless our meeting with trust and respect. Then we moved to a beautiful white gazebo where we chatted and ate, and over coffee the discussion began.

I assumed that in order to work out how we would direct a women's health research centre, where social change was our goal, we would start by examining our work to date to see how we could better facilitate the processes of identifying and addressing women's health issues. Then we would need to explore who we were partnering with, and whether we were making the right connections. We would have to discuss how well we were working together to get experiential reports, whether we had really found the experts on each topic to interpret the information, and whether we were doing the right kind of packaging – for the government, media or other women – so that change would result. We had a lot of work to do to find the balance between all our different and complicated ways of doing research, and central to all our discussions should be the issue of expertise and interpretation, of whose voice counts.

But the discussion in the gazebo was not about connections or voice, it was about policy and policy research. For perhaps an hour, I listened to the word *policy* going back and forth across the table. The different speakers all seemed to understand each other, but I had only the vaguest idea what they meant by the word, and understood even less why we were taking time from our precious two days to talk about it.

When people refer to 'policy research' they seem to mean conducting research so that we can advise and inform government. The implication is that this is a *kind of research*, and different from the participatory action research that community groups usually try to do. It is treated as a method of doing research. It is not. Informing policy can be one of the *outcomes* of research, but it is not a type of research, except that government officials often seem to consider academic research done on people-as-objects to be 'policy research'. By contrast, feminist research is about process, with special attention paid to who the partners are in a research project and how issues of power and privilege are handled. As feminist research is, by definition, research for social change, attempting to inform and change policy can be, and usually is, one of its many goals. Surely, policy research is not about why or how we do research, but a description of one part of the dissemination of results? Our work is about connections: the connection of people to each other; the connection of people to research; and the connection of research to change. The possibility of making social change through informing government policy is just one of these connections.

Diana Majury began her 78-page report with the words, 'Policy is an amorphous concept' (Majury, 1998). In an in-house document, Carol Amaratunga, the Director of the MCEWH, observed:

> It is evident from the work of Diana Majury that policy occurs at many levels, that it is multidimensional, and that policy development varies from situation to situation ... policy formation is by and large an *ad hoc* process which is influenced by a combination of determinants (i.e., influence and power), and is rarely based on rational evidence-based decision making. (Amaratunga, personal correspondence)

Yet here we were, discussing policy and policy research as if it were defined, concrete and our proper focus and process. Fortunately these women are my friends and colleagues and I was able to interject, 'I'm sorry, but I don't have a clue what you are talking about.' They explained that because Health Canada, our source of funding, wanted our research to be 'policy research' we had to figure out how we were going to do that. 'And what *is* policy research?' I asked. No one answered. For this group of academic, government and community-based women, the concept might be amorphous, but the funder's response to our Plans of Action had made it clear that it wanted the Centre's work more focused on policy. As our funder, it assumed the right to insist on such a focus. So here we were, letting the government set our agenda. And that is a mistake.

The discussion about policy research is, in a fundamental way, about partnering – that is, who the research is by, for and about. We do not want to bite the hand that feeds us – albeit with our own tax dollars – and we do want to persuade government to do many things differently when it comes to women's health. But we think differently from government officials, have different functions, aims, dreams. Their agenda is not our agenda. They need research reports that explicitly address and attempt to inform government decision making. While such papers are useful, they are not our principal focus. As members of community-based, non-government organizations we shouldn't feel forced to adopt their agenda, or their words. The most important question for us is not what is policy research, but how do we use research to facilitate change and what, in reality, creates social change.

A process in which the participants are equal partners in the research is a better agent for change than any policy report. One of the best illustrations of this is Archibald and Crnkovich's chronicle of how they struggled with issues of privilege and control when they worked with the Inuit women's organization, Pauktuutit (Archibald and Crnkovich, 1995). Significant change occurred – and probably would not have if the Inuit women had not taken control of their own process. They listened, not to the white researchers or to the Department of Justice, but to each other, and acted according to their own dictates. The researchers supported the Inuit women, even when they advocated changes that the researchers did not agree with, because they believed that research must be rooted firmly in the community, and that the women who owned the problem were the best agents for change. The 'evidence' may not be visible in our terms, but only to the women connected to the issue. Our work is to facilitate the process of collecting this knowledge and working together with the participants as advocates of change, ever vigilant of the fact that we are interpreters. Archibald and Crnkovich see it this way:

> As white women raised in the dominant culture, we are frequently expected to perform the role of 'translator' or 'intermediary' between Inuit women and the public policy officials they deal with. Although we are members of the dominant society, our knowledge about Inuit women, their culture, and their lives is 'valuable' to the government officials who have

the power to make the changes the Inuit women are seeking. This is probably a matter of being more comfortable conversing with people who share the same first language and a similar culture, but it can have the effect of undermining the Inuit women present and increasing the status of the white researcher. (Archibald and Crnkovich, 1995: 112)

Archibald and Crnkovich recognize that they are under the pressure of being seen as representative of the groups they work with when they try to influence policy change, and they make a conscious effort to resist this pressure:

> Yet there is still a danger that the role of intermediary or translator can be seen as, and become, the role of a 'representative' of the organization. An outsider who crosses this line and sees herself as a 'representative' is, in our view, exploiting her relationship with the women with whom she shares her research work. (Archibald and Crnkovich, 1995: 113)

In order for change to occur, the research participants – that is, the women who live the research problem – along with the policy makers, 'outside' researchers, consultants and community developers, must be equal partners in the process. This often means that the research problem should be identified by the participants, and that the participants should have a voice in decisions about how the research is to be conducted, and in the analysis, interpretation and dissemination of results. This is an exceedingly difficult and therefore rare occurrence. Most research, including feminist research, is designed with little input from the people who will participate in the study. The projects usually have a principal investigator (an advisory committee sometimes plays this role) who controls the process but does not have time to support the researcher adequately; the latter is often a paid employee who also did not have any input into the design. The subjects/participants are seldom 'partners', for they rarely participate in any way other than to attend a focus group or interview. 'Outside' researchers, consultants and community developers often think they know how to do all phases of the research, and ignore the input of the participants.

The process of equal participation is community development work and creates change in itself. This is not the view held by most government officials. When bureaucrats with the federal government department, Status of Women Canada, went across the country in 1996 to consult about their 'mission', I lined up at the buffet table behind some of our visitors from the nation's capital, and we chatted about research as we filled our plates. 'What you must understand, Barbara,' one said, 'is that action research and policy research are two very different things.' What she meant was that policy research was something academic women could do, while action research was community-based. The dichotomy is false. In order for our research to effect change, it needs to be a combination of academic, community and government skills and knowledge. The fact that government does not operate on this assumption is why it is dangerous for women's groups to allow the government to set our agenda.

Whose Theory?

At the retreat, we agreed to move away from the unresolved discussion about policy research and we began to look at social change (Duffy and Momirov, 1997). We took the topic of violence against women and attempted to analyse what changes had occurred over the past 20 years, and what had stimulated them. Based on our experience and on our reading of publications such as Linda MacLeod's study of some of the violence prevention projects funded by the Canadian government (MacLeod, 1994), we acknowledged that dramatic change has taken place. Many of us were old enough to remember walking in Take Back The Night marches past men who jeered and threw beer bottles, and when the police response was laughter. Since then, public perception, community action and government policy have changed. We tried to identify who had stimulated the change and concluded that advocates, researchers and policy makers all played important roles. But it did not happen by women focusing on policy. Instead we had started with our lives, the real lives of women, and moved on from there, and along the way we developed theories which helped us conceptualize the problem and influence policies at every government level.

The movement challenging violence against women was one of the ways in which women began to understand the impact of objectifying research subjects and the danger of treating research participants as merely objects. In her work, Norma Jean Profitt (1997) discusses the fact that in the struggle to end violence against women, those activists who acknowledge their own experience of violence usually feel they are treated as inferiors by activists who do not admit to experiencing violence. The impact of the objectification by 'professionals' on people who have first-hand experience, and the need for those with experience to be included as partners, were illustrated recently in a situation that occurred at a community policing conference.

In a workshop, a police officer who was a trained hostage negotiator and instructor of conflict resolution and crisis intervention, outlined his theory about the similarities between the experience of being taken hostage and 'the battered woman syndrome'. His presentation was followed by an actor's dramatic enactment of what it is like to be trapped by 'relationship terrorism'. The purpose of the dual presentation was to demonstrate the similarities between victims of hostage-taking and family violence and the difference in society's reactions to them. The officer explained that when a hostage-taking incident is over, the police are trained to reassure the victim that everything will be all right, that they are safe, and that even if acts of sexual aggression, submission and degradation had to be endured, the victim acted appropriately. By contrast, victims of woman abuse are questioned about why they stay with men who are violent towards them. He concluded the workshop by encouraging the audience to look at domestic violence as relationship terrorism and to intensify efforts to break the cycle.

After the two presentations by the police officer and the actor, a member of the audience, Lorraine Berzins, responded:

> I have been the victim of a hostage-taking myself. As I sat there listening and comparing it to my own experience I found (the officer's) way of characterizing what I experienced very dehumanizing, demeaning, and infantilizing of the victim. His theory reduced a very complex multi-faceted experience to pathological categories. This human interaction which for me was very personal and also contained positive elements was interpreted as a 'mental aberration'.
>
> It is important to say this because I think victims of 'wife abuse' and 'relationship abuse' may feel this way too and ... you are not really going to make it easier for them by doing this.... It may in fact be experienced as distorting, hurtful and traumatizing. It is once again falling into the old trap of the 'experts' claiming the power of telling the victim what she has experienced, defining for her what her experience has been about.....[2]

This kind of 'expert power' is a huge force and it can be tremendously damaging. If the only way for a victim to get the support she needs is to have to go along with a distorting interpretation of her behaviour, it will drive her into silence about what has really taken place. She may feel too afraid to reveal all the other complex dimensions. Yet she knows things we can't possibly know unless she tells us. Only through her can we learn what we need to understand about these situations, and about what could be truly helpful to the people struggling with the problems, and about what could truly help us with prevention.

Again we are reminded that it is of dubious value, and even damaging, when people who do not own a problem assume ownership without adequate partnering. This situation speaks to the need to make sure that those who authentically own the problem have some role in the theorizing about it, and a conscious effort is made to make sure they are always part of the presentation of those theories so that the theory is grounded in experience. These are basic tenets in community development work.

Whose Process?

One example of a group of women who partner with community developers/researchers and still manage to own their own problems and search for their own solutions is the group I quoted at the start of this chapter. The Women Down Prospect formed almost a decade ago when ten women in Lower Prospect, a coastal community in Nova Scotia with a population of about a hundred people, conducted research to identify the determinants of their health and ways to make changes in their own community and their own lives.[3] It was participatory action research community development: the women controlled the project, the money was theirs, the directions were theirs. The group has expanded and changed over the years, and is not without struggle and conflict, but it is still together, still participatory and without hierarchy, still doing research with all decisions made democratically. By taking turns at the tasks, participants are learning skills like chairing meetings and writing minutes, meeting with bureaucrats and conducting interviews. The ability of the women to be involved in research and community development work, to talk about their lives and articulate their needs, has grown over the years, every woman at her own speed. They have carried out research projects; have produced newsletters and videos; have upgrading programmes for adults in the village; are in the process of partnering with other groups to make computers accessible to the larger community, and are making the local elementary school a more accessible space for everyone. They continue to work to identify their needs and the ways that things can be changed to make life in an economically depressed coastal community healthier and richer for everyone.

I lived in the village from 1976 until 1986, worked with the group, and with their assistance studied the Women Down Prospect group for my Master's thesis (Cottrell, 1995). One group member and I have more formal education and more experience with community development than the other members, and both of us have struggled with how to be members of the group without controlling it, especially when the women themselves look to us as the 'experts'. The central argument of my MA thesis was that:

> Research practitioners and group facilitators tend to use their authority, knowledge and expertise to control and manipulate the research process, especially when, as is usually the case, they have more formal education and exposure to the research process than the other women in the group. Often this dynamic occurs without the research practitioners realizing this is what they are doing, and without realizing that the impact of their power positions is that they disempower, or at least hinder the empowerment of

other women involved in the research process. This is contrary to the very ideals of feminism.

This brings up the issue of leadership. When is one disempowering, as opposed to helping? After an evaluation meeting of one of the Women Down Prospect projects, I wrote in my journal:

> I sat through the session trying to decide if I should say what's on my mind. Is it acceptable to put it on the table, or will the women be offended? It's so important to me not to annoy them, or put them down. I decided it is important to articulate my concerns so I take the chance. When it is my turn to speak, I say how uncomfortable I am that the group had not taken ownership of the project and relied on me to make decisions. Theresa immediately jumped in and accused me of being unfair and impatient. She said the women were learning many skills and building their self-confidence, were beginning to take control, and may eventually be ready to work on their own, but for now they value help and guidance. Others agree it is important that someone with more experience and skills in action research take the leadership role, and Carol says that on occasions when she was unable to reach me she was able to make decisions for herself and is proud of herself for it. Annie reminds me that she made a decision, and even in the face of my annoyance, she stuck to it! We both laugh at that.

If the situation is handled very carefully, and if there is respect for those who own the problem, 'outsiders' can be advocates. Sometimes, because they are too ill or too poor, women who own the problem cannot be their own advocates. Often, advocacy of change is a group rather than an individual action. Then the question is, who can be advocates, and how? Barnsley and Lewis write:

> We believe that both types of change – the short term changes that can ameliorate the worst consequences of women's oppression and the longer term changes that can ultimately eliminate it – are motivated and driven by women as a group. Change is a bottom up process. We must recognize that the organizations which are closest to the day to day lives of the majority of women are best placed to define the changes that women need and the strategies that are necessary to realize those changes. It follows, then, that in working for social change we give primacy to the perspectives of community-based organizations. (Barnsley and Lewis, 1996: 6)

What role can other women's groups realistically play for groups such as the Women Down Prospect? Perhaps we could become knowledgeable about policy and policy changes that would improve the women's lives. But our focus has to begin with women's experience. The government is not wrong in requesting that we do policy research. To improve women's health, many policies need to be changed. Poverty has been identified by both the Women Down Prospect and the federal government as one of the major determinants of ill health. Perhaps it would be helpful if we were to identify which policies keep people poor and how, and who the players are, so that we can get the key policies changed. But we must start with the recognition that women in poverty own that issue.

Working together is a key issue. The Canadian government is right to encourage partnerships, but we need to take control of the process. Often the government as funder decides when women will and will not partner. Partnerships make sense. When the federal government funded an analysis of how women's studies students could intern in Atlantic Canadian, Indonesian and Caribbean community-based organizations, community-based women in Halifax were distressed to discover that the Canadian research team was made up entirely of academics. The Canadian research team did not include community-based women because the funders would not permit it. In a similar case, writing about a four-year collaborative research project funded by the Social Science and Humanities Research Council (SSHRC), the coordinator acknowledged that the terms of their grant, which restricted support for participation to academics, were to the project's detriment: 'These restrictions prohibited us from including partici-pants with more grassroots backgrounds and limited the diversity of our Network in ways that frequently made us uncomfortable' (Sherwin, 1998: 18). In both of these cases, the research would have benefited from a broader partnership.

This is not to deny that many problems emerge when academic and community-based women attempt to work together. If partnerships are to be required, we all need to be more aware of what we are getting into. As Barnsley and Lewis (1996: 5) wrote, 'These partnerships are discussed in terms of the mutual benefits to be gained by both sides of the partnership, but seldom are the pitfalls and tradeoffs that can develop made clear.'

Not least of the key issues identified by the CRIAW report is that the very definition of women as community-based or university-based creates difficulties. In some ways this is another false dichotomy because some community-based women have graduate degrees and even teach univer-sity courses, while some university-based women are active in community groups. Ultimately though, the division is valid because it is a matter of privilege. When university-based women claim to be community-based, they are eclipsing the authority of others and disclaiming the privilege and authority that accrues to them as professors. When I suggested this at a recent meeting, women who are senior professors argued that it is male professors who have the status. In the context of the university this may well be true, but status is relative, and I challenge any female professor to go to a bank with, for instance, a community development worker and see who is treated as more valuable, or to consider whose research is valued more. If a woman gains status and money because she is based at the university, it is inauthentic for her to put aside that identity when it is convenient to assume the credibility of community. Most community-based agencies are poor and the women associated with those organizations have limited access to resources, but they can speak with some authority on behalf of the disenfranchised and others who have limited access to resources (Roberts, 1998).

In partnerships there are frequent differences of opinion about how information should be reported. Most academics want results in a form that will lead to publication in a peer-reviewed journal, while community-based women want more direct action. Scholarly journals may contribute to knowledge and the way the world is conceived, but I suspect a recent article in *Maclean's* magazine did more to stop the re-victimization of victims of woman abuse in the military than any number of articles in scholarly journals could. Perhaps the military were shuffling in that direction, but the magazine article moved the military with the speed that victimized women need.

Differences in status also reflect community-based women's relatively limited access to resources. Community organizations are already stretched to their limits and can rarely afford the time and costs of participation, and that means that successful partnerships require appropriate resources allotted for full community participation. But all too often the funder, usually the federal government, wants proposals written and implemented at speeds dangerous to any participatory process. The proposal for the MCEWH was written by university-based women and evoked rancour from women in the community who felt they had been used rather than consulted, but those who submitted the proposal felt that 'Given the mandate and requirements imposed by the funder, it is a testament to everyone involved and to their sheer tenacity that the proposal was submitted at all within this short time-frame' (Cottrell *et al.*, 1996: 80). One of the participants said that the letter of intent was a 'workathon imposed by the deadlines required by Health Canada'. She was aware that their information 'contained feminist language and yet ... violated those very feminist principles by the short time line they imposed' (Cottrell *et al.*, 1996: 83). In that case, Health Canada, however unintentionally, set up women to fight among themselves and it continues to set up applicants to include 'name only' partners in their applications.

Conclusion

If we take seriously the idea that all feminist research is research for change and all research, even research which will ultimately inform policy, must be based on a community development model, then we are making a commitment to allowing the process to unfold. And that takes time. The first wonderful, strong, exciting Women Down Prospect project was funded for six months. It took us three years. Its strength was based on the knowledge that it could move slowly, and I doubt that the group would have survived had we been forced to complete the project in six months. And the issue is so much larger than not permitting sufficient time:

> [Health Canada's] approach was institutional and academic and lacked understanding of community development.... In fact, the time line imposed by Health Canada was a severe barrier that overlaid and impacted on all of the barriers and activities in this process. The guidelines were designed to put the money into an institution rather than into the community while the institution was asked to 'network' with the community and involve them as 'partners' without any understanding of the community development processes or the time that would be needed to accomplish this task. (Cottrell *et al.*, 1996: 91)

When the government insists on projects having a 'principal investigator' they are using the language and concepts of academics, concepts with which many non-academics are uncomfortable. Although many of us have had experiences where this is not so, at the community level we tend to think more about group work and to be less individualistic, so when community-based groups do research we form advisory or support committees and put all our names on the document, in alphabetical order, while academics are more likely to want to claim lead authorship because of the impact of such things on their applications for tenure and promotion. Such differences can lead to major problems. It sounds simple enough to say that all partners must have a common understanding of the need for the research, and of each other's roles, but many projects, some of them described in the CRIAW report, are fraught with difficulties because of a lack of this understanding.

The academics on the MCEWH Steering Committee heard me when I said I didn't see the point of their discussion of policy, and there was no resistance to adapting the workplan to accommodate my concern, although one woman said honestly and with a frustrated sigh, 'Okay, let's write into the agenda the discussion of what research is, and put it to rest for once and all.' We didn't put it to rest, but we did have our conversation about how change occurred in the movement opposing violence against women. At the end of the discussion, one of the academic women said, 'I want to say that in the last two hours the discussion was led by the community-based women, and those of us attached to the university and the government have largely been listeners, and it has been some of the most valuable discussion we've ever had as a group.' This public acknowledgement by an academic of the value of input from community-based women is an example of the ways we on the Steering Committee try to be true partners, not spurious, because-it-looks-good-for-the-Centre partners. It is intensely affirming when we recognize each other publicly even though, in spite of our best attempts, we continue to experience many of the struggles identified in the CRIAW Report. The academics sometimes feel their work in the community is dismissed; the community-based women sometimes feel that the academics want to wear all the hats, including ours.[4]

On the MCEWH Steering Committee, we encounter both the problems and benefits of partnering. We have (and are) a lot of partners! The Centre is sponsored in part by a university and half of the Steering Committee are university professors; we are housed by the local women and children's hospital; we have provincial government, institutional and community representatives on the Committee (and community representatives who teach at universities, and bureaucrats who are active in their communities). The MCEWH Advisory Committee is a group of over 50 women representing many communities. We all have different agendas, but we know enough now to try to be allies. The Steering Committee retreat began with Terri's prayer that we listen and be respectful of each other, that we see each other as a gift. As well as recognizing the gift of each other, we all have to learn to acknowledge where we do have power and privilege. Whether our base is community or university, institution or government, the vast majority of the women around the table are the 'educated, articulate, well-dressed, heterosexual, and not-too-forceful white women, who are not too young or too old or too "pretty" [who] have by far the best chances of being heard in consulting rooms, classrooms, courtrooms, and the offices of various bureaucracies throughout the affluent Western world', as Lorraine Code puts it (Code, 1991). At the same time as we are respectful of difference, we must hang on to what is important to us: seeing each other's points of view does not mean that we must abandon our own belief in the need for equal partnering in work for change. It isn't easy, but we continue to work towards an ideal of good partnering, because we are getting better at it, and our work is stronger for it. When I look back over the history of the MCEWH, I see a diverse – albeit not diverse enough – caring and concerned group of women in the – sometimes painful – throes of a learning process. Because we all want a better world, we work to respect and trust each other, and from a rocky and turbulent beginning, we've managed to grow into a stronger force for change. I have experienced a quality of shared commitment to change, and I have grown through it. In the words of one of the Women Down Prospect group, our work is:

> Building Community. That was one of the main amazing things that came out of the project.... Along with the individual learning of skills and building self-confidence, learning how to work together as a group, we also built our community. (Meta Research, 1998: 10)

Notes

1. The Maliseet are a tribe of North American native people who are associated with the St John river in New Brunswick, Canada and Maine, United States. They call themselves 'Welustuck', which means 'of the beautiful river'.
2. Taken from the draft report, *Community Partnerships: Together We Make a Difference. Report of the 12th Annual Crime Prevention Conference*, Fredericton, New Brunswick: Crime Prevention Association of New Brunswick, 1998.
3. The women chose this name because they are known in surrounding communities as, for example, 'Dolly from down Prospect'. This makes it clear that the women are from Lower Prospect rather than Upper Prospect, a village a mile away by boat and thirty by land.
4. However, indications are that since the Centre received almost US$2m in endowments, its status has risen somewhat in the academy.

8 • Women Organizing for Change: Transformational Organizing as a Strategy for Feminist Development

Collette Oseen

In the spring of 1998 I went overseas as a participant in a CIDA project[1] and all of the difficulties of being a feminist doing development rapidly became apparent. Those things I had glossed over before I left dogged our footsteps like ghosts: an inadequate budget, which signalled our limited importance within the project (even though the funding had been given on the basis of our full and equal participation); colleagues who weren't comfortable calling themselves feminists; other colleagues who saw us merely as a necessary addition in order to get funding, but not to be seriously included in the project. Our marginality within the initial proposal process and then within the process of implementation was heightened and underlined by our experiences in China. The partner overseas institution gave our component grudging acceptance, and this was mirrored by the indifference of the Canadian institution. The principle which CIDA itself states as its second priority after basic human needs – 'the full participation of women as equal partners in the sustainable development of their societies'[2] – was routinely ignored by both institutions. One illustration of this was the paucity of the budget for our section and our inequality as participants.

Of course, it had not been the intent of the project that women be minor participants – our only role dutifully to carry out the small tasks flung to us while the men ran the show and collected most of the goodies – but it seemed to us that that was the result. The whole situation was an organizational problem that seemed to exemplify the common problems found in most organizational texts or in the popular press: that in order to succeed, women must act like men; that in order to get anything done, women must find a male mentor/protector and just work within the system – 'getting along to go along'. Faced with having to work within rigidly hierarchical systems that rewarded obedience to men rather than feminist commitment to change, in a context that appeared to be covertly hostile to feminist goals, it was a sobering introduction to what little I was actually going to be able to accomplish.

In the project we were marginalized, both in terms of our lack of access to money and by our subordination as participants, conditions which were inextricably intertwined and mutually reinforcing. How could we have prevented this? There is no cookbook for translating feminist development policy into the successful realization of feminist development projects, although there is a great deal of literature pointing out how difficult that transition is (Young, 1997: 367). I would argue, however, that there are organizing strategies, which are political in intent, that can lead to better results. These politically adept organizing strategies are best understood within the context of transformatory organizing, which focuses not only on meeting women's short-term practical or material needs, but on meeting women's long-term strategic interests: on transforming male–female relations from relations of domination–subordination to relations characterized by women's freedom and ability to shape the world in ways that suit them.[3]

In other words, the means and the ends are inextricably intertwined – transformational organizing strategies used by women doing development are the means through which male-female relations are transformed in the larger society. Organizing strategies that are about advocacy are embedded in the ways we get things done, within the context of how we relate to each other. Hierarchical relations inside our organizations, existing alongside rhetorical commitments to eliminating hierarchical relations between men and women outside, are not merely inconsistent; rather, the presence of the one guarantees the failure of the other.

Within this context of transformational organizing strategies as the means of achieving the ends of women's long-term strategic interests, I want to focus on the two areas that I think most need most attention if feminist development projects are to succeed: equal access to money, and rough equality among the participants – in other words, the intersections of money, sex and power. These are not uncommon problems within development projects; lack of money, and the failure to address who has power and why, are characteristics of most development projects dealing with women.[4] Without money and rough equality between the male and female participants (or sexually specific subjects),[5] what can you 'put into play', to use Foucault's phrase? Ultimately, what can you accomplish?

In this chapter I want to look at the development project I was involved in from two intersecting perspectives. One focuses on power and money – the budget, as it was and as it might have been; and the other focuses on power and people, or on the organizing strategies we used and those we should have used. The budget we worked within set the stage for how the project was to be conducted; our organizing strategies were the means through which the project was to be realized; neither were adequate for what we wanted to achieve.

Setting the Stage: the Budget

My first focus is the budget, its initial allocation, and who controls the ongoing allocation of the budget monies. Money is a proxy for power; it's not only about who has computers, or how many visits overseas your section rates, or how long these visits are to be, but about who actually controls the project. The power of money can't be hidden or justified by calling it 'resources'; it has a symbolic value as a carrier of power relations between the sexes that can't be overlooked. In Buchanan's evocative phrase, money is Frozen Desire (Buchanan, 1997): the budget reveals whether women are equal participants or mere add-ons to meet funding requirements. In our case, the component dealing specifically with women was not funded equally to the others. Feminist analysis stresses that unequal budgets may fulfil women's short-term needs, but it is only by ensuring that women have equal funding that male–female relations can be transformed from inequality to equality (Visvanathan *et al.*, 1997; Parpart and Marchand, 1995; Braidotti *et al.*, 1994). Money talks, and only an equal place at the table will provide us with the means to redefine development in a way that suits us, or will allow us to question – using Luce Irigaray's (1985, 1994; cf. Goux, 1994) evocative phrase, 'the reign of the masculine neutral' – men masquerading as the neutral human, to whom the bulk of development monies and advantages flow.

In my project, the budget for a three-component development project – one component focusing on women, two components on the 'gender neutral male' – was not divided equally. Clearly, we might hope that a few of women's short-term practical needs would be met, but an unequal budget made it impossible for us to address women's strategic interests, as we identified them. The unequal division of the budget sent a clear message that our component was less important, and indicated that women are a mere addition to the main business of development, which is to meet men's needs as if they were gender neutral humans – the human without a sex, who is actually male. CIDA's guidelines try to ensure that women should be integrated into the development project as a whole, and this, as well as the goal of transforming male–female relations, requires a budget roughly equal to the others. Money is power, and anything less than rough equality, no matter how it is justified, consigns women to the margins of the development project, as it did in the project in which I was involved.

Ensuring that the budget is allocated equally is a matter for the funding agency; by withholding funding they have the means to ensure this. Equality would be more readily achieved, however, if the funding agency was involved in the initial stages of writing the budget, by establishing and enforcing clear guidelines: for example, that all project personnel be paid the same when working overseas; that women's sections should not have to rely on volunteer efforts where the others do not; that the number of visits to ascertain conditions be roughly equal. These kinds of guidelines would prevent job classifications from being used to obscure the fact that men hold the better jobs. In another development project with which I was involved, there were wide differences in terms of education and experience among the male participants. The decision was taken to pay everyone equally in order to foster solidarity. It was a practical and preventive solution to what the men decided could develop into a divisive situation. They felt that equal pay was the prerequisite for solidarity, commitment, and responsibility. This was a good principle, but when it came to the parallel situation between men and women in my project, it was not followed.

I need to stress, however, that actual involvement by the funding agency is essential. If they simply indicate a policy or guideline, it is like a principal telling the bully not to beat up the little kid in the schoolyard, and then walking away. An equal budget allocation doesn't just happen as the result of stated guidelines; it's the result of discussion, and ultimately, of rejection of the budget if it does not meet those guidelines. Reallocating budget money after the budget has been accepted is too difficult, especially because participants have to continue in a viable working relationship. Budget equality, as a principle, has to be stressed, adhered to and monitored from the beginning, not after the fact when the various sections are already committed to spending what they see as *their* money.

Both the initial budget allocation and then the ongoing budget allocation for the duration of the project have to be carefully and systematically attended to, in terms of means as well as ends. If the ends – whether integration or transformation – are going to be achieved, the means have to be consistent. An egalitarian budget allocation system needs to be installed. If the project has a pyramidical organizational structure in terms of allocating money, it will not lead to egalitarian relations among the various sections. In my recent experience, the director of a three-sectioned project, in which one of the sections was devoted to women, had sole signing authority. It would have produced more egalitarian relations if each of the section leaders controlled the budget for her/his particular section. Women participants at a breakfast or lunch meeting don't want to have patriarchal relations reinstated when the male director picks up the tab; it's too much like the husband paying the bill. It also echoes development projects of the 1960s in which the administrators, mimicking the wise and altruistic patriarch, ensured that the women of the family got the necessary pin money (Young, 1993: 18).

These intricate relations between money, sex and power which work to create and recreate relations of domination and subordination between men and women, so apparent in the above scenario, need to be carefully attended to if they are to be subverted. Ensuring that the women's section of the project is equally funded and can control its own budget is a form of subversion, creating the egalitarian organizing strategies necessary for transformation of male–female relations both inside the development group and outside in the larger world. Women can't do development in ways that suit them when they're making do, patching, resewing and cutting down, while the project sections devoted to the neutral male are all out buying new suits.

Means to the End: Transformatory Organizing Strategies

This brings me to the second focus of this chapter: the transformational organizing strategies we needed to employ if we were going to be able to do development in ways that suited us, rather than as marginalized participants within a development project directed at the 'neutral male'. On our arrival in China, we worked with our counterparts, the members of a small women's programme located within a post-secondary institution, to clarify our joint vision regarding the development of a short-term educational programme for older, unemployed women.

In preparation for this, the women involved as Canadian participants focused on what we needed to do, drawing up a roster of who was to do what, deciding on the contents of our lectures, preparing factual material for the meetings, and so on. In other words, we focused on information. We were so concerned about ensuring that our information was full and complete that we completely overlooked thinking about the process: about how we were going to go about achieving what we wanted. The clarification of our joint vision didn't sound nebulous, but without careful attention to how we were going to do this, it was. We failed to ask ourselves about the process, about how exactly we were going to clarify our joint vision with our counterparts, about how we were going to bring about the realization of this vision. Nor did we attend to our own organizing processes beforehand as we went about gathering information and preparing the factual material for our discussions. Lunch is not a substitute for analysis and political strategizing, and things just don't happen at meetings, even with agendas.

For us, our focus on efficiency, lists and deciding who did what and when left out the most important part of the equation, the 'how'. Because we had not constructed a shared political strategy before we left for our overseas meetings, we found that we could not do it when we arrived for our meetings. It was as if we were in separate racquet ball courts: I could hear the other ball in play, but I had no way of returning it. We laid out our factual information, our counterparts laid out theirs, but we existed in separate rooms. There was no process that could unite us and bring us together in joint involvement to decide what the educational programme was to be, and how we were to go about realizing it. What we had prepared was essentially annotated agendas. Without the means to strategize together with our counterparts, the decisions could not be made by us as a collectivity. We exchanged information, politely, but the joint effort eluded us, as did the larger goal of meeting women's long-term strategic interests. In the absence of our ability to come together to strategize politically, the pre-eminent organizing strategy, the joint project remained stuck at its most limited level.

What we needed to do was to develop our ability to strategize politically, both before we left, among the Canadian participants, and while we were there, with our counterparts. Exchanging information is not joint action; particularly in development projects. We need some way of figuring out how to work together in order to get something done. We can't just leave it to chance, e-mails, and dinners together. As Helen Brown (1992) has stressed, working together is not the result of social spontaneity or inspired anarchism; it requires thoughtful attention to the process of organizing in order to get something done.

I want to examine that process of organizing, and for the purpose of this analysis, I want to pull apart this process, although I ask you to keep in mind that the parts of process to which I am going to refer separately are inextricably linked. Without the presence of any one of these parts, the whole process would stand much less chance of success. Having stated that, I would like to focus, first, on the four-step organizing process of Lewis and Barnsley (1992) as the basis for the development of a political strategy; then on the mindful teaching, learning and sharing of all organizing skills which Helen Brown (1992) and Kate Young (1993) explore as the basis for political strategizing; and, finally, on Luce Irigaray and her ideas of 'entrustment'.

I will sketch briefly the four steps in the development of politically adept organizing strategies to give you a sense of the importance of the process, and how it might be used in a development project. This process, with its explicit focus on the involvement of all participants, is particularly suited to women who do not share the same language but who do share a task, as was the case in our project. We needed an organizing process which would bring us together and provide us with ways of expressing ourselves which didn't privilege the spoken word. Lewis and Barnsley provide methods of organizing that involve drawing or writing as a way of ensuring that everyone is heard as the organizing strategy takes form, invaluable when you neither speak the same language nor share the same backgrounds. Most importantly, this process can provide a forum which, in the act of developing a strategy for getting something done, creates a space where we can, perhaps, feel freer to talk – or to draw – all the other issues which usually remain undeveloped and unsaid because of politeness and the avoidance of conflict.

The first step, or grounding the issue, allows women to understand the issue from the basis of their experience of it, and literally to draw that experience as a way of locating the issue in terms of their own under-standing of it. Without fear of judgement or censure, we can ask what we think this issue is about, validating our own experiences of it and providing a map which forms the basis of the next step, analysing the issue. This second step involves, once again, a drawing, in this case a web chart which provides a space for women to lay out causes, and causes of causes. It is a form of public analysis which rectifies the urge for the simple, quick fix as it works to focus, consolidate and clarify the issue. In our case, we lacked the means to address what offering a short-term educational programme might mean for either the Canadians or the Chinese, just as we lacked a sense of the historical context. Lacking a process other than quick synopses, we really had no way of coming together to do shared policy analysis, or of bringing to the surface different visions as part of the process of acknowledgement, rather than as incidences of potential conflict.

The third step, the development of a political strategy, arises out of the shared assessments, analyses and accommodations of different points of view which are the necessary preliminaries to joint action. This third step, however, is not just simply deciding on an action, but drawing out the pros and cons of a number of actions, deciding on possible responses by both allies and opposition, and deciding on how we might respond as a group, in the context of short-term and long-term goals. This political mapping needs to be done, and like the earlier step with its emphasis on the complexity of the causes leading to a particular definition of an issue, it emphasizes the interrelationship of power and action. The final step described by Lewis and Barnsley is devoted to laying out strategic responses to the possible outcomes of various actions, as well as a detailed evaluation of the strategic action chosen, which provides the basis for subsequent actions. These are steps which would have been invaluable for us if we had used them because they serve two functions: the ostensible one of developing a strategy to get something done which is detailed and politically adroit, and one that is less obvious, but equally important: the development of solidarity between and among the women charged to work together to carry out a particular development task. When women working together are separated by an ocean, a culture and a language, the development of solidarity is a crucial aspect of any project timeline.

Overlaying this four-step organizing process in the pursuit of a political strategy is the skill sharing which must accompany it (Brown, 1992). These are organizing skills which are not privileged one above the other, or assigned to a person or a position, but taught to others and learned from others, including the skill of leading and the skill of political strategizing. Just as the organizing process described above develops solidarity as it develops political analysis and strategizing, so does the process of skill sharing. The teaching to others and the learning from others of skills – such as information sharing and consciousness raising; policy analysis and the creation of shared scenarios; networking and the creation of interdependencies; decision making, consensus and responsibility building and leading; culminating in the sharing of the skill of political strategizing – are fundamental to the creation of a non-hierarchical social order. Brown's point is that if we do not learn how to strategize politically in egalitarian ways, if we do not figure out ways of getting things done that do not re-establish hierarchies, we are doomed to participate in the continuous recreation of hierarchical relations between men and women. In other words, our reality has to match our rhetoric.

The last organizing process I want to examine is that of 'entrustment'. The organizing process explained by Lewis and Barnsley depends on egalitarian participation in the service of political action; Young and Brown focus on non-hierarchical participation in the shared skill of political strategizing as organizational skill sharing; Irigaray talks about how sharing is actually accomplished by two women, in a process that she refers to as *affidamento* or entrustment (Irigaray, 1994; Whitford, 1991; Milan Women's Bookstore Collective, 1990). She describes the relationship between two women, the one who wants and the one who knows, neither of whom can accomplish separately what they can accomplish together – or, as I see it, the essence of political strategizing in the interests of feminist development.

According to Irigaray, if, for example, the skill of leading or political strategizing is to be shared, the act involves the teaching by one woman and the learning by another. That involves entrustment, which is more than just an organizational act aimed at a common goal. It is a political strategy, in that it embodies what has been unrepresented, the relationship between two women who are not the same, who are not equal, who are different. Entrustment gives us a way of thinking about a relationship between two people which neither requires difference as between a greater and a lesser, nor demands the erasure of sameness, where one must become the other in order to be equal. In our present symbolic structures, we have no representation of women who are different. In this form of relationship we do not have to be the same as the other, and erase ourselves, nor are we required to be different, and therefore greater or lesser. We can be different, without hierarchy. We can be beside the one who knows, in pursuit of what can only be accomplished together. Entrustment is crucial to the creation of the non-hierarchical social order, which enables the ability to strategize politically to achieve shared goals.

When I evaluate what we did in our project, I realize that we needed to be much more strategically and politically minded than we were; advocacy without political acumen isn't going to succeed. We also needed to establish conditions of rough equality between the participants, and having achieved that, we needed to reach the conditions of entrustment, if we were to achieve the transformational change to which we aspired. Irigaray's analysis deals directly with the competition and fear that afflicts so many women in an environment where it's much easier to go along with powerful men than to put one's trust in another woman. But individual success is no substitute for collective advancement, and entrustment gives us a way to move towards our goal without abandoning or being abandoned by each other. Entrustment is not merging with the other, the fear of the less powerful towards the more powerful woman, nor is it mere situational pragmatism. Instead, entrustment recognizes that if women are to succeed they have to have some means whereby they can transform the subordinate relations they live in.

We already practise entrustment unknowingly; we need to make it more specific, to recognize it as the foundation for political action. Funding agencies are not outside this process; Hester Eisenstein (1995) has pointed out the absolute necessity of working with what she terms 'femocrats'. These are women within the official bureaucracies, and she argues that they need our help just as we need theirs. Looked at like this, a relationship between feminist development activists and 'femocrats' might well meet the condition of entrustment (Goetz, 1996).

This same process of entrustment needs to be used with women partners in overseas development projects, as the only way to overcome the fear and competition for scarce resources, and the marginality that has been written into the projects. Such success as we did achieve was the result of the relationships we established with each other. At first there were the tentatively shared experiences which always form the basis for trust, with the awkward attempts to find common ground. While these took place in the context of a nearly complete lack of access to resources, which hampered our attempts, they did underline how powerful are women's attempts to ponder together the sources of our oppressions and to find solutions to them. Needless to say, these tentative explorations of commonalities, the basis for entrustment and then political strategizing, were carried out when no men were present. This seemed to be a condition for subversive political activity.

This highlights the other dimension of inequality in overseas projects. Even if a women's section within a larger project is equally funded and autonomous, it must work with a group of women who are not, and who have been even more marginalized in the process of developing the project. We need to examine inequalities of resources and power between the overseas and Canadian partners, and between the overseas men and women partners. This should include a thorough analysis of resources available. For example, do the male partners have access to computers, while the partners for the women's section do not? This constant examination of who has access of resources, who has power within the organization as indicated by resources, and what that implies, is necessary if development projects are going to succeed. At a minimum, entrustment as a basis for political strategizing rests on the opportunity for women to speak. That is enhanced where women feel that it is to their advantage to strategize with other women, something that is easier to carry out in women-only groups. If our women partners are in an environment where they are already so fearful and so marginalized that they cannot speak openly to each other, the development project cannot succeed. In this context, we need to develop organizing processes which specifically counteract the silence of oppression and specifically build women's solidarity in shared acts of political strategizing.

Conclusion

I have argued in this chapter that if women coming together to 'do development' are to succeed in transforming the structures of domination, and to address women's long-term and strategic needs, then we must pay careful attention to our organizing strategies. Conventional hierarchical ways of organizing prevent women from learning how to overcome inequitable relations between themselves or to challenge effectively the inequitable relations within male-dominated projects or the wider world. If we are going to be able to 'do development' in ways that suit us as feminists, then we must first confront and overcome the processes of marginalization in our own organizations, in order to confront and overcome these same processes outside. Using a number of patterns of feminist organizing, I focused on Irigiray's idea of entrustment as especially useful in enabling us to think how to create non-hierarchical, participatory relations that will lead to the most important organizing strategy – the skill of political strategizing. Organizational processes are about power, and we must not ignore this if we are to succeed as feminists doing development rather than just women dutifully carrying out projects aimed only at making the cage in which women exist a little prettier.

Notes

1. This is a five-year Canada–China linkage project. It was the joint creation of two post-secondary institutions, one overseas and one Canadian, and was divided into three components, one focusing on an environmental management programme, one on reform, and one on the joint development of a short-term educational programme on women's entrepreneurship. The main focus of our section was on this last element.
2. See CIDA website: http://w3.acdi-cida.gc.ca/cida_ind.nsf
3. Kate Young points out that development has focused on women's material condition rather than their position relative to men (Young, 1993: 43); on poverty rather than on oppressive male-centred social structures (Young, 1993: 130). Transformatory organizing means that we need to focus on women's strategic interests, or the transformation of the structures and processes which give rise to women's disadvantages (Young, 1993: 134).
4. As Kate Young has pointed out, 'At the project level women's components are usually poorly financed and either limited to welfare areas of decision making, reemphasizing women's reproductive roles, or focus on forms of income earning which are marginal, unstable or poorly rewarded.... Gender relations and the distribution of rewards and burdens of development are rarely if ever addressed' (Young, 1993: 132–3).
5. The dichotomy between sex and gender, biology and culture, misses the inextricable relationship between the two; I prefer to use the term 'sexually specific subject' (Elizabeth Grosz, following Luce Irigaray).

9 • Taking Development in Our Hands: a Reflection on Indonesian Women's Experience[1]

Nori Andriyani

In July 1997 the Asian monetary crisis, which first struck Thailand in February 1997, began to attack Indonesia. The prosperity that the New Order government had promised was unravelling fast. The monetary crisis triggered the cracking of President Suharto's totalitarian ruling foundations. Led by the student movement, popular forces mounted increasing pressure on Suharto to step down during the first part of 1998. On 21 May 1998 Suharto resigned and Indonesia has since embarked on a new era of power struggles that will determine the country's future.

During Suharto's New Order regime (1965–98) the term 'development' was used as a weapon to repress people as well as a means to gain people's support. Suharto's government had always accused the previous regime, the Old Order (1945–65), of focusing too much on politics; riddled with political conflicts, it was said, the Old Order had ignored development. Suharto's New Order government, on the contrary, did focus on development. But to maintain development, political stability was needed. And for Suharto, political stability meant repression. Thus it was not surprising that Suharto's New Order government used the term 'development' as a weapon to maintain power.

Indeed, for a time, this policy was successful. People were assured of getting sufficient rice, basic health services and primary-level education. People could also see that roads were being built; electricity and telephone lines became available; and tall buildings sprouted up in Jakarta, the capital city. The term 'development' was only applied to physical development. People forgot, or tried to forget, that this development also meant the enrichment of the elite: the bureaucrats, the military officials and a minority of business people (McDonald, 1980; Bourchier and Legge, 1994; Vatikiotis, 1993).

After Suharto's downfall in May 1998, Indonesia entered a critical phase. At the time of writing (February 1999) it is still uncertain whether the factions which support the *status quo* will remain in power or not. One thing is certain: a window of opportunity has opened up. There is now more opportunity for a genuine people's movement to flourish. The Indonesian women's movement is currently flourishing in this opening up of the Indonesian society.

This chapter is a reflection on the efforts made by Indonesian women to make changes for the better during the Indonesian New Order era and after the regime's downfall, particularly efforts by women activists who are based in women's NGOs. I myself have been involved in the Indonesian women's movement in various roles: as an individual woman activist, as a founder of a women's NGO, and as a project officer of various women's programmes in development projects for about 13 years.

I begin with a brief review of how funding for women's projects arrived in Indonesia. I will describe how the international women's movement affected the introduction of concerns about women and hence funding for women's projects. Next, I will present and analyse my own experience of organizing the NGO Yayasan Perempuan Mardika (YPM). I will then compare my first experience at YPM with recent efforts by women activists during the present political and economic crisis that Indonesia is undergoing. Through these experiences, I try to reflect on the importance of women taking control into their own hands. In the YPM experience control was taken out of our hands, while in the more recent experiences control remains in the hands of the women themselves.

The Arrival of the Idea of Women in Development

Indonesia under the New Order regime is a clear example of a country that 'benefited' from the modernization approach to development. The West was so relieved when finally left-wing movements in Indonesia were crushed by the New Order regime that, when Indonesia then opened its doors to foreign investment and aid, it poured in from the industrialized countries. Modernization and development soon became government catchphrases (Liddle, 1994).

By the late 1970s critiques of the modernization theory as the key to development began to be discussed in Indonesia. University students learned about 'dependency theory' and Paulo Freire's popular education for the oppressed. NGO workers debated how to implement adult education or participatory action research. Grassroots development became the catch-phrase for those who criticized the government's approach to development.

One form of resistance to the government was the establishment of NGOs (lembaga swadaya masyarakat or LSM) which had a very different understanding of development from that of the government. After the 1974 wave of students protests was crushed, NGOs became the only outlet for radical ideas of development.[2] Establishment of these Indonesian

NGOs also coincided with an international trend that placed development high on the agenda. Therefore their growth was supported by international funding agencies. By the 1980s the argument that women should also be included in development began to circulate among Indonesian NGO workers, an idea that has flourished since.

By the early 1980s the feminist demand to be included in development began to be heard in Indonesia. The concepts of 'Women in Development' and later 'Gender and Development' began to circulate. The terms 'gender', 'women's role' and 'patriarchy' became popular. Gender training courses were held and 'gender analysis' became common.[3] Women NGOs were established and mixed NGOs introduced women's sections or placed a priority on women target groups. Even the government reflected this new concern to include women in development. In 1978 a Ministry of Women's Affairs was established. This was, in part, the result of pressure from international agencies to include a gender perspective in government policy and projects (Lindsay, 1997). This also explains some of the funding provided to both the government and NGOs by international agencies.

Part of the concern to include women in development efforts was merely cosmetic. Women's sections or activities that focused on gender issues were established merely to impress the funders, but this same concern nevertheless resulted in the establishment of women's NGOs throughout the country. In my opinion, most of these women's NGOs now reflect genuine efforts to improve women's position in Indonesian society. I shall now describe some earlier and more recent experiences of these women's NGOs.

Good Intentions Ain't Good Enough: the YPM Experience

Origins in the students' movement

After Suharto crushed the earlier student protests in 1974, there was a long silence.[4] But the mid-1980s to early 1990s saw a resurgence of the student movement in Indonesia. I was immersed in that movement. During my first year at university in 1983, enrolled in the department of sociology, I immediately linked up with other concerned students who preferred discussing real social political issues with each other rather than being bogged down by sterile lectures. The links between discussion groups became wider, linking students of different cities. The various student discussion groups held small lectures, inviting the few remaining radical scholars, who introduced socio-political theories that were unthinkable within formal university courses.

Of course mere discussions bored us. We wanted some action. So, like many other groups of students, we started a small development project to 'link with the masses'. Ours was in a village in West Java. As we became involved in 'development', student activists were determined not to replicate the mistakes we saw made by the 'established' NGOs, many of whom were closely linked to the government.[5] We criticized these groups for not being political, for selecting projects in safe areas, for not empowering the people, and, worst of all, for merely 'selling poverty'.

Soon, discussion groups and small development projects became too small a pond for our bubbling political consciousness. So we 'took to the streets'. It was the disputes over intensifying land grabbing in the rural areas that initiated large-scale student support for the masses in the late 1980s. Students rallied with peasants or attended the trials of indicted peasants. They rallied at the parliament (DPR) and at the government offices, and were joined by other radical groups in society.

Establishment and end of YPM

This protest experience had a big impact on me. It was a feeling of being at one with the people, the powerful feeling of being together, and I was exhilarated at the strength that we found to fight against injustice. The whole radical experience (not just the 'street protests') turned my mind upside down. I no longer wanted to be merely a wife and career woman but to ensure that my life would be dedicated to something more, like serving the people and fighting for justice, freedom and democracy.

I was not alone. There were quite a few young women like me. Naturally we banded together. We moved from one resistance movement to another. We stayed in touch even though all of us were studying or working. In mid-1991 I was one of a group of five women in Jakarta who agreed to continue our radical work by developing a long-term plan. We decided to focus our work on industrial women workers because their number was increasing and they are, as a group, heavily exploited.[6] We believed that aside from the economic perspective, a feminist perspective was needed within the labour movement.

We opted to establish an NGO, the Yayasan Perempuan Mardika (YPM), because we needed the funding. Forming a 'licensed' NGO is the only channel by which popular movements can gain funding in Indonesia. At that time we didn't bother about the legal structures that this entailed. We were sure that what was important was the design and running of the programmes. We saw the establishment of a legal NGO merely as a formal requirement by the funding agencies, the banks, the government and other agencies. We just came together to the notary's office to sign the documents and there it was. It was so easy. Looking back now, I realize that, even though we thought that having a licence for our NGO and having a relationship with funding agencies were only to meet legal requirements, and a means to acquire financial support, we were actually being moulded into the established development structures.

As soon as we got confirmation of funding we started work in high spirits. Our programmes covered a wide range of activities. We designed and delivered adult education programmes for workers on various topics, including labour law, political economy and gender issues. We aimed at helping the workers to organize themselves. We wanted to see more women worker activists in the labour movement; we dreamed of setting up a small but comprehensive documentation, research and campaign centre on labour issues; we wanted to generate public support. We certainly aimed to do *a lot*. Probably too much. On top of that we had to recruit people, set up the institution and learn about management and the nitty gritty of running a professional outfit.

Looking back, I realize that we were crazy. Although there were five foundation members, only two were willing to work full-time, including me as coordinator. Recruiting members was no easy thing. The ideal YPM staffer was a progressively political feminist who was willing to work in a new NGO. She must be prepared to have an uncertain future and no career path, and be happy to receive a small wage. She would also have to move from her comfortable surroundings at home to live with the workers. In short we looked for middle-class educated women who were prepared to commit class suicide – something that even we, as the founders, could not do.

Meanwhile the funding agencies were on our backs. Naturally they wanted regular reports. One donor even wanted more sophisticated financial reports. It drove me crazy, having to learn about financial accounting. We also had to come up with statistics – how many workers did we actually facilitate, how many groups were we able to assist in the establishment, what were the outcomes of the education programmes?

Besides our planned programmes, we also had to deal with the unplanned activities, such as assisting workers in disputes, getting legal aid, aiding sick workers, and meeting the pressures put on us by the military, such as attending their summons for 'interviews'. The programme we set out to do was more than we could handle. The professionalism needed to run an organization was lacking and, most of all, the level of political commitment we required of ourselves was bogging us down. Therefore it was not surprising that by late 1992 YPM was in trouble. Things were not running as planned; everyone began to become uneasy. By mid-1993 the bubbling kettle blew up. Everyone just literally screamed at everyone else. But we were not ready to give up and we began a process of restructuring. By the end of the next year we were making serious efforts to identify and train women who would take over

YPM in 1995. But we were still strict in our commitment to work for the women workers. We required that organizers live with the workers in their community, and we dispensed with activities not directly related to the workers at the grassroots. In August 1994 I left the country on a scholarship for a graduate programme on women's studies, returning to Indonesia in April 1995 to do field research for my thesis about women workers' activism. By this time we were engaged in a debate about the failure of our restructuring programme. There were also financial irregularities and a refusal to allow professional auditing. The situation was not good, and the way we became personally hostile to each other was even worse. Communication was no longer possible. In January 1996 some of the founders sought the legal dissolution of YPM.

Struggle for Democracy Through NGOs?

How could this happen? What went wrong? What did we do wrong? We had good intentions, how could we fail? We truly believed that our small, politically progressive organization could make a contribution in the struggle for democracy by uniting the voices of women workers. I asked myself those questions again and again. I just wanted to run away, start my life all over again, and be reincarnated! But I knew I had to analyse the situation to be able to get my life back and to make sense of what happened.

So this is my analysis. We are the products of our history. Since the rise of the New Order in 1965, people's experience in organizations had been very limited, since popular organizations were heavily controlled. Even among the educated middle class, the formal education system provided no experience of modern organizations.

After the banning of suspected left and nationalist political organizations in 1965, the next generation of activists (1970s) opted for NGOs as an alternative form of organization. These NGOs mostly worked on economic development issues, thereby generating a social but not a political perspective. That is understandable considering the political pressure on the people's movement at that time. The organizational structure assumed by these NGOs is generally conventional, with the founders sitting on the board of trustees, board of directors or similar body. This board sets the policies, appoints the executive staff, and approves the budget and evaluation reports. The NGO is therefore unable to work as a participatory democratic organization, but is bound to be based on hierarchy, control and directives – and how can we model democratic principles if we do not practise them? YPM adopted this conventional structure. It reflected our background as young women with little or no organizing experience.

When we tried to establish a more democratic working relationship, we failed.

Our roots are also middle-class, and this characterized our work. We were buoyed by our abundant funding. We flattered ourselves that we were far more modest than the Big NGOs (nicknamed BINGOs), but still we showered ourselves with facilities like telephones, fax machines, computers. And every day we wanted more. Our telephone bills soon rose to one million rupiah (US$500) per month. Compare this to the fifty thousand rupiah (US$25) a worker needs to rent a room monthly! We became dissatisfied with simple computers: we wanted coloured notebooks. We paraded like executives. We would fly or take cabs to meetings instead of huddling in a bus or train as we had done. Our middle-class origins were also the main reason why we did not keep our focus on the women workers at the grassroots. We enjoyed the spotlight of public forums. We liked seminars, exchange programmes and training programmes more than being with the workers where they needed us. We did not want to move our office closer to the workers' community, but offered all sorts of justifications to keep our office in the nice neighbourhood in the city. Worst of all, we gradually failed to listen to the voice of the workers. We only listened to our own voice as our interests became more and more institutionalized within the NGO. It was not surprising that efforts to open up the management of YPM to include labour activists or to include women workers as members met with fierce opposition. And when some of us wanted to be honest, to admit our failures and seek progressive solutions, the result was only intense and deep conflict that led to the breakdown of the organization.

Don't the donors care? Don't they know what is going on? Maybe they kept on giving aid because they believed in us. Maybe they were too ashamed to admit that they had made a mistake in giving funding to us. Maybe they just didn't care as long as they could claim that they were funding a women's organization that was struggling for the workers (a rare species among the male-dominated NGO community, and one of only two such NGOs in Indonesia). Whatever the reasons, excessive funding made us dependent. We were also burdened by the demand for professionalism (which is not wrong, but we were not ready for it). A lot of our time and energy went on meeting donors' requests for a certain type of financial report or running a management improvement programme. While there is no doubt that management training was important, we had no way of handling it in the context of our ideals.

YPM started with a desire to build a genuine partnership with grassroots activists, but our structure as a legal NGO forced us into the mould of the funding agencies. We lost control of our own organization. It takes guts to admit to our failure, and I can only hope that our experience will alert fellow activists to the need to critique the NGO movement, and the constraints of relying on external funding. While there are obvious advantages to having relations with international funding agencies, including financial support and a push for improvement of management capabilities, there is the clear danger that such funding will lead to dependence and the loss of control. YPM's experience should not be viewed merely as our internal problem, but as reflecting wider obstacles within the NGO movement in general and within the women's movement in particular.

Women Unite: Experiences in the Crisis

I now want to turn to my involvement in the Indonesian women's movement since the economic and political crisis that started last year (1997). In the current Indonesian economic and political crisis there is evidence of an increase in women's unity. The economic and political issues draw women together to address their problems. Individual women at the grassroots and women's organizations were all concerned to try to address the issues that have a direct impact on women. In this section I would like to discuss how women have controlled the 'development' work that they have been doing as the crisis has forced them to come out, unite and take control of these issues.

The economic crisis of 1997 caused a massive increase in the cost of living. By early 1998, the price of foods, medicines, medical services, educational needs and transportation had increased by 100–300 per cent since the onset of the crisis the previous July (Suara Ibu Peduli newsletter, various issues). Such increases made life impossible, especially for poor women. Women's groups thus addressed the issue of basic food prices as a matter of urgency. Women set up buying clubs and cooperatives. Two groups of middle-class women in Jakarta pooled their capital to purchase goods in bulk and sell to the community at low cost.[7] Similar groups of women sprang up in other Indonesian cities.

Suara Ibu Peduli: from domestic to public

One effort by women to organize around the food issue brought to the fore a group calling itself Suara Ibu Peduli (The Voice of Concerned Mothers). I want to focus on this group because they obtained widespread media coverage and support from the public, and their movement had consequences far beyond the food issue.

Suara Ibu Peduli (SIP) gained immediate media attention when, on 23 February 1998, they organized around 20 middle-class women, who were mostly NGO activists, to stage a peaceful protest at the heart of downtown Jakarta. The protest raised the issue of the increase in the price of milk by over 100 per cent and its adverse impact on women and children. The protest was immediately curbed, and three leading protesters were arrested and later put on trial for disturbing the peace (*Jurnal Perempuan*, May–July 1998, supplement). The protest gained widespread support from the public and enormous media coverage, inside and outside Indonesia.

The media played an important role in ensuring the high profile of that protest.[8] For days SIP and its leading women protesters, particularly Karlina Supeli, made the news. Inside and outside SIP there was a debate regarding the strategy of the protest. One group thought that it was good to gain wide support, and this could be done with the 'help' of the media that continuously carried SIP's news. They realized that the media loved the idea of mothers defending their children because of the increase in the price of milk. They could use this version of the protest to show that the economic situation under Suharto had become so severe that even mothers had taken to the streets. The media also loved to focus on Karlina, as she represents the ideal type of the new Indonesian mother: beautiful, educated 'and still she puts her family first'.[9] SIP argued that to use the word 'mother' as the name of the group was a tactic to portray that all mothers in Indonesia were very angry. They argued that the idea that mothers were concerned over the country's future would appeal to the public – and it did.

Another group in SIP, however, was concerned that focusing on the sight of concerned mothers crying over the lack of milk for their children would encourage a backlash against the women's movement. This group suggested that the word *perempuan* (women) be used instead of *ibu* (mother). This group argued that not all women are mothers and yet the increasing price of milk is the concern of all women. This group also argued that for a long time the women's movement has tried to portray to the public that women's role is not just to be mothers but workers and community leaders as well. Therefore this group was not happy with the fact that the media covered SIP's efforts purely from the perspective of the mother image and role. Indeed, subsequent media focus on women's involvement in the struggles leading to Suharto's downfall has continued to stress the mother role.

Suara Ibu Peduli's main activities have been in pooling donations from the public to purchase milk at factory price and distributing it to low-income families. Donations poured in and women from various class backgrounds offered to help and participate in different ways. Branches for milk distribution were set up. Media coverage on Suara Ibu Peduli has died down, but its activities continue. One important consequence of both the activity and the media coverage is that one of Suara Ibu Peduli's leaders, Karlina Supeli, has become very well known to the public as a 'respectable' woman leader, voicing grassroots feminism. Her frequent public appearances ensure that a feminist interpretation has often been aired in public discussion, both before and after the fall of Suharto. This high profile has also ensured that SIP has continued to play an active role in the continuing student protests against the Habibie government.[10] During the students' occupation of the parliament buildings in May 1998, it was women's support (including SIP's) in providing food and medical aid to the students that was reported by the media. This may have obscured the number of women students who were involved in the movement, some of them in leadership positions, and many of whom gave speeches at political rallies or to gatherings of students.

Suara Ibu Peduli's success teaches us that women actually have all the resources to organize, without having to depend on funding agencies. When there is a real need, such as the increase in milk prices, women can unite themselves, pooling their energy, time and money. Suara Ibu Peduli never asked for external funding, although they were happy to accept donations from inside and outside the country. But because they received money freely, they could assert control over all aspects of their organization. Indeed, it is clear that precisely because everyone knows that Suara Ibu Peduli is strong, money comes from the public and funding agencies, as well as from individuals and groups.

We must also learn from Suara Ibu Peduli's efforts that taking up a domestic issue like the price of milk can be very political. When the media reported the initial peaceful protest, the government was forced to acknowledge that the milk issue had to be taken seriously. The visibility of SIP also meant that other women could see that there was something that women could do to help make changes for the better. When the leaders of Suara Ibu Peduli's protest were arrested, the public rallied to their support. Suharto's government looked bad in arresting mothers who were only concerned for their children's welfare. Thus, SIP's activities have an important theoretical implication in broadening the definition of politics by showing the link between domestic and public issues.

Volunteer team for rape victims

President Suharto, who had been in power for 32 years, was toppled on 21 May 1998. But his stepping down was surrounded by bloodshed and destruction. Suharto's final days started with the killing of six university students from Trisakti University who were demonstrating peacefully in favour of reformation in politics and economy on 12 May 1998. The army's attack on the students (many others were injured at Trisakti and other universities) was followed by riots, looting, killings and rape throughout Jakarta for three days. For many months, Indonesians had feared the breakdown in order that would accompany the change of regime, and this confirmed their worst fears. As usual, women had been particularly aware of the dangers, and it was they who suffered most in the May Riots.

The occurrence of the rapes was slow to reach the media, and the full extent was never revealed in Indonesia. It proved to be an intensely controversial issue. Information about incidents of sexual molestation and rape during the May riots in Jakarta was passed by word of mouth, especially among women's groups, and it was only much later that the full facts came out. While rape is notoriously difficult to 'prove' it has been established that some 1,500 women suffered during the three days in Jakarta or in other cities in related riots, and that there are 168 confirmed cases of rape among these. The vast majority of the victims are Chinese ethnic women, an appalling outbreak of the latent racism towards this group in Indonesia.

The rape issue during the May riots in Jakarta angered many women activists. It was soon clear to us that the majority of victims would not come forward and that there was little support for those who did. We also became increasingly clear that this was an issue of women's human rights. Together with other women activists I was involved in the setting up in early June 1998 of the Violence Against Women Division of the Humanity Volunteer Team (usually referred as the Volunteer Team),[12] to provide support for victims and their families and to raise public awareness about the racism and sexism embodied in the attacks. The Volunteer Team started from scratch; there was no money to start our work, and we depended on the resources of Kalyanamitra, a feminist NGO whose members were involved in the Volunteer Team.

The Volunteer Team began by carrying out preliminary investigations into the rapes, relying on information from victims' families and religious leaders. Information about sexual molestation and rape during the May riots in Jakarta was released to the media and support immediately flooded in. People came to be volunteers and donations were received in small and big amounts. The issue of the rapes during the May Riots continued to be controversial, however, with both the government and the army denying their very existence and lengthy discussions in the media about whether such rapes were even possible. The result was that victims were even less willing to come forward, which perpetuates the problem of the lack of 'proof' (Suryakusuma, 1998). In turn this has placed the Volunteer Team and other supporters in a difficult position.

The decision of rape victims and their families to keep silent is very understandable. There are strong indications that rape was used as a method of terror during the Suharto regime. The Volunteer Team gathered information that the rapes were conducted by a group of men who were not locals. After such rapes, victims are understandably terrorized. Terror was also inflicted on the Volunteer Team and other NGOs working on the rape issue in the forms of threatening phone calls and stalkings.[13]

Part of my job in the Volunteer Team was disseminating information and looking for support, in Indonesia and overseas. In late June 1998 I had to travel to Canada for my work. On my way home, I visited friends in Vancouver who arranged for me to meet with the Vancouver Forum, a group of Chinese Canadians concerned about the victimization of Indonesian Chinese during the May riots. Cooperation between the Vancouver women activists, the Vancouver Forum, the Volunteer Team, and a Jakarta-based women's crisis centre, Mitra Perempuan, brought a Canadian psychotherapist, who had experience of similar work in Bosnia, to Jakarta to provide training in counselling trauma victims. Again resources drawn from a variety of sources supported this training. Funding came from the participants and the organizations involved. This is another example of they way in which individual women and women's groups can respond to a real need. They communicate, they organize and they get support from other women and women's groups. They get funding this way, and they remain in control of their organization and its activities.

Conclusion

My intention in this chapter has been to reflect on three different efforts by groups of Indonesian women to improve their situation. Their efforts are crucial to mainstream development strategies or efforts. Without women, no worthwhile development can take place. Reflecting as a feminist and as an activist, however, I find that I must be critical of myself, the Indonesian NGO community, and the international funding and development agencies. These reflections lead me to question what development really means, and especially what it means for women, and for feminists doing it.

Development, for sure, means more than physical improvement, such as better food, clothing, buildings, working equipment, machinery or capital. Development also means that various, less tangible needs are met: the need to have a say and be listened to; the need to follow our chosen path and to have dignity.

Coming to my conclusions has been a long and painstaking process for me. I have read and discussed other critiques of development, yet only through living these experiences and being ready to be open and critical have I realized where the mistakes lie. At the same time, learning about our mistakes and those of others has also been empowering: we know what to do and what not to do in the future, and we know where our strength is.

My first experience organizing the YPM was an experience of failure. Considering that experience, it is clear that even with the best of intentions to meet the genuine needs of women workers, when the need is moulded into the funding agency's interests then the result is the loss of control by the activists. Whether YPM liked it or not, it had to play according to the rules set by funding agencies.

In the experiences of SIP and the Volunteer Team, control remained in the group's hands. When control is firmly in the hands of the NGO, even if funding is sought the NGO is more on a par with the funding agency. The lesson learned from these experiences is that it is possible to organize independent women's projects, without direct funding interference.

People can, and always have made efforts to develop themselves. Groups have always had an understanding about what 'development' will best help those living at the grassroots. The examples provided by SIP and the Volunteer Team show groups of Indonesian women responding to real needs that emerged as a result of the political and economic crisis in Indonesia. A crisis situation forces developments and encourages potential that may not come out otherwise, but we must learn that the potential has always been there. When women take control of development, it is free of outside interference and this increases the feeling of ownership. It is this kind of development that we all want to build.

Notes

1. A part of this chapter appeared in *Inside Indonesia*, May 1996, with the title 'The Myth of Effective Little NGOs'. The word 'myth' used in the title was meant to refer to the notorious saying that 'small is beautiful'. Local NGOs are considered small and effective development vehicles by funding agencies. With the case of YPM I was trying to show that small does not always mean beautiful; it can also mean weak.

2. The Suharto government gave the term *malari* (*malapetaka lima belas Januari*, or the 15 January Disaster) to the peak day of these student protests.

3. That this apparent victory for feminism was often a double-edged sword is not the focus of this chapter.

4. Apart from another, smaller, upsurge of student efforts to criticize the Suharto regime in 1978.

5. That is why we mocked them as *plat merah* – or 'red plate' – NGOs, with reference to the colour of the licence plates carried by government-owned cars.

6. We focused on women workers at least in part because of the Marxist theory that argued that industrial workers are (or should be) the most politically progressive section of the proletariat.

7. See Nova, 2 September 1998. Suara Ibu Peduli activities are documented in their newsletter, published every two months.

8. Foreign media tended to exaggerate their reports – for example, the *Newsweek*

coverage, 9 March 1998, headed 'Moms in Revolt' – but even Indonesian media made it clear that SIP activities were not seen to violate women's traditional role as mothers.

9. Karlina has what Indonesians call an 'Indo' face, part Indonesian and part European or American. Many famous Indonesian actresses exemplify this model of beauty. Karlina is also famous as the only female graduate in astronomy in Indonesia.

10. They have developed a 'logistical' support operation for the student demonstrations, providing food, drink, basic medicine and transport back-up as formidable as that of the army. It is, of course, within the traditional parameters of 'women's work' and this has continued to be a point of discussion; see Myra Diarsi, *Jurnal Perempuan*, June 1998, supplement.

11. The most conservative estimates were made by the government-sponsored Task Force. Even they estimated that well over a hundred women were raped, and many others attacked and injured in the riots.

12. The Humanity Volunteer Team itself was initially set up to address the victims of Suharto's crackdown on the Indonesian Democratic Party in July 1996.

13. This culminated in the murder of one young activist in the Volunteer Team on 9 October 1998. Police have successfully implicated a young neighbour in the murder, and have resisted any suggestion that it was politically motivated.

PART III
Integrating the Local with the Global

10 • Falling Between the Gaps

Fenella Porter and Valsa Verghese

This chapter looks at the experience of working in an international feminist organization during the period 1990–5, in the light of some key questions: What is feminist? More particularly, what is an international feminist organization and what is global feminist work? In exploring these issues, we will focus on a process that informed these years for us: the move of our organzation from Geneva to Uganda. The questions of feminism and what it is to be feminist in different contexts will be explored in a complex dance with another important set of dynamics: What and where is international? And what is the relationship between Northern/Southern feminisms and 'development'? How far can we engage with development constructively? And how far can we compromise without selling out?

Isis WICCE (Women's International Cross-Cultural Exchange),[1] an international feminist resource and documentation centre, was until 1993 based in Geneva, Switzerland. In 1993 it was moved to Kampala in Uganda, with consequences for the identity of the organization and its relationships with the local and international women's movements, and with donor agencies. The period 1990–5 was a time of great changes in feminist theory and practice, as well as in development. The post-Nairobi (1985) surge in awareness of women's issues through women's studies, women's activism, women's advocacy initiatives and national and international networking was finally beginning to bear fruit. There was an acceptance of women's issues in the international development discourse. In the build-up to the UN Fourth World Conference on Women in Beijing (1995) there was greater collaboration between government bodies and NGO organizations in many countries, and words such as 'empowerment' and 'gender' became more acceptable and, soon, part of popular jargon. National and international funding was also available for regional pre-conference events and for participation in the Beijing Conference. But all this apparent acceptance of the principles of gender equality was actually quite 'theoretical', especially in the areas of human rights violations, and social and economic discrimination and injustice.

It was also during this period that a number of major development agencies began to experience budget cuts. Donors like CIDA (Canada), which were known to support women's organizations with feminist agendas such as Isis WICC, stopped most of their grants to women's organizations outside Canada. Other major governmental donors began a process of decentralization and reorganization. For example Holland, Germany and Sweden opened regional offices to liaise with 'Partner Organizations' who received grants from them. Another trend was the shift in donor support from international (feminist) women's information networks – which tended towards more feminist transformational perspectives – towards support for development work which accommodated an analysis of gender relations but did not set out to transform the economic, social and political structures of gender inequality.

Another development was the fairly rapid cooption of the 'women's agenda' through the opening up of job opportunities in gender departments of governmental, international and NGO development agencies and the multiplication of Women's Studies departments in universities around the world offering degrees and training courses in 'gender'. All this led to a rise in people espousing the terminology of gender whose motivations were purely academic and (in the worst cases) monetary rather than political. This had the effect of diluting and sapping the transformational and political energies of the feminist movement. Much of the work on 'gender' today is far removed from the early feminist political activism and research of the 1970s and early 1980s, which were closely interlinked and based on a clear critique of global patriarchy and its detrimental impact on women world-wide, united through a commitment to change, and fed by the voluntary energies of women acting together.

The 'gaps' in the title of this chapter are those between feminist vision and ideology, and how 'legitimate' activity is understood in development discourse – that is, what is understood as 'gender and development'. The discourse of gender and development may once have been a radical and transformatory agenda for feminists, but the way in which it has been taken on by mainstream funding agencies and governments in 'development' discourse pushes the radical politics of feminism to the margins.

When 'Women' Becomes 'Gender'

Other chapters in this volume have expressed the idea that the motivation behind the espousal of 'gender' can sometimes be seen in its complete rejection of the language and political identity of feminism (see Ines Smyth in Chapter 2). Women in Development (WID) became Gender and

Development (GAD) for good reasons, and for many of us GAD is the more radical agenda, seeking to address the basis of inequality between men and women, and locating 'development' in social transformation. But this is a difficult approach to take on for many 'mainstream' development agencies, encapsulating as it does ideas of challenging and transforming structures of power and elitism.

Gender and development discourse can be seen as a positive attempt to address women's inequality, and an attempt to 'include' feminist thought in development ideas and practice. In many cases this has had enormously positive results, with organizations such as Oxfam formulating an operational policy on gender equality and mounting genuine attempts to implement the policy through their programmes. In academic development discourse, 'the constitution of gender as a category of analysis even in mainstream academic scholarship is a political achievement' (Udayagiri, 1995). On the other hand, the way in which 'gender' is treated by many mainstream development organizations seems to seek to de-politicize it to such an extent that it has become a 'technical' element that needs to be 'ticked off' the check-list (Porter and Smyth, 1998). This is evident in the way in which 'gender training' and 'gender planning frameworks' are doled out to eager development professionals, who then instantly declare themselves 'gender-sensitized'.

This alarming tendency is not even a return to the less transformatory agenda of Women in Development (WID), when women were marginalized as a separate group. Attempts to 'include' can normalize and standardize ideas and discourse, which undermines politics (such as feminism) and smothers diversity and dissent (Porter, 1998; Jackson, 1998). It is more of an attempt to coopt the GAD approach by 'including' it in development discourse, smothering the politics as part of the terms of 'inclusion', and thereby keeping the development process non-threatening.

The feminist movement was not prepared for this cooption by the mainstream and today still lacks a coherent strategy to counter it.

On the Margins of 'Development'

'Development' is a fundamentally conservative agenda (see introduction to this volume), tied as it is to improving the economic status of countries, communities or individuals – rather than transforming the *status quo*. Feminism as a political and transformatory discourse has a natural 'home' on the margins of development from where it challenges the very basis of development discourse. On one hand, feminists working in development (whether as 'gender specialists' or not) risk exclusion from the mainstream of economics; on the other hand, by working from within development they also risk exclusion from feminist debates and support structures, and the transformatory energies of the women's movement. They can often fall into the gaps between feminism and development. What is needed is not to 'bring feminism in from the margins', but to ensure that the margins are places where feminisms and feminists can thrive and make a difference, remaining connected to transformatory energies and political discourse. This is the political agenda from which 'gender specialists' can become disconnected.

> [M]arginality is not something which should be relegated to the past when we were the victims of exclusion. Marginality is not simply a symptom of oppression, but a site which can be chosen as a location for radical critique, creativity and openness. (Davis, 1997: 195)

Organizations such as Isis WICCE, by remaining firmly within the political arena of the international feminist movement, operate on the margins of gender and development discourse even at its most radical. Isis WICCE was part of the debate of moving development discourse from WID to GAD, working from a critical perspective of feminist analysis with many other organizations within an international global agenda that was developed during and after the international decade on women (1975–85) and the international conferences of the 1990s. Once 'gender' is no longer considered to be about politics and transformation, however, our foothold in the development process becomes unsafe and either we fall into line behind the depoliticized version or, eventually, we fall off. In many ways the movement for the incorporation of gender concerns into development discourse has been overtaken by its own success. The terminology has been accepted by mainstream development, but without the substance of transformation.

If the marriage of gender and development could become a reality, and if mainstream development could begin to take on board real feminist transformation and a genuine commitment to gender, then development would begin to bring about genuine sustainable and positive *change*. But in order for this to happen, there is a need to recognize that gender is about a transformation of the roles and relationships of and between men and women, and of the social, economic and political structures within which these roles are played out. We also need to recognize that this cannot be achieved overnight, and that, in order to be sustained, the changes will necessarily be slow and require evolving strategies that involve both women and men, and that address their respective and mutual needs.

Some Theoretical Perspectives

There are many tensions around how 'feminist' is defined in different contexts. In particular Northern feminist analysis has created a hegemony which has defined Southern feminisms as the 'Other': exotic, strangely rooted in 'culture', and powerless. This is in opposition to the way in which Northern feminists define themselves and their struggles – strong and radical, the voice of 'global feminism'. Mohanty criticizes Northern feminists' use of the term 'women' to denote 'powerless' in the Third World, rather than investigating the ideological and material specificities of the situation that are the cause of women's powerlessness (Mohanty, 1988: 80). Thus Mohanty argues the case for all analysis to be rooted in the specifics of particular situations. Mohanty's analysis uses Foucault's insights into discourse, power and knowledge to pick up on postcolonialist orientalist[2] tendencies in development, and in particular gender and development discourse.

Although this presents a very real challenge to feminists working in the field of gender and development, particularly in academic circles, Mridula Udayagiri points to its failure to address the way in which feminist politics can actually engage with development policy and practice (Udayagiri, 1995). Furthermore, for feminist organizations such as Isis WICCE, working as part of an international movement, feminists are not exclusively Northern but include all those who cut across the regional divide and try to arrive at a common analysis of patriarchy in its many manifestations in different contexts. They strive to develop effective strategies and tools that address the diversity but do not lose sight of the common goal. Their goal is permanent change in the form of justice, development, freedom from discrimination and peace for men and women of all societies.

Isis WICCE

Isis WICCE is an international feminist resource and documentation centre, running an exchange programme (now known as the Exchange Institute) for women activists from different parts of the world around a particular theme or issue, and producing a biannual publication, *Women's World*. Isis WICCE's work is based on the belief that in order to be able to change their oppressive realities, women need to become aware of the nature, causes and consequences of that oppression, and break their isolation. To do this, they need access to relevant information about the status of women in their own and other societies, the common factors causing the inferior situation and status of women in most communities, and how women are organizing to change their situations and striving for freedom from discrimination. Isis WICCE's objectives, strategies and actions were based on a global feminist perspective.

Isis WICCE, as a global feminist organization, aims to facilitate women's networking, and the empowerment of women to become effective agents of change. The activities of Isis WICCE create different channels of communication through which women empower themselves by exchanging information and experiences, and by contributing to the collaboration, support and solidarity between women activists, researchers and movements world-wide. Initially this was accomplished through publications and an information and communication service. Issues such as violence against women, women's health and development were addressed as priorities; the media, and their role in perpetuating the biases against women, were also an important focus. Later, the cross-cultural exchange programmes for women activists were begun, to strengthen these efforts and offer women activists the opportunity to make direct contact with each other, to travel to other cultural situations and see how similar issues are dealt with, and to share and learn from each other's experiences and knowledge.

The activities of Isis WICCE were funded and still continue to be funded by major development agencies based primarily in Europe. Our values and objectives were formulated in the 1970s within an emerging international feminist movement. Our identity, our programmes and our funding base developed over time as an organization operating within the international women's movement, questioning processes of 'development' and working towards equality and social justice for women all over the world.

In 1993 Isis WICCE moved to Africa with the intention of strengthening links with the women's movement in that region; enabling women there to have more direct access to the resources of the documentation centre; and enabling us to serve the documentation and information needs of the local, regional and international women's movement. In order to implement the move an International Advisory Committee of representatives from leading women's/feminist organizations, with a substantial representation from Africa, was set up to identify the needs for the region, the location of the organization and strategies for the smooth implementation of the move. Following this, a feasibility study was conducted covering countries such as Zambia, Uganda, Namibia, Zimbabwe and Tanzania. Kampala in Uganda was selected because the women's movement there was extensive and active, the government was stable and supportive of women's issues, the infrastructure was being rebuilt (after years of civil strife) with a substantial influx of Western aid, and the existing communication and banking facilities were adequate for Isis WICCE to function effectively.

Once the location was identified, the process of closing the office in Geneva and the move of documents, equipment and the entire resource centre to Africa took place. The registration of the organization in Kampala, the location of suitable office space and the recruitment and orientation of an entirely new staff were undertaken by a Transition Committee, led by a Transition Coordinator, who handed over responsibilities to the first Board of Isis WICCE, Kampala. The regular donors of Isis WICCE, the Netherlands Foreign Ministry, the Norwegian government development agency NORAD and the Swedish International Development Agency (SIDA) were major donors supporting and financing the move.

The move had certain implications for the identity of Isis WICCE, however, as well as for its programmes and funding base.

What (or Where) is International?

Whilst 'transitional funding' was secure for the first couple of years in Uganda, a large part of the work to set up the organization and its programmes in our new home was to seek new funding sources that would allow us to continue the work in Africa in the longer term. There were considerable tensions around seeking funding from development sources, however, as our work was still 'international' in focus, and had a clear feminist political message.

Our move to Uganda coincided with a process of decentralization that was suffusing the donor community. Thus, by moving to Uganda, Isis WICCE was, in a way, reflecting donor priorities. At the same time there was no space identified within this process for international organizations to work in developing countries. It seemed that once we had moved to Uganda, we were no longer eligible for 'international' funds. We were now a 'local' organization and needed to seek funds from the national or regional offices. This we did. When we approached many of these national/regional offices, however, we were told that because we did not focus specifically on Uganda and Ugandan women we were still 'international' and therefore did not fall into their funding priorities. For example, on a visit to the country representative of SIDA (Sweden) in his office in Kampala, it was clear that whilst he was receptive to the idea of Isis WICCE moving to Uganda, he did not see how our activities fitted in with the way in which he would disperse his funding, which was for local 'projects' in Uganda. His advice was to seek funding centrally from SIDA.

It seemed that we were falling into the gaps, and that Isis WICCE as an organization with an 'international' focus did not qualify for 'development' funds unless it developed local or regional projects. A major part of the reason for moving Isis WICCE from Geneva to Kampala was to work more directly with women in Africa, and our work, whilst remaining international in focus, aimed to ensure that this was indeed the case. In many ways it was our responsibility to ensure that the programmes and the organization were rooted in the needs and the agenda of the women's movements in East Africa, and in Uganda in particular. This reflects Chandra Mohanty's understanding that all analysis must be rooted in the specifics of a situation in order not to homogenize the category of 'women' and make sweeping assumptions about power and powerlessness. But by being rooted in a (Southern) situation, we were discovering, it is no longer possible to be 'international'. Now we were in the domain of 'gender and development', which (according to some donor priorities) is different from 'international feminist' – and Isis WICCE fell into the gaps somewhere in between.

This is not to say that there were not enlightened and supportive donors. There were; and many of our relationships with funding agencies were cooperative and rewarding. There was a genuine concern amongst donors, and many feminists working within donor agencies, to support the work of organizations like Isis WICCE. There was clearly far more to be done, however, to move the donors *as institutions* from accepting the terminology of 'gender and development' to taking on a transformative and feminist agenda. For an organization like Isis WICCE, finding where our identity should 'fit' in funding proposals was problematic. The message clearly was that whilst it was acceptable to have an international and feminist focus in Geneva, now that we were based in Uganda our focus was expected to narrow to one country and to reflect 'gender and development' discourse – which in their understanding was quite different. And here lies the tension: the donor definition of what constitutes acceptable work in gender and development risks effectively silencing the voices of international feminist organizations in the South.

Mainstreaming: on the Edge Again

The time of the move from Geneva to Kampala (the early 1990s) was a time when funding agencies themselves were beginning to experience a squeeze on their own financial status. In an attempt to prioritize funding relationships, many organizations cut back on their relationships with women's organizations, while the financial squeeze set off processes of re-structuring, through which organizations lost their specialist, and often politically motivated, gender units. Gender was not seen as a priority at this time. Although many organizations were cutting back, however, the motivation was supposed to be a desire to ensure that the entire organization took on responsibility for understanding and addressing gender inequalities in each development programme. This was called 'mainstreaming'. No feminist in development would argue with the need for this to happen, but the problem was that it so often became rhetoric with no cor-responding commitment to transformation of the very structures of the organizations and the work that they carry out (Porter, Smyth and Sweetman, 1999).

> [M]ost donor agencies, particularly bilateral ones, act primarily as 'brokers' of development. They are tightly constrained by the policies of their own governments and have only a limited capacity, or even desire to influence practice and effect societal changes in the developing countries where they work. The social relations of gender are labelled as falling into the realm of culture and strong advocacy for a rethinking of gender relations would be seen as unwarranted 'cultural interference'. This reluctance in turn is reinforced by the high proportion of senior male staff in donor agencies, many of whom do not necessarily see the current social relations of gender as fundamentally problematic. (Rathgeber, 1995: 207)

Mainstreaming meant that sources of funding for feminist transformation work were diverted towards development work into which gender analysis had been incorporated. Donors preferred to fund government or United Nations programmes, or those of the UN's specialized agencies, and traditional development organizations, in the hope that they had the potential of impacting on a larger section of the population. Donor priorities also shifted away from education and awareness raising and advocacy (which is transformational) to economic projects for poverty reduction, social welfare and rehabilitation in post-conflict situations. But how can these organizations be effective agents of change, when they have stripped the word 'gender' of its political and transformational significance?

In practical terms of seeking funding for the work of a feminist organization, mainstreaming also meant that we no longer had a thematic foothold. As we were an organization working with women to eliminate gender injustice and challenge the whole process of development, we did not have a 'development-style' thematic focus (such as health, environment or micro-credit). The poverty agenda of development claimed to address gender issues within poverty reduction measures. If we had been working more specifically on anti-poverty strategies *for women*, we might have found it easier to target our funding proposals developmentally, 'from a gender perspective'. But gender subordination is not an 'element' of poverty. By mainstreaming gender in development strategies, the process of development itself remains unchanged, and unchallenged:

> [T]he concept of poverty cannot serve as a proxy for the subordination of women, [and] anti-poverty policies cannot be expected to necessarily improve the position of women .... [T]here is no substitute for a gender analysis, which transcends class divisions and material definitions of deprivation. (Jackson, 1998)

Gender in Context

In Uganda, as in many other countries influenced by donor agendas, 'development' discourse is common currency, including a 'commitment' to gender. The commitment of the Ugandan government to gender equity is well recognized, and since the NRM (National Resistance Movement) came to power women have been included systematically in all systems of representation. 'Women issues' are discussed with fervour, and the President and the First Lady lend their personal support. In 1994, the then Minister of State for Gender was appointed Vice-President: an enormous boost to the already sophisticated and powerful lobby of women in the Ugandan government. It appeared to us, however, that the concept of gender was understood as emphasizing the integration of women into the development process rather than the fundamental transformation of social relations between men and women. Government officials would frequently declare themselves to be 'gender-sensitive', which we found ironic in the face of the daily struggles of the Ugandan women's movement to ensure women's equality with men.

For example, the alliance between government and donors such as the United Nations Family Planning Association (UNFPA) on issues such as reproductive health followed the agenda of population control rather than the more transformatory feminist agenda of ensuring women's control over their own bodies. *The National Population Policy for Sustainable Development* (1995) is clear in its commitment to enhancing the status of women as an integral part of the policy. This manifested itself, however, in promoting products controlled by the (male-dominated) medical establishment, such as Depo-Provera and Norplant, whilst severely restricting women's access to abortion. Attempts to distribute contraceptive pills to women were catastrophically unsuccessful. The 'pill plan' did not include accessible information for women, nor were the distribution attempts accompanied by an understanding of intra-household decision-making power, and efforts to ensure that women actually controlled their reproductive choices within the household. Feminist understanding of women's reproductive health is linked intricately to women's power to control their own bodies and their lives, and the need for reproductive rights to accompany any efforts to reduce women's fertility. But in the arena of 'reproductive health' in Uganda, there was no room for this approach to be freely expressed. Thus the language of 'gender' was coopted by government and donors, and feminism was left with little space in which to argue and develop alternative approaches.

In many ways elements of the Ugandan women's movement are rooted in the resistance struggle that brought the NRM to power, and is therefore closely associated with the government. This association has brought many benefits to women in Uganda, and represents a politics of intricate negotiation and compromise. As in every culture, the perception of feminism may be coloured by different priorities, but the principles remain the same. Such a close relationship with the government, however, limits the ability of the local women's movement to develop alternative, and perhaps politically provocative, approaches. 'Gender' in Uganda has been adopted by the government/donors to such an extent that it has left little autonomous space in which politically motivated feminist groups are able to question and challenge this definition. Women's organizations with a political and overtly 'feminist' and international agenda risk falling between the gaps as well, and being marginalized in a context that is apparently supportive of 'gender'.

So What Is Feminist?

Uganda has a sophisticated and active women's movement, and as an outside organization coming into the country, Isis WICCE needed to find its place within this movement. Mohanty argues that 'it is only by understanding the *contradictions* inherent in women's location within various structures that effective political action and challenges can be devised' (Mohanty, in Visvanathan, 1997). Finding a place in the Ugandan context not only needed an understanding of the context and the political structures we found ourselves in, but also a re-examination of ourselves and what we represented as an international feminist organization based in Uganda.

Isis WICCE moved to Uganda complete with boxes of books, journals, files and computers – and a completely new staff. It was a question of taking on a new identity whilst remaining true to the objectives and mission of Isis WICCE in Geneva. This, of course, was not possible. But there are degrees of 'not possible'. Isis WICCE's aim has always been 'to eliminate injustice based on gender discrimination, and to improve women's economic, social and political situations. To reach these objectives, the centre exchanges information, promotes ideas and actions and develops solidarity networks.' This has remained the case in Uganda. It was not really the aims and objectives that were in question, however: it was more a question of 'image'.

Isis WICCE's staff was predominantly Ugandan and, with time, the organization found a place within the women's movement in Uganda (which was already active internationally). Even before the move, it was a priority to ensure that the activities of Isis WICCE were needed in Uganda, and were not simply duplicating the work of some other organization. Once we were based in Uganda, this became even more important, and our activities over time became more relevant to the Ugandan context, as well as maintaining an international perspective. As in Geneva, Isis WICCE also recruited non-national staff members to Isis WICCE Uganda. Within the organization this strategy worked well, and there has been a rewarding process of negotiation of what it means to be a feminist organization in different parts of Africa, in other contexts in Europe, North America and Asia, and internationally. Many of our networking partners and collaborators have also appreciated an internationally staffed organization. But many others considered that if Isis WICCE was to move to Uganda, then it should 'look' Ugandan. Here again was a tension – between how we wanted to look to reflect and carry out our mission, and how other people (Northern, often feminist and often in donor agencies) felt a 'real' Southern women's organization should look – that is, homogeneously 'Other'.

There are clearly accepted norms of how feminism looks and behaves in certain contexts. Isis WICCE, in taking an international and politically feminist organization to a Southern country, challenged norms of international development discourse in both funding agencies and the local political context, and in some ways in the women's movement itself.

Conclusion: Challenges for Feminist Organizations in Development

There is as much of a continuing need for the political project of feminism in Africa as in the rest of the world. Balanced by the need to root such work in a specific situation, it is vital to keep a clear feminist vision so as not to lose the political usefulness of this identity for international feminist work.

Operating on the margins of the mainstream and at the vanguard of a movement for equality has become a way of life for feminists. As we mentioned at the beginning of this chapter, the very constitution of 'gender' as a category of analysis has been a huge achievement of which we are rightly proud. The terms of 'inclusion' do need to be more carefully examined before we leap right into the mainstream. When looking at the recent trend of talking about 'social exclusion' in Europe, both Jackson (1998) and Porter (1998) have found that inclusion into the mainstream isn't all it is cracked up to be. In fact the concept of 'social inclusion' holds implications of making people 'includable' and thereby smothering dissent and diversity. This isn't what feminists need. The margins are free, and in them feminists are able to operate creatively to challenge the very basis of the mainstream.[3] What *is* needed is more acceptance of the legitimacy of the margins and ways in which challenges from the margins can be heard.

This is already beginning to happen, for example around UN World Conferences. Despite the repressive efforts of the Chinese authorities, over 30,000 women and men from all over the world attended the NGO forum at Huairou, and through various means we were able to get our voices heard on the world stage. Mainstream development agencies funded women's attendance at the Fourth World Conference on Women so that they could influence the process of the conference and network with other women's groups from around the world. But we need more than special one-off funds for trips to conferences: we need long-term relationships in which our voices can be heard all the time.

By refusing to take on mainstream definitions of 'development' and 'gender', organizations such as Isis WICCE are able to retain a vision of transformation from the margins. This vision is necessarily modified, however, by the constraints of seeking funding and working constructively with other partners, both from the conservative mainstream of development and from the various elements of the women's movement in both Northern and Southern contexts. There is a real role for feminist organizations such as Isis WICCE, in both the North and the South, to bring feminist voices into development, but the choices we make are strategic as well as visionary, and feminist work in development is often a process of negotiation and compromise.

Notes

1. Isis WICCE was established as one organization called Isis in 1974 with the basic aim 'of collecting and disseminating information of all kinds on the women's movement and to provide a service to women and women's groups around the world'. This basic concept remained firmly grounded as Isis evolved into two separate organizations in 1983 – Isis WICCE in Geneva (which moved to Kampala in 1993), and Isis International in Rome. In 1984 Isis International Santiago was opened in Chile by staff of the Tomme office returning home from exile. And in 1990 Isis International in Rome packed up its resource centre and transferred its documentation and activities to Isis International in Manila. (Taken from Marilee Karl, 'Isis: 25 years, still going strong', in *Impact*, a special publication of Isis WICCE, Uganda, 1998).
2. For the origins and use of this concept, see E. Said, 1978.
3. Liz Stanley, in her introduction to *Knowing Feminisms*, articulates a similar idea about the 'borderlands' of academia, and the unwitting freedom this sometimes bestows on feminist academics.

11 • Globalization and Development at the Bottom

Joyce Green and Cora Voyageur[1]

In Canada, large numbers of women, and extraordinarily large numbers of aboriginal women, together with their families, are experiencing unemployment, underemployment and economic marginality. In 1995, more than a third (35 per cent) of all Canadian women lived in poverty (National Council of Welfare, 1998). The United Nations Human Development Index (HDI) shows that Canadian wealth and well-being disproportionately evade women and aboriginal peoples (1998). Yet Canada, as a member of the G7, is one of the seven wealthiest industrialized countries in the world. The Canadian economy is strong, despite a tremulous global economy. The Canadian government is bound by constitutional and international equality guarantees to protect women's equality and aboriginal rights. Given the apparent availability of economic resources and the legal iteration of rights standards, how is it that women and aboriginal people continue to suffer from such economic marginalization?

We argue that the colonial and sexist practices of the Canadian state fuse with contemporary neoliberal ideology[2] to produce a political consensus on government withdrawal from public spending. This leaves the most marginal sectors of society without state-supported minimal levels of health, hearth and wealth. Neoliberal ideology also privileges private corporate development of natural resources, in ways that injure not only, but especially, aboriginal women. Thus, while state welfare is minimized, economic development in Canada also fails to aid those who are economically marginal, especially where these people are already disadvantaged by racism and sexism.

This chapter uses the feminist method of 'looking to the bottom of the heap, to see who is buried there' (Gretchner, 1991), to see how globalization and development play out. In Canada women of all backgrounds and aboriginal people of both sexes are disadvantaged economically. Although women have made inroads into male-dominated fields and have narrowed the gender income gap slightly, there are still significant differences between the economic positions of men and women in

142

Canada, with women earning about 70 cents for every dollar earned by men (Status of Women Canada, 1999).

Women are more likely to be poor than are men. A National Council of Welfare report[3] states that there are more poor women than poor men in Canada and that the poverty rate is consistently higher for women. The data show that women's poverty rates for the period under review are between 4.3 and 5.4 per cent higher than men's (see Appendix C). The incidence of poverty is even higher for disabled women, aboriginal women and visible minority women (Status of Women Canada, 1995).

It is the economy that is dominant in neoliberal ideology, which is itself a dominant ideology among Canadian opinion leaders and governments. Neoliberal ideology in turn both explains and advocates the current phase of capitalism, globalization.[4] Are these forces benefiting aboriginal women? We look at the data showing how those at the bottom of the economic heap – women and aboriginal peoples – are doing. Then, we look at the case of the Innu people in Newfoundland, whose traditional and unceded land includes the extraordinary mineral wealth which may be developed by the International Nickel Company (INCO) at the mine known as Voisey's Bay; and at the Lubicon Lake Cree, whose social disruption and impoverishment is a direct consequence of resource development by government-authorized corporations on Lubicon unceded lands. We conclude that development has not benefited aboriginal women to any significant degree: rather, it has contributed to the erosion of viable community economies and social structures, corroded the environment and marginalized women and children.

Neoliberalism and Globalization

Globalization is treated by media and politicians as if it were, like the weather, immutable. Political and economic analysis in Canada suggests that we are vulnerable to the effects of globalization, but that we have little power to contest the conditions under which globalization exists. On this view, political resistance and the construction of alternatives is futile. Globalization, however, is far from neutral, nor is it an ineluctable consequence of air masses aloft.

Globalization is tied to development, its connotations suggesting a rising trajectory of economic and cultural growth, carrying human well-being with it. It has an aura of historical inevitability about it. Like globalization, development is taken to be an incontestable feature of human existence. Both emerge from the practices and the propaganda of capitalism.

Two strands of contestation suggest that development and globalization are problematic. Feminist analysts have mounted a sharp critique of the inequitable nature of capitalism and development, linking it to patriarchal social relations, the invisibility of women's unpaid labour, and the hyper-exploitation of women's paid labour (Waring, 1988; Simmons, 1997). Critical analysts have shown the colonial practices of capitalism; the easy appropriation of indigenous lands and resources assumed by states and corporate interests; and, occasionally, the questionable virtues of the capitalist paradigm itself.

Colonialism continues in Canada in the form of contemporary global capitalism, and as indigenous peoples were sidelined by so-called 'development' when the state was initiated, so the majority of citizens are now peripheral to political and economic power. Women in both categories are affected more negatively, and have less power to contest the changes, because of women's disadvantaged position in both colonial/settler and contemporary indigenous societies.

Even mainstream communities have suffered under neoliberal regimes, and women and children have been disproportionately injured. The federal government of Canada, under Prime Minister Jean Chretien, has cut spending for social programmes and abandoned federal support via the Community Assistance Programme (CAP) for provincial governments to deliver social programmes. The consequences for Canadians have been increasing economic and social polarization. Child poverty in Canada is at a 17-year high with almost 1.5 million children living in poverty (National Council of Welfare, 1998: 12). Now, Canada has been censured by the United Nations for its rising disparity of wealth and poverty, and for the skyrocketing incidence of child poverty (UN Committee on Economic, Social and Cultural Rights, in *Herizons*, 1999).

Aboriginal people in Canada are marginalized from mainstream social and economic life, and neoliberal practices have done nothing to change this. Indeed, state and corporate economic practices have left aboriginal communities out of any processes that might create wealth or social well-being. The intersection of sexism, racism and colonialism in a neoliberal political climate ensures a very high probability of immiseration for aboriginal women.

Engendering Development

Feminists have demonstrated that women hold a less than equitable portion of the world's wealth, but do a majority of the unpaid work. Women have less political representation and influence as well. For example, in 1995 only 18 per cent of Members of Parliament (MPs) were female (Arscott and Trimble, 1997: 2). Not surprisingly, given this under-representation, policy-making bodies and state policies take little account of women. Women maintain reproductive, productive and community management roles, but have little power to manage these roles authoritatively and little official account is taken of them (Moser, 1989): women's work is invisible in the official reckoning of economic activity and directed development (Waring, 1988). Too often, development planners assume that increased economic (remunerative) activity will produce gender equality (Moser, 1989). Accordingly, women are drafted or coerced into the paid economic sector, where they provide cheap labour. At the same time they continue to be responsible for the reproductive and social servicing work that has always been invisible (Dacks, Green and Trimble, 1995). The failure of politicians and bureaucrats to adopt a gendered policy analysis results in a 'women-blind' policy that imposes additional burdens on women, while failing to address their gender-conditioned needs. According to Sunera Thobani, 'There is no acknowledgement that the current model for economic growth and globalisation, based as it is on "free" market principles and reducing the role of government in redistributing wealth, devastates the lives of women' (1996: 48). Certainly, there is little acknowledgement of the problems development produces for women and aboriginal people in the Canadian context.

Appropriating Aboriginal Wealth

The story of Canada is the story of capital's evolution, in uneasy conjunction with the evolution of civil society that is imbued with both the conditions of historic capitalism – that is, racism, sexism and colonialism[5] – and contemporary contestations of these conditions. Canada is rooted in colonialism, an economic process associated with capitalism. Canada was initiated in racism: a structured and theorized racism, encoded in law and politics, which defined indigenous nations as non-existent for the purpose of international and British common law. That is, they were theorized to be so different from the standards of civilization that they could not contest the Crown's sovereignty, first invoked as a colonial relationship and then represented by a domestic government in the emergent state of Canada. Deemed subjects but not citizens until 1960, aboriginal peoples were utterly peripheral to the state and to its driving economic impulse: first mercantile, then staples capitalism, and now commodities, industrial and investment capitalism. Aboriginal lands and resources, however, were central. Canadian political, economic and social development is a consequence of the colonial relationship and the appropriation of indigenous lands and resources (Green, 1995).

The government has taken special interest in what remains of Indian lands – 'reserves' under the Indian Act – in relation to the remaining natural resources. The inventory drawn up by the Department of Indian Affairs – Mineral Resource Potential of Indian Reserve Lands – consists of 45 volumes with approximately 18,000 pages and 10,000 maps. The report is defined as 'records of all available material on the geology, geophysics, geochemistry, economic geology, and mineral operations of a reserve and a surrounding area' (INAC, 1990).

According to the report, approximately 30 per cent of the 2,267 Indian reserves (which encompass 2,671,564.7 square hectares) have either moderate or good mineral potential (see Appendix A). By 1990 the Indian Lands Registry, an office of the Department of Indian and Northern Affairs, recorded 564 mineral-related permits, leases and/or agreements (INAC, 1990: 7). The private sector undertook 72 per cent of the mineral agreements while provincial governments accounted for 14 per cent and municipalities for 6 per cent.[6] Clearly, non-aboriginal interests continue to benefit from development of the last vestiges of aboriginal resources.

Indeed, provincial motivation to settle outstanding land claims and questions of aboriginal title seems to be linked to interest in clearing the path to resource development. The federal and provincial governments are interested in settling aboriginal rights and land claims in order to create the conditions for investment confidence, and to protect 'third party interests' (that is, non-aboriginal property). Especially following the Supreme Court of Canada decisions in *Sparrow* (1990) and *Delgamuukw* (1997), with their acknowledgement of pre-existing and outstanding indigenous interests, governments have moved to make treaties, settle land claims and negotiate specific settlements. Meeting these legal and constitutional obligations paves the way for resource development and related activity in Canada's economy, which is based on resource commodities.

Remarkably, in 1982 the new constitution recognized and affirmed the 'existing aboriginal and treaty rights' of the aboriginal peoples of Canada. This reluctant gesture by the state[7] to acknowledge something – though not sovereignty – has been interpreted by most observers to be fundamentally about self-determination within the Canadian state.[8] It was not, however, to be decolonization, because the land and resources appropriated by Canada were still largely constructed in law and theory to be outside the negotiating parameters. Indians might be 'given' land settlements by the state, but they would not be able to reclaim their traditional territories, nor would they be able to claim a share of the wealth generated from those stolen lands.

Indeed, most negotiations suggest that colonialism continues, in a kinder, gentler, more localized fashion.[9] And, while granting full citizenship status to Indians in 1960, the state has never seriously attempted to meet aboriginal people's basic citizenship and human rights, as measured by socio-economic and political indicators. With the lands and cash settlements they might obtain, however, Indians are expected to develop their social and economic infrastructure; that is, to engage in development.

Bad Attitude

Most non-aboriginal Canadians have been oblivious to the colonial relationship, though they have benefited from it. Indigenous peoples have been rendered so invisible through policy, law and culture that their absence from settler socio-economic and political institutions is not cause for comment. Non-aboriginal Canadians typically hold erroneous stereotypes about their aboriginal fellow citizens. In fact, many Canadians believe that aboriginal people are responsible for their own low social and economic position in Canada. The 1996 poll commissioned by the Department of Indian Affairs found that 'almost half of Canadians believed Aboriginals had equal or better standards of living than the average citizen. And, 40 per cent believed natives had only themselves to blame for their problems' (Aubry, 1997: A9).[10]

The discrimination experienced by aboriginal people is fuelled by many sources, one of which is the media. Voyageur (1993) found that the media presented conflict-based aboriginal stories[11] in 70 per cent of their coverage during the period under review. Benjamin Singer's content analysis of aboriginal-based stories in Canadian newspapers for a five-year period (1971–6) found that stories predominantly showed Indians in two ways: in negotiation with the government over one issue or another; or in conflict with the government (Cooke, 1984). In 1980, Peter Pineo rated the social standing of 36 ethnic and racial groups, and found Canadian Indians ranked the lowest on the social ladder along with four other non-Caucasian groups. Katie Cooke's (1984) study of the image of Indians held by non-Indians found that Indians were viewed as different and possessing many undesirable characteristics and values. She also noted the many cultural sources that reinforce the negative stereotype of Indians: newspapers, television, movies and textbooks. Perhaps the most disturbing revelation was that Indians are seen as irrelevant to Canadian society (see also Stymeist, 1975; Dunk, 1991).

Globalisation and Citizenship

Let us return to capitalism and its present evolution to the form we call 'globalization'. Globalization of capital – especially investment capital – has expanded the arena in which to seek profitability and, simultaneously, has granted transnational corporations and investment brokers more leverage over states. Governments are attentive to the interests of capital because of 'investor confidence', guaranteed by favourable evaluation of domestic policy choices by international bond rating agencies like Standard and Poors or Moody's; and because the ability of investment capital to move instantaneously gives to it the power to destabilize national currencies and undermine national economies. These practices are normalized through multilateral trade regimes, which erode state sovereignty and, therefore, government policy flexibility to maintain the conditions for citizen and human rights (Cox, 1995; Gill, 1995; Teeple, 1995; McBride and Shields, 1997; Schneiderman, 1999).

States are headed by governments, political constructions which are theoretically the advocates of the public good. Citizens of the state are supposedly the *raison d'être* for government policy choices. Since the 1948 Universal Declaration of Human Rights, governments have had a central role in protecting human rights and creating their preconditions, further supported by the international conventions on economic, political, cultural, civil and social rights and by other rights instruments. Yet governments now routinely make policy choices that favour the interests of international capital to the direct detriment of citizens – and justify these choices by invoking 'the economy' and TINA: There Is No Alternative. Citizens largely accept these explanations without much critique.

In this process, state governments are aligned with capital, not with citizens. As capitalism consolidates its current global regime, its practitioners have moved to institutionalize the relation of states to capital through multilateral trade agreements and transnational regimes such as the World Trade Organization (WTO) and the currently dormant Multilateral Agreement on Investment (MAI).

The purposes for which governments are constituted, and the core of rights and relationships foundational to citizenship itself, are obliterated by this new regime. Governments that persist in orienting policy to citizen needs over those of 'the economy' or the advice of bond rating agencies and the WTO are likely to be disciplined. Lowered credit ratings, devalued currencies and unattractive bond rates, together with a loss of 'investor confidence', quickly bring these governments to heel.

Citizens are utterly inconsequential to this new relation, except as producers and consumers. 'Development' is synonymous with profitability, not with social and political indices measuring well-being and democratic participation. Now, more citizens are treated like Indians by the state, because citizens as such are peripheral to the state's grand obsession with a dominant and decontextualized economy. This economy is more detached from societal interests because of its global arena for production and investment; and because an increasingly large portion of its activities –

currency trading, derivatives speculation, bond markets and investment capital – are entirely unrelated to material production or social interests. The profitability equation is divorced from social goods such as employment standards and numbers, environmental and health protection and other social needs.

Government restructuring to conform to this new regime includes privatization, deregulation and a retreat from public spending on the social services that are foundational to human and citizen rights. All of these changes have resulted in measurable declines in living standards and quality of life indices for many Canadians, especially for the most marginal sectors of society.

Corporate downsizing (elimination of jobs) exacerbated the bleak economic climate. Federally regulated companies under the Employment Equity Act reduced their workforces by approximately 8 per cent between 1990 and 1993 (Voyageur, 1997). The jobs of private sector employees were also terminated, many by profitable companies seeking even greater profitability (Green, 1996).

Even where the economic fundamentals for capital growth are sound, the IMF, the WTO and other sultans of capital confidence continue to badger states to choose domestic policy options congruent with ever-greater measures of profitability. Little by way of critique of these processes has been made available to the general public. The 'fifth estate', the media whose constitutional rights to freedom imply their centrality in democratic practices, are almost entirely privately owned. The interests of privately owned media are determined by profitability. This situation promotes a 'cultural colonialism' and a 'cult of modernity' (Petras, 1997: 183). A uniform political discourse is presented, while dissent is marginalized. This constraint on debate and opposition undermines citizenship. In the words of Robert Cox, 'The death of politics is the death of the citizen, which is the death of democracy' (1995: 9).

Development for the Innu and Lubicon Lake Cree

The Innu nation

Consider the specifics of the Innu and Inuit people in Labrador, in whose traditional and unceded territory lies the vast mineral concentration at Voisey's Bay. The Innu and Inuit have been ignored by provincial and federal governments, apart from some desultory attention following media coverage of the social pathologies endemic at Davis Inlet, particularly youth substance abuse and suicide rates. The colonial state has shown little interest in human rights or 'development' for the Innu and Inuit.

The discovery of the biggest nickel deposit in the world near Voisey's

Bay has changed all that. Wealth has flowed around the find: its identification, registration and sale; the exploration rights paid to the province by the nickel giant INCO; the servicing of the emerging infrastructure – all this has attracted multi-millions of dollars, although the Innu and Inuit have been sidelined in the process (Lowe, 1998b). It came as something of a shock to state and corporate parties when the aboriginal landlords suggested that development would not proceed without land claims settlements and a negotiated share of the pending wealth. But during the negotiations, the international commodities market suffered from global capital instability and a glut of commodities on the market. Nickel fell to its lowest price in a decade. Although a tentative settlement has been negotiated between the Innu and the federal and provincial governments, INCO began to wonder publicly if the site was worth developing, given falling commodities prices and the possibility of cheaper production elsewhere (in Indonesia, for example, where aboriginal rights and labour and environmental issues are less constraining). The impetus to settle up with the Innu and Inuit fizzled. Clearly, the commitment of the colonial state to contemporary justice for indigenous peoples is linked to its interest in corporate activity, not in justice *per se*. Nor is economic development so enticing if it includes indigenous people on equitable terms. That shaves the profit margin, no doubt.

Mineral exploitation was always a dubious benefit for the Innu. There were no guarantees of corporate commitment to local hire and training policies. 'Local hire' policies are based on the premise of locally available skilled workers, not on commitments to training. 'Locals' are sometimes hired as menial labourers with little commitment from the employer on the conditions or length of employment. This situation causes conflict between local people and the companies.

In the case of the proposed INCO development at Voisey's Bay, the environmental integrity of the land would be compromised, thereby affecting the indigenous communities. The Tongamiut Inuit Annait *Ad Hoc* Committee on Aboriginal Women and Mining in Labrador argued that women in the communities around the mine will be affected profoundly by impacts of the development. Gender has not been taken into account, however, in the environmental assessment review of the costs and benefits of the project. Similarly, the socio-economic impact assessment conducted for Shell's proposed Muskeg River Mine Project looked at potential employment, increased population and regional economic benefits, but did not incorporate a gendered analysis (Shell Canada Limited, 1997: 33).

On 17 February 1999, the Labrador Inuit Association (LIA)[12] tied its tentative support of Voisey's Bay to satisfactory negotiation of a comprehensive land claim. The LIA also noted concern with environmental implications of the project (*Globe and Mail*, 1999).

The Lubicon Lake Cree

The Lubicon Lake Cree in northern Alberta, by virtue of aboriginal title, claim lands to which the province claims Crown title and constitutional control of resources. The resources in question are oil, gas and forests. The corporate exploiters of these resources, which are almost exclusively transnational corporations based elsewhere, pay royalties to the province, which in theory at least uses this wealth on behalf of 'all Albertans'. The consequence for the Lubicon is the destruction of the land they claim and, therefore, of their economy based on hunting and trapping.

The Lubicon fall within the territory covered by Treaty 8, but are not signatories to the treaty. It seems that when Treaty 8 was being negotiated the Lubicon people were hunting elsewhere, and this was of no concern to government until oil and gas were identified on traditional Lubicon territories. The Alberta and federal governments then took the position that the Lubicon did not really exist as a distinct socio-political entity; or, alternatively, that their claims were mitigated by a variety of events between 1899 and the 1970s. Alberta had no problem in claiming the resources, and then selling various multinational corporations the exploration and exploitation rights on them. The corporations in turn paid royalties back to the provincial government. Non-native Albertans have welcomed the profit in provincial coffers without examining where it comes from, or at whose expense.

Nor will the province and the federal government conclude negotiations for a just settlement. The Lubicon found negotiations thwarted at every turn. Band membership has been a sticking point: the Lubicon insist on defining their members, including some people whom the federal and Alberta governments don't recognize as having 'status'. This, of course, is a consequence of the patriarchal provision in the pre-1985 Indian Act, which tied band membership to 'legitimate' patrilineal descent and marriage (Jamieson, 1978; Green, 1985; Green, 1992; Weaver, 1993; Green, 1997) and so is directed especially against women who 'married out' and against their children. The federal government has also engaged in divide-and-rule tactics to divert support from the Lubicon leadership, contributing to community disintegration. Twice now it has created 'new' bands, the Woodland Cree First Nation and the Loon River First Nation, from 'status' people, some of whom were associated with Lubicon, and then moved to settle claims with these new bands, while taking the new negotiating position that the Lubicon Cree membership numbers are shrinking. Agreement on the membership issue was only reached in the spring of 1999 by the Lubicon, Alberta and the federal government, clearing the way for negotiation on other issues.

In 1983, the Geneva-based World Council of Churches wrote a letter to then Prime Minister Trudeau, condemning the Alberta government and 'dozens of multinational oil companies' whose actions were 'genocidal' in their effect (Goddard, 1991: 86). In 1988 the federal government refused to honour a negotiated agreement to pay US$100 million compensation to the Lubicon for lost revenue resources on their lands. To further exacerbate the Lubicon woes, in 1988 the Alberta government permitted the multinational Diashowa to 'harvest' trees from the land under dispute. The trees supply wood to the Alberta Pacific (Alpac) pulp mill near the town of Athabasca in north-central Alberta. During the government-sponsored public hearings into the pulp mill, the provincial government and Alpac promoted the mill by saying it would provide employment in the region. The environmental impact assessment (EIA) process cited 600 full-time positions for supplying wood to the mill, but further investigation showed that only 35 would be full-time Alpac positions. The majority of the jobs would be filled by independent loggers, haulers and contractors; many would be seasonal (Richardson *et al.*, 1993).

The Lubicon, self-sufficient until 30 years ago, find their traditional economy has been devastated by 'development'. Now, they are a welfare community with a rising suicide rate along with other measures of social pathology and a tuberculosis epidemic characteristic of the last century. The Lubicon example is illustrative of the processes the state uses, in the name of those who elect the government, to oppress and exploit indigenous peoples not a century ago, but today. It is an example of resource-based economic development, benefiting some and injuring others.

In her stinging indictment of the impact of resource development on the Lubicon Cree in Northern Alberta, Rosemary Brown shows that community women were profoundly affected in all aspects of their lives. Not only had local resource development changed the Lubicon community from a subsistence economy to a wage labour economy but it had also changed the gender and social dynamics within the group. Women experienced a 'decline in the practice of many traditional productive skills, a shift to paid labour or welfare, changes in housing, household technology, changing diets and methods of food preparation, and growing incompatibility between productive and reproductive roles' (Brown, 1997: 195). Further, the traditionally egalitarian relationships between men and women were altered, with women shouldering more of the responsibility for economic, familial and community matters (Brown, 1997).

Conclusion

The Canadian commitment to aboriginal peoples and to women is thin at best. The long-standing indices of social inequality and social pathology in aboriginal populations show the lack of state commitment to the fundamental human or aboriginal rights of these people. The extraordinary social, political and legal inequality of Canadian aboriginal and non-aboriginal women with men shows a similarly cavalier attitude towards women's human rights. Globalization and development have not benefited either category, much less the category of aboriginal women, while these people continue to be unequal in their political ability to change these measures of inequality.

Governments fail to employ gendered analysis in public policy making, either in in-house offices such as the federal Status of Women Canada or by supporting and incorporating the analysis of more independent organizations. As evidence of the state's refusal to support women's analyses, advocacy and projects, consider the federal Liberal government's undermining of the National Action Committee on the Status of Women (NAC) by withholding core funding and imposing funding criteria designed to gut the organization of its political autonomy and economic ability to implement it (Rebick, 1999). Consequently, government development policy fails to take into account the different social locations of men and women, and of aboriginal and mainstream citizens. Corporations have not felt any pressure to do their own gender and race analysis, so the policy arena continues to be innocent of consideration of women and aboriginal people.

As primary care givers with respect to their families and communities, women end up coping with the results and effects of development decisions made by male-dominated governments and business interests. Women and their organizations, which receive very little financial support from governments or industry, will be left to pick up the pieces. Women, particularly aboriginal women, stand to gain the least and lose the most from development decisions that typically exclude them. Gender and aboriginality must be taken into account in all discussions concerning community, bush and industry life; in services and facilities; in politics and community development; in harvesting and land use; in hospital and medical facilities; in determining individual, collective and aboriginal rights; and in tackling social problems such as violent crime and family breakdown (Tongamiut Inuit Annait *Ad Hoc* Committee on Aboriginal Women and Mining in Labrador, 1977). Remedying this should be a top priority for governments and their corporate cousins. Even neoliberal analysts should understand that incomplete analyses lead to costly and inappropriate policies. The crudest economic calculus would be more precise for including gender and race considerations.

Fifty-one years after the Universal Declaration of Human Rights, in the era of globalization, what is it that we can say about advances for aboriginal and women's rights? Neoliberal governments are more concerned with 'development' as a practice of facilitating the private exploitation of public and aboriginal resources than with rights or justice. In this ideological environment, aboriginal rights are costed out by colonial governments in a discourse reflective partly of justice, but more of clearing the path of development of legal and governance hurdles, while women of all origins remain utterly invisible.

Appendix A

A reserve's mineral potential is rated on a three-point scale (low–moderate–good). Table 11.1 indicates the mineral potential of Canadian Indian Reserve Lands.

Table 11.1: Mineral Resource Potential on Canadian Indian Reserves by Region and Overall Rating, 1990

Region	Overall rating			Total
	Low	Moderate	Good	
Atlantic	46	19	3	68
Quebec	19	9	3	31
Ontario	82	69	38	189
Manitoba	65	27	12	104
Saskatchewan	87	47	9	143
Alberta	73	20	7	100
British Columbia	1,194	356	56	1,606
Northwest Territories	1	1	0	2
Yukon	15	5	4	24
CANADA	1,582	553	132	2,267

Source: Indian and Northern Affairs, Canada
http://www.inac.gc.ca/natres/canada.html p. 2

Appendix B

In 1997 the United Nations Committee on Economic, Social and Cultural Rights criticized Canada for failing to meet its obligations under the Covenant on Economic, Social and Cultural Rights. The criticisms included (but were not limited to) the following:

- The federal government created the conditions for erosion of Covenant standards, and of accountability for meeting them, by abandoning social rights to the provinces when it eliminated the Canada Assistance Plan (CAP) and replaced it with the Canada Health and Social Transfer in 1996.

- The shortage of adequate housing and high levels of unemployment and suicide, especially among young people, in aboriginal communities.

- Significant reductions in provincial social assistance programmes, the unavailablility of affordable appropriate housing, and widespread discrimination create barriers for women leaving domestic violence.

- Canada's ten largest cities have declared homelessness a national disaster.

- The number of food banks has almost doubled between 1989 and 1997, and still they cannot meet the increased needs of the poor.

- In 1993, approximately 4.5 million Canadians lived below the poverty line. By 1996 that number had increased to 5.1 million, and continues to climb.

Appendix C

Table 11.2: Poverty Rates in Canada by Gender, Year, Percentage and Ratio, 1980–96

	Number of poor (in thousands)			Poverty rate[14] (%)		
Year	Women	Men	Difference[15]	Women	Men	Difference[16]
1980	1,565	1,058	507	18.0	12.7	5.3
1981	1,567	1,063	504	17.8	12.6	5.2
1982	1,624	1,160	464	18.1	13.6	4.5
1983	1,836	1,334	502	20.1	15.	4.7
1984	1,817	1,304	513	19.7	14.9	4.8
1985	1,754	1,240	514	18.8	14.0	4.8
1986	1,677	1,197	480	17.7	13.4	4.3
1987	1,673	1,176	497	17.4	12.9	4.5
1988	1,664	1,081	583	17.1	11.7	5.4
1989	1,534	1,001	533	15.5	10.7	4.8
1990	1,622	1,079	543	16.2	11.3	4.9
1991	1,767	1,234	533	17.3	12.7	4.6
1992	1,804	1,289	515	17.4	13.1	4.3
1993	1,949	1,398	551	18.5	13.9	4.6
1994	2,011	1,434	577	18.1	13.4	4.7
1995	2,059	1,556	503	18.2	14.3	3.9
1996	2,143	1,555	588	18.8	14.1	4.7

Source: National Council on Welfare, 1998. Catalogue Number H67-1/4-1996E p. 86

Notes

1. The authors thank Dr Marion Jones, Department of Economics, University of Regina, for her helpful critique of this chapter. Responsibility for remaining errors, analytical frameworks and conclusions rest with the authors.
2. Neoliberalism is an economic ideology advocating a retreat by the state from spending on social programmes and from state activity in the economy in a regulatory capacity (including labour and environmental legislation) or as a player in economic sectors. It should not be confused with neoconservatism, which is a social ideology advocating a more hierarchical, inequitable and authoritarian society grounded on the patriarchal family.
3. This report uses Statistics Canada data. This particular citation covers a time period from 1980 to 1996.

4. Globalization consists of the emerging global economic order dominated by fluid capital, instantaneous communications technologies, financial deregulation, disaggregated production, multilateral supra-constitutional trade agreements and agencies, and relatively immobile, tractable labour forces mindful of competitive advantages.

5. Colonialism as used in this paper refers to the inequitable relationship in which the wealth of one society is appropriated by another, which also legally, socially and culturally subordinates its victims (Green, 1995).

6. The remainder were made up of bands (3 per cent), federal organizations (1 per cent) and other unknown entities.

7. The First Ministers were opposed to the constitutional recognition of aboriginal rights (and of women's equality rights) and only acceded after arduous political struggles by aboriginal peoples (and feminists). In these struggles, aboriginal women who held feminist analyses were targets of both colonial and indigenous patriarchs.

8. The most recent example of this may be found in *Delgamuukw v The Queen*, SCC 1997, which explains that aboriginal title is derived from the historical fact of pre-existence to the Crown's claim of sovereignty, but is never constructed as legitimately oppositional to the exercise of Crown sovereignty. Aboriginal title amounts to a right of possession, perhaps in some cases of exclusive possession, and to rights of usage of traditional lands, sometimes to the exclusion of non-aboriginal usage, but it is not seen in law to occupy the space of the state's sovereignty.

9. For example, Canada negotiates specific rights only at the price of the aboriginal participant giving up the constitutionally recognized 'inherent' rights. Extinguishment of aboriginal title, explicitly or implicitly, is a precondition to settlement in every land claim and governance negotiation in Canada. The state insists on it. And the 'self-government' powers contemplated by the state range from simple delegation of administrative powers, through to limited recognition of governing jurisdiction over a limited class of subjects and exclusively over indigenous peoples, with the proviso that provincial and federal legislation, in the event of conflict, will supersede aboriginal powers.

10. In an earlier study, Rick Ponting (1987) found of non-aboriginal Canadians' attitudes toward aboriginals that the average Canadian did not consider aboriginal issues important. Respondents chose protecting the environment and reducing the national debt as top priorities while aboriginal issues trailed a distant third, but still ahead of women's rights. According to Ponting, although they did not deem aboriginal issues important, Canadians tended to be more sympathetic than antagonistic toward aboriginals. Those antagonistic towards aboriginals stated that aboriginals already received too much financial aid from the government.

11. Conflict-based stories included land claims, constitutional conflicts, defamation, and self-government issues.

12. The LIA should not be confused with the Innu Nation; the two are ethnically and politically distinct, and are involved in separate claims processes.

13. Mineral types include: metallic, non-metallic, aggregate, peat and water.

14. Poverty rate is the percentage poor people (those living under the poverty line) represent of the total population.

15. Difference is obtained by subtracting the number of poor men from the number of poor women.

16. Difference is obtained by subtracting men's poverty rate from women's poverty rate.

12 • Labour Rights, Networking and Empowerment: Mobilizing Garment Workers in Bangladesh[1]

Habiba Zaman

In the past 25 years, the world has witnessed a marked expansion of export-oriented industries in Third World countries, which now employ millions of women workers. This process of industrialization has often been masked as development, but has been bolstered by structural adjustment programmes of bilateral and multilateral donor agencies (for example, the International Monetary Fund, the World Bank, the Asian Development Bank, the United States Agency for International Development). To enhance export-led industrialization, such donors played crucial roles in backing economic liberalization in a number of key areas such as export promotion, free markets, removal of trade barriers and industrial licensing. The framework for this industrialization in many developing countries was a new international division of labour, the relocation of production from developed to developing countries, the establishment of export-oriented world market factories and the massing together of millions of young women workers as cheap labour in garment factories.[2]

The impact of this export-led industrialization on women workers has had a mixed reception in the current literature: the epithets range from 'cheap labour' to 'flexibilization of the labour force' (Mitter, 1986; Standing 1989), from 'adverse impact' to 'benefits' of industrialization (Elson and Pearson, 1984; Lim, 1990; Ward, 1990), and from 'docile and subservient' to 'active' labour force (Tiano, 1994; Ward, 1988, 1990). This chapter explores the impact on women's consciousness manifested in network building and multiple forms of resistance strategies in the workplace and in society. Although much attention in many Third World countries has rightly focused on women's paid work in export-oriented garment industries, an equally important issue in women and development studies remains largely unaddressed: the experience of women workers, particularly regarding their rights as labourers, their strategies for survival, and their struggles to advance and organize. Feminist analyses to date are contradictory on this issue. One point of view argues that the export-led garment industries have adverse impacts on Third World women, resulting in the erosion of their rights and exacerbated by their docility, patience and lack of unionized experience (Beneria and Roldan, 1987; Roldan, 1993). Consequently, employment for these women, rather than freeing them from oppressive forces, intensifies and reinforces their secondary position and marginalizes them in the society (Elson and Pearson, 1989; Kung, 1983; Ward, 1988; Young, 1988). This view perpetuates stereotypes and negative images of Third World women and makes an unwarranted generalization across spatial and temporal contexts (Tiano, 1994).

Another point of view is that employment in garment industries liberates Third World women from economic constraints and marginalization and provides these women with certain kinds of strength and solidarity across class and gender lines (Lim, 1983; Safa, 1995; Westwood, 1984, 1988; Wolf, 1991). Further, the experience of women workers in the workplace interconnects with formal and informal organizations between or among workplace, community and the family (Morgen and Bookman, 1988).

The gap between these two points of view is slowly narrowing with the emerging of an analysis both of forces of exploitation and of strategies of resistance, network building against exploitative forces, and organization for women workers' rights (Chhachhi and Pittin, 1996). This chapter continues the analysis, considering industrialization to be – at the same time and because of its mode of exploitation – conducive to increasing and improving women's rights, especially labourers' rights, and to networking and empowerment in general. Using the results of field research I conducted in Bangladesh, I use garment workers' experience to assess the implications of paid work for Third World women workers, especially for their work conditions, their organizational links – formal and informal – and their empowerment. I argue that these women's multiple identities and specific social locations as women and garment workers create distinctive forms of activism and political consciousness.[3] Further, I suggest that women's networks with other women, as well as with women's and labour organizations, create a 'double consciousness' as women and as workers.[4] This double consciousness generates multiple forms of individual acts, resistance and various kinds of movements against the nexus formed by the state, multinationals and local entrepreneurs. In my view, it is important to remember that despite the presence of exploitative socio-economic forces in Bangladesh, these women workers' experience in the workplace can lead to women having greater roles in network building, and to the enhancement of women's rights.

Review of the Issues and Their Implications

Several recent works reflect on a wide range of arguments around the issues of women workers' economic power and status, their real or presumed docility and their struggles to improve their collective lives. In her study of Mexican women workers, Tiano (1994) found that women workers, despite structural and societal constraints, are not passive victims of the complex oppressive forces embedded in capitalism, imperialism and patriarchy. Women workers in general, despite varying levels of consciousness, can act as their own agents 'to engage in daily struggles on a personal or collective level to improve their lives' (Tiano, 1994: 221). Parveen and Ali (1996) recommend a multidimensional approach in dealing with women workers, arguing that there are class, gender and broader human dimensions to the issues of worker rights. Gandhi (1996) describes the emergence of innovative women's unions in the unorganized sectors in India for the purpose of establishing worker rights in society. Unlike the formal and well-established worker institutions, these innovative organizations encompassing both working-class and middle-class women have manifested their protests through militant acts and street demonstrations. Despite her contentions, Gandhi has focused more on the role of the innovative women workers' unions or women's groups rather than on their networking and multiple resistance strategies to achieve rights as women and workers.

The analysis that follows is based on exploratory research I carried out in Dhaka, the capital of Bangladesh, through two consecutive trips made during the summers of 1996 and 1997, a total period of four months.[5] Using primarily the snowball technique, I interviewed 20 garment workers with the aid of tape recorders and open-ended questionnaires.[6] In addition, I used various secondary published materials[7] and notes from both formal and informal meetings with women's groups concerning the rights of women in general and of garment workers in particular.

Feminization or Flexibilization of the Labour Force?

Every morning, between six and eight, hundreds and thousands of women garment workers in Dhaka walk through the streets – a scene not even imagined 20 years ago. These workers are migrants from rural areas and have moved to the city for employment, because job prospects for women in the countryside are scarce and, when available, are either non-remunerative (paid in kind) or low-waged (Alam, 1985; Paul-Majumder and Zohir, 1994). According to one estimate (*The Daily Sangbad*,

1992), about 85 per cent of the workforce in the garment industry are women who have moved (primarily from rural areas) in search of work, thus breaking the traditional isolation of Bengali women in *purdah* (seclusion).[8] In urban areas, domestic work, hitherto a major source of employment for in-migrants, has largely been replaced by work in garment industries run by both local industrialists and multinationals. Employment in the garment industries has given many workers their first opportunity to earn wages several times higher than they could have earned as domestics (Paul-Majumder and Zohir, 1994).

In the mid-1990s, it was estimated that women made up 69 per cent of garment industry workers (Bangladesh Bureau of Statistics, 1994) and that number is likely to be even higher in 1999. According to Standing (1989), this feminization of the labour force is due to several factors such as deregulation in industries, erosion of labourer rights, insecurity in jobs, and the nature of work. Standing argues that feminization and the flexibility of the labour force have caused displacement of male workers by a female work force. Elson forcefully contests this view, however, and points out that 'flexibilization does *not* necessarily lead to direct substitution for men in types of work traditionally done by men; nor does it necessarily lead to a rising female share of paid employment in manufacturing industries' (1996: 40).

In the case of Bangladesh, I argue that socio-economic forces, particularly poverty and unemployment among rural women and the nature of jobs in the garment industry, are largely responsible for increased women's employment in factories. In other words, new job opportunities in the city are responsible for rising women's employment in the urban areas, together with several push factors. These include the displacement of women and their labour from rural areas due to increased use of mechanized devices in post-harvest operations; the rapid rise of rural–urban migration as people search for jobs in the cities; and an increase in female-headed households due to separation and/or divorce and/or death of male heads, particularly among low-income families (Islam, 1991).

Sisterhood and Resistance

'Women's work never ends' is a statement which is absolutely true for garment workers. All the women I interviewed reported that the expected norm is a regular nine-hour work day (8 am to 5 pm), without any day off. Each work day normally includes a one-hour lunch break from 1 to 2 pm, although some women reported only half an hour for lunch break. All reported that they do overtime regularly, meaning that the average work day is about 12 hours, from 8 am to 8 pm. Respondents in Paul-

Majumder and Zohir's study (1994) also reported work days of eleven or twelve hours. In order to meet deadlines for production and supplies to the world market, the workers I interviewed said that they are often required to work late hours – up to 10 pm or, in some cases, even 2 am. No consistent overtime rules exist for garment workers; they are often notified the same day, during work hours, that they must extend their work hours. Sufia described her usual work during a peak period:

> I work from 8 am to 10 pm. I get overtime payment and it's about Tk 400 –500 a month. I also work at night time – from 10 pm to 3 am. This is different from overtime and is called 'night duty'. I get Tk 30 per night. I sleep in the factory after night duty and return home in the early morning. Then I take a shower, cook and eat and start my work again at eight the same morning.

Overtime is hardly ever shown on individual time cards; this is one way for employers to avoid existing industrial laws[9] and undercount overtime payment. Several workers also reported great irregularity and frequent delays in the payment of overtime and sick leave. Ruksana said:

> I had been sick for four days. On my return to the office, I applied for sick leave on the company's prescribed form. Later on, I discovered my monthly salary had been deducted by four days. Upon inquiry, I was told that my supervisor did not sign my form [the supervisor had left the office for unknown reasons]. Hence the general manager deducted four days' pay from my salary as it was not approved by my previous supervisor.

Moly reported another kind of irregularity and extraction in her factory:

> Three days late is counted as one day absent. If I say anything, the supervisor responds, 'Can't you come on time?' ... The supervisor also deducts Tk 10 from my monthly salary and Tk 3 from my overtime payment .... The worst thing is we don't get paid on time. We work for money!

Moly was conscious of her expected gender role: 'Men protest. As women, we don't. For this reason, men are not hired in the factory, but we are.' Her story sheds light on the presumed docility and submissiveness of women workers, attitudes which may partially explain the feminization of the labour force. During my research, however, I documented many incidents of resistance by the women workers against abusive practices by the management. These incidents suggest that, despite women workers' multiple roles and long hours in the workplace, the intersection of their work and social networks has resulted in multiple forms of resistance and organized movements. These women are vocal about hazardous and deplorable working conditions, poor physical and civic amenities, irregularity in monthly salary and overtime payment, and lack of organized unions. Their responses and resistance strategies are manifested in a number of ways – both informal and formal.

Everyday Resistance in the Workplace

Most of the workers I interviewed were aware of their oppressive situations and their personal resistance strategies towards workplace abuses were numerous. The following are three examples. First, if receiving verbal abuse for the quality of their work, most women reported that they asked their supervisor to stop the abuse and demanded that the supervisor show them how to perform more efficiently. Second, three garment workers missed work the day I interviewed them and did it quite happily – a subtle example of collective resistance. Third, some workers reported that on occasion they demanded their supervisors pay their overdue monthly salary. Salma said:

> We say, stop your abusive words; give us our exact payment, then we'll leave the place. [Using slang language] the supervisor says, 'Did I appoint you to get you out? Mind your own business.' ... Line workers [those who work on the floor] have understandings. The worst are supervisor, floor-in-charge, manager. We can't enter into the General Manager's or Director's office. They work in their own offices. No worker is allowed to enter into their offices as they are always guarded by security personnel [darwan].

It is evident that women workers use diverse and individual resistance strategies to fight against exploitative situations.[10] The informal network system, such as walking together to and from the workplace, living in close proximity to each other, and working in the same factory, also facilitates exchanges of information on their rights and interests.

Formal Resistance: Protests and Demonstrations

Since the resurgence of the garment factories in the 1980s, garment workers have been organizing and rallying around workers' issues. Work experience in the factory has sparked in many workers a new working-class consciousness. One of the focal points for worker' grievances is fire safety. Laila, one of the woman I interviewed, was very conscious of fire hazards and aware of the necessity for united protests:

> In our factory, we have only one entrance door at the front gate. When fire occurs, we all try to run through the same door at the same time. Incidents of fire happen quite frequently. Nobody protests regarding this issue! Because the workers are not united!

Many workers I talked to had participated in protests and meetings involving their own rights or the rights of women in general. The following excerpt from an interview with Bula, Sabiha and Urmi indicates that women workers are aware of and involved in various rights issues concerning women:

During the non-cooperation period [a political strategy by the opposition party to discredit the government in 1995–6], I had no job; then, I participated in demonstrations. With others [co-workers], I chanted slogans: 'We want jobs, we want jobs, we want to live through our jobs'.

During the *hartals* [strikes], I participated in protest meetings. We walked through the streets and chanted slogans: 'Want jobs, want jobs'. Journalists spoke with us. We said, 'We want to be alive!'... I have good feelings about demonstrations. ... Then, a [general] election was held and after that, there was no *hartal*.

I participated in demonstrations for the murder of Reema, and the murder of Yasmin [two highly publicized murders]. For this, I went to a place [women's organization] near Sangsad [Parliament building] ... They did not give me money, but we had Coke. ... The police did not allow the demonstrators to go forward.

Between 1990 and 1997, as many as 50 garment factories in Bangladesh were reportedly affected by fire, mostly caused by electric short circuit; 87 workers died and about 1,000 were injured.[11] Of all the fires so far, the worst broke out on 27 December 1990 at Saraka Garments on the outskirts of Dhaka. Thirty workers, 25 of them women and children, died in the fire (Simu, 1995). According to the workers, there was no fire exit – Saraka and many other garment factories lacked minimum safety precautions.

To protest against these shocking deaths, the garment workers called for a *hartal* on 1 January 1991. According to Alam, '20,000 women garment workers from various factories marched through the streets of Dhaka demanding compensation for their dead and wounded sisters, a government investigation into the accident, and the application of proper safety measures in the factories' (1995: 41). With the assistance of the police and muscle-men, the management tried to stop workers from organizing, but for a while it was a futile effort. Feminist and activist Farida Akhter of UBINIG (Policy Research for Development Alternative) remarked:

Women *are* getting more aware of their rights. Some problems – like the prevalence of violence against women workers – have started to get a little better. I don't subscribe to the view that women in Bangladesh cannot be organised because of family pressures and so on. Despite the appalling conditions we come across everyday, I *am* hopeful that women garment workers can win improvements; and that more owners will see that it is in their interest to have a healthier and more satisfied workforce. (Jackson 1992: 28)

An important outcome of this spontaneous movement by garment workers was the establishment of a broad-based trade union organization called Garments Sramik Karmachari Oikya Parishad (The United Council of Garment Workers). The United Council organized a mass demonstration in which garment workers from 60 different factories participated and drafted a plan of various demands to improve the conditions of garment workers. Some of the main demands included: (1) written employment contracts for all workers; (2) provision for maternity leave; (3) one day (Friday) weekly holiday; (4) eight-hour work day; (5) payment of overtime hours; (6) child-care facilities for women workers with young children; (7) transport facilities for women workers, especially night-shift workers; (8) regular on-time payment of workers' wages; and (9) protection of child labourers from arduous work and long work hours. The Council has opened up a new era for garment workers in terms of empowerment and resistance against harassment and intimidation of workers in the workplace. A further development was the formation of Bangladesh Sramik Oikya Parishad [Bangladesh United Workers' Council] on 14 July 1997, by nine Garments Sramik Federations (Garment Workers' Federations) (*Garments Katha*, 1997). It is thus clear that women workers through their networks provided support to political activism in order to protect their rights as industrial workers.

Linkages with Women's Groups

Throughout the 1990s, various women's groups, trade unions, and NGOs have been actively involved in promoting the rights of garment workers in Bangladesh through seminars, conferences and workshops. 'Women Industrial Workers in Bangladesh: Current Situation and Future Prospects', a seminar held during 21–23 October 1992, drew a wide cross-section of people, including women's groups and women workers from twelve industrial sectors (including the garment, textile, fabric, tea plant, telephone, and pharmaceutical industries).[12] In her presidential address, Professor Latifa Akanda of Dhaka University, a member of Women for Women (the internationally respected women-oriented research group), compared women's labour with human blood, as not having any distinctive features in terms of nationality, gender and religion. Akanda was also critical of gender-based discriminatory practices in the area of work and wages. Another speaker, Ayesha Khanam, General Secretary of Mahila Parishad (a feminist/women's organization), stated that she considered the women workers' movements to be part of the national women's movement. She added that while the Bangladesh Constitution guaranteed equal rights for both women and men, in practice women [workers] had been deprived of these rights. Khanam also drew attention to the apathy of the state towards the protection of the rights of women workers set out in the United Nations Declaration of Human Rights.

Farida Akhter of UBINIG also spoke at the 1992 seminar. As well as being a major source of strength for the women's movement in Bangladesh, garment workers were identified by Akhter as a social force which had been changing social expectations and values continuously. She questioned the so-called development policies of the World Bank and argued that they paved the way for relinquishing labourers' [women's] rights. More positively, the Bangladesh government, by using the skills of the garment workers, could compile a national plan for industrial development with an indigenous rather than an export-oriented emphasis. Shirin Akhter, a trade union activist, summarized the barriers to women in the trade union movement (which, she stressed, nevertheless played a key role in helping alleviate women workers' problems): military rule, anti-worker laws, reactionary/right-wing policies and the undemocratic procedures of the state.

In this three-day seminar, the garment workers were divided into a number of discussion groups which focused on their lack of rights and on procedures to achieve their rights. In all, 120 women workers participated. They adopted 30 agendas regarding their rights which have been endorsed by many women's groups and trade unions. The relevant agendas in that context were: (1) a single trade union for every industry; (2) a woman who loses her job due to her involvement in union activities has the right to take legal action against the employer or factory owner; (3) representation of women garment workers in every trade union; (4) women workers to be searched by women only (at the time, they were searched mainly by men); (5) security and protection during night shifts. The garment workers skilfully articulated their demands and the seminar could be seen as a broad-based political forum that combined lobbying with strategies. This seminar projected a new path for women in Bangladesh, one in which achieving women workers' rights will expedite women's liberation from all kinds of oppressive forces.

In July 1996, to celebrate 25 years of Bangladesh as an independent country, a national seminar at Proshika Manikgang was sponsored by four NGOs: Nijera Kori, the Association for Land Reform and Development (ALRD), UBINIG and the Society for Environment and Human Development (SED). There were six workshops in a three-day seminar (3–5 July), and one of these centred on women workers in industries. Participants in the workshop, which I attended, included garment workers, activists, labour leaders, trade union members and lawyers. The seminar called for the implementation of the eight demands of the Garment Workers Federation. The participants also demanded that a number of policies be implemented: the government's promised minimum wages for garment workers; four months' maternity leave; establishment of day care in factories where 50 or more women workers are employed;

separate toilet/rest/prayer rooms for women, and so on. The main demand was that industrial and labour laws be implemented immediately. The links with various women's groups and trade unions had obviously fostered a sense of sisterhood among the women workers.

Feminist Strategies in Linking with Garment Workers

Women's groups and feminists/activists have supported garment workers to improve labour practices through an agenda of gender equality. The advocacy of these groups has been manifested in a number of ways. In 1992, Mahila Parishad, a 29-year-old grassroots women's organization in Bangladesh, published a 17-page strategy report for the advancement of women in Bangladesh in the run-up to the year 2000. The report poignantly described the conditions of garment workers: 'The export oriented garment industry earns 50 per cent of the country's foreign exchange; 41 per cent of the female labour force is engaged in the garment industry; women are given no contracts or legal protection; women's wages are generally 66 per cent of men's wages' (Bangladesh Mahila Parishad, 1992: 10). A left-oriented feminist organization believing in establishing the rights of women, Mahila Parishad continues to advocate garments workers' rights in its documents as well as in its actions, such as organizing protest meetings and demonstrations.

UBINIG has published regular features on garment workers in its bi-weekly newsletter, *Chinta*. *Chinta* exchanges information and features with Third World Network, an international networking group, and thus paves the way for garment workers' voices and concerns to cross national boundaries. In the first quarter of 1996, *Chinta* published these headlines: 'No more slavery! Demand Friday as a weekly holiday: Garment Workers' Movement'; 'Accidents in garment factories and questions regarding workers' security'; 'Nine killed, fifty wounded: Who's responsible?' 'Situation of garment workers during non-cooperation movement'. UBINIG's reports and features established garment workers' issues as women's issues at the national and international levels. At the national level, UBINIG organized workshops on garment workers. In its 1986 workshop, 'Export-Oriented Development: Industrial as well as Labour Policies and Women Garment Workers', participants came from Women for Women, the International Labour Organization, the Ministry of Industries, the National Women Lawyer's Association, Mahila Parishad, Caritas, the Consumer Association of Bangladesh, and factory owners and workers from different garment factories. Throughout this workshop, common themes emerged, such as the establishment of an effective trade union and of gender-sensitive labour policies. Ten years later, in 1996, garment workers' demands have still not been met and they continue to articulate their demands in various women's forums.

Whatever their differences, women's groups supported garment workers' demands to remove the quota system. In 1985 Britain and France imposed quotas (2.23 million and 1.7 million a year respectively) on Bangladesh's exports of shirts (Jackson, 1992: 29). The United States followed the same path, imposing similar quotas on imports of clothes (Jackson, 1992). Women's groups questioned this quota system and viewed it as First World countries trying to control Third World countries' production through unilateral decisions. The result would be that the Third World would be more vulnerable in the international power structure. Women's groups support of garment workers' rights has provided a mass consciousness about the rights of garment workers. In addition, women's groups have supported garment workers in maintaining pressure on the government and factory owners to address some of the workers' labour demands immediately.

Networking beyond the National Boundaries

As I mentioned earlier, *Chinta*, a feminist bi-weekly journal, has been exchanging features and reports about garment workers with Third World Network for many years. In 1987 the *Asian Women Workers Newsletter* reported:

> A national meeting of garment workers ... was organized by the Bangladesh Garment Sramik Federation in February to initiate dialogue amongst the garment workers about their daily problems to fight for legitimate demands. (1987: 7)

In 1997, the *Asian Women Workers Newsletter* was still vigilant:

> Injuries are more frequent as workers become tired from over work. The long term effects of working in such a dusty fibre-filled atmosphere, made worse by the higher levels of production.... Fire is a constant hazard in these large unregulated buildings filled with flammable materials yet no precautions are taken. (1997: 5)

Reports on garment workers in Bangladesh are widely evident in international news forums, indicating that women workers can put forward and define their own agendas in concert with their international sisters. These reports have shown the capability of women workers to build networks and linkages with related groups within and outside Asia, for solidarity and support. In recent years, one significant outcome of this networking has been appeals to the general public to write to the appropriate person or authority expressing concern, protest and solidarity. For example, in 1998, *Maquila Network Update* published this request:

The National Garment Workers Federation in Bangladesh (NGWF) is denouncing working conditions at M. Hossain Garments in Bangladesh which produces for the GAP [a US-based company].... According to the NGWF, the company is not paying the minimum wage.... The NGWF is requesting that protest letters be sent to the GAP [US address and name of the Vice President was given] asking them to ensure that the principles outlined in their code of conduct are respected. (1998: 6)

Conclusion and Recommendations

The growth of the garment industry in Bangladesh has resulted from the global relocation of capital as well as the availability of a cheap labour force, particularly female labour. The research discussed in this chapter clearly indicates that the socio-economic gains achieved by women through employment are overshadowed by exploitative practices such as lower wages, gender discrimination, harassment, job insecurity and hazardous work environments. Yet these women workers cannot be considered quiescent and docile. They use various tactics and strategies on an everyday basis to fight harassment and gender discrimination and to establish their rights in the workplace. In order to sustain their social gains and also to further improve their lives, the women workers are moving beyond the factory and national boundaries to make alliances with women's and other activist groups, including labour unions. One fundamental reason for this reaching out is that the needs of women workers are not confined to the workplace alone. Women's rights issues are generic and require a wider understanding of the needs of all workers, taking into account the need for dignity, health and safety in the workplace and the community. As a feminist-academic, one cannot ignore women workers' rights in the research and development context. My contact with the garment workers through this research is a deliberate link as I believe that the struggles of women garment workers in Bangladesh are part of the much larger issue of subordination and rights of women across nations.

As evident in this chapter, the garment workers in Bangladesh are organizing themselves to broaden their networks to mobilize further and to establish their rights. As feminists, I consider that we have a role to play in further strengthening their efforts. This will require involvement and some form of activism to promote rights issues both nationally and internationally. I offer the following recommendations toward that end.

1. A deliberate link with the garment workers, women's groups, trade unions and other advocacy groups at the national level is required. This link will broaden awareness on the women workers' issues and build up effective solidarity with them.

2. There should be a continued exchange of materials and information among various groups interested in women's issues. This may enhance their consciousness and help them to question the discrimination in industrial and labour practices.

3. Feminist groups working with women industrial workers should organize national seminars and workshops to educate policy makers as well as industrial entrepreneurs on issues such as health, child care and labour practices in an attempt to make them aware of the working conditions of women and the need to address these effectively.

4. Women's rights are in effect political issues. Therefore, there is a need to deal with these issues politically through lobbying – writing letters, signing petitions and political campaigns by feminist groups – to create pressure on the government to enact pro-women legislation, and particularly to protect the rights of industrial women workers.

Notes

1. The author is grateful to the editors of this volume, and particularly to Ellen Judd for her insightful comments in revising an earlier version of this chapter.
2. Elson (1996) has elaborated on this shifting trend with a wide spectrum of references.
3. My analysis in this chapter has been influenced by the writings of Chhachhi and Pittin (1996), Morgen and Bookman (1988), and Safa (1995). Although Morgen and Bookman use the concept of multiple responsibilities, Chhachhi and Pittin talk about multiple identities. I believe these concepts intersect.
4. The concept 'double consciousness' was used by Morgen and Bookman (1988) as well as by Safa (1995) to describe the experiences and empowerment of working-class women engaged in a wide spectrum of activities ranging from acts of individual resistance to mass mobilization.
5. This field research was funded by a Simon Fraser University President's Research Grant (PRG), 1996–7. I gratefully acknowledge the generous support of the PRG; I am solely responsible, however, for any analyses and comments made in this chapter
6. In addition to the snowball technique, Hasina Khanam Lata, my sister and compatriot, was instrumental in locating the interviewees. My long-time involvement in research in Bangladesh facilitated the process. I gratefully acknowledge the time and support of the garment workers who were interviewed for this research. Despite their hectic work schedules, they welcomed me to their homes (especially during the daytime when men were not around). All the taped interviews of the garment workers quoted in this chapter have been translated from Bangla [Bengali] to English by me.
7. Farhana Azim Shiuli, my research assistant, a student in the Master's programme in the Department of Anthropology, Dhaka University, collected most of the secondary materials. I have translated the Bangla materials into English.
8. In earlier research, I found that these women break the 'cultural norm' of *purdah* and consequently challenge patriarchal authority in their villages (Zaman, 1996).
9. For details, see Hossain, Jahan and Sobhan (1993); Paul-Majumder and Zohir (1994).

10. For further discussion of this strategy, see Andriyani, 1996.
11. These statistics are based on two reports: (1) Simu, Sima Das, 'Garments', *The Weekly Chinta*, No. 24 (3 September 1995); (2) Reza, Kazim, '*Poshak Shilpe Agun Atanka*' [Tension about fire in the garment factories], *Robbar*, 10 August 1997, pp. 18–23. The reference to the number of people killed appeared on p. 22.
12. *Chinta*, a local feminist journal, published an issue titled *Bangladesher Shilpayan O Nari Sramik* [Industrialization in Bangladesh and Women Workers] (*Chinta*, 15 November 1992). In this issue, *Chinta* elaborated on the activities of the seminar and summarized the statements of prominent speakers. I have retranslated all the statements published in Bangla.

Part IV
Working with Global Structures

13 • Women Organizing Locally and Globally: Development Strategies, Feminist Perspectives

Peggy Antrobus
Linda Christiansen-Ruffman

Doing Development

This chapter focuses on the experience of two feminists – one from the Caribbean, the other from Canada – who have worked at 'doing development' in different capacities over the past 40 years. Peggy Antrobus got her degree in economics and professional training as a social worker from British universities in the 1950s and 1960s respectively. She has been 'doing development' in the Caribbean since her graduation in 1958. Linda Christiansen-Ruffman, a professor of Sociology at a Canadian university, first encountered the practice of Third World development while working as an undergraduate research assistant in Africa in 1963.

Since those beginnings both have worked with women's organizations at local, national, regional and international levels. In this chapter we want to highlight the convergences and divergences of our lives and work, interweaving it with our experiences of international trends in development, including International Women's Year in 1975 and its subsequent evolution. We describe how our feminist consciousness and analysis changed our understanding of the policies, strategies and practices of 'development', and we indicate the potential for collaborative work between women from the South and women from the North, and between activists and researchers.

Peggy's story, 1950s–1960s

Growing up in the small islands of the West Indies in the 1940s as a member of a family of public servants, I had first-hand experience of the social and political processes leading up to adult suffrage and independence. The political parties which forged that path had close links with the labour unions that had emerged from the wave of social unrest in the region in the 1930s. For these former British colonies, independence was the outcome of a social movement whose ethos was justice for the majority of people, who had been exploited and marginalized by the post-

175

emancipation plantation economies of the region. In the Westminster-style democracies of the Commonwealth Caribbean (CARICOM), all political parties gave priority to laying down the framework for broad-based socio-economic development.

On winning a scholarship to university at the end of my schooldays in the early 1950s, I chose to study economics, endorsing the priorities of this period. We believed that economic development was the other side of the coin of political independence and that economic growth was a linear process which could be guaranteed by the 'right' combination of land, labour and capital. Although development economics was not on the curriculum, W. Arthur Lewis's (1955) classic was on the reading list, and I felt proud to be a West Indian, and even more validated in my choice of subject. Lewis was my role model for a career in public finance.

On graduation I entered the Jamaican public service as a junior adminis-trative assistant in the Ministry of Finance. Optimism about the future of the region fed confidence in our ability to bring about a better life for all. Poverty elimination (not alleviation) was the central objective of the development programme.

Even so, without reflection, I embraced what I saw as the imperatives of gender. I abandoned my ambition to work in public finance because of the difficulties of combining the roles of wife and mother with a career as an economist in the public service. Instead I accompanied my husband to Britain where I underwent post-graduate training as a social worker. It seemed a more 'appropriate' choice. Afterwards I served as a field worker in an applied nutrition programme implemented by the Commonwealth Save the Children Fund on the Caribbean island of St Vincent. Working as part of a team with my paediatrician husband, I trained and supervised a small group of village women as field workers in a programme aimed at reducing infant mortality and improving maternal and child health.

In 1967, after only three years of this work, I left to become a full-time mother to our first child. Two years later I was invited to help the government of St Vincent set up their first community development pro-gramme. It was seen as part of the preparation for statehood, and I received my orientation in this work from a United Nations adviser as well as from the government of Guyana, which had launched one of the most comprehensive programmes of community development that I have ever encountered. Here, in the context of the newly independent govern-ment's programme to establish a 'cooperative republic', was a truly 'bottom-up' approach to development, determined by priorities set by communities.

Linda's experiences of development, 1960s

My first encounter with the challenges of development was in Africa, where I worked as an undergraduate research assistant. In South Africa we collected documents of non-white political parties, which had been banned by the government three years earlier, and we also studied the emergence of the Bantustans. In Tanganika (now Tanzania) I got caught up with the excitement of independence movements and President Nyerere's optimistic vision of African development, similar to the 'bottom-up development' described by Peggy. While I was certain that we were doing important research in Africa as outsiders, I was dismayed by the number of North American journalists and researchers with ethnocentric and distorted interpretations of events. I felt ambivalent. I wanted to be there as a researcher and scholar of Africa and, at the same time, I felt that as an outsider I could not and should not be there as an 'expert' on a culture and society I hardly knew. I decided that, first, I needed to become an 'expert' in my own part of the world.

At Columbia University Graduate School, I based my PhD dissertation in Canada rather than in East Africa. I also began to study community activism in USA, and, increasingly, Canadian urban and rural communities. First I was simply an observer of grassroots activities, but through the women's movement I began to participate more actively. For example, in the early 1970s I joined a group distributing newly legalized birth control information. Part of that work resembled Peggy's bottom-up approach to development; we hired poor women as field workers and later proposed that their representatives be involved in decision making on our board.

A job at a school of Social Work in Canada (1968–70) provided a setting in which to apply and enrich my knowledge of community development and to challenge text book interpretations. I learned the limits of sociological knowledge and reconsidered the concept of expertise. Sociology's key concepts did not fit the local realities, but without a feminist perspective my analysis was distorted and I did not understand the full picture. Without a fuller understanding of how power operates in scholarship, I was confused by the apparently contradictory assumptions and meanings of development.

The First Two Development Decades (1960s and 1970s)

In retrospect, our experiences show that community development was one of the strategies used by people 'doing development' in the first development decade of the 1960s. Despite the mainstream orthodoxy which equated 'development' with economic growth or material progress, we did not assume that the benefits of growth would 'trickle down' to those sectors of the population which were poorer, or less well equipped to be involved in the rising tide of 'progress'. We had direct contact with the poor at the grassroots, a style which foreshadowed the second development decade.

While international development was dominated by the idea of economic progress, the second development decade stands out as having a more political focus on the state's role in enabling development. During that decade, assumptions about economic progress held by development 'experts' were challenged, partly by a new generation of Third World economists. The search for 'alternatives' to growth-oriented strategies was reflected in the call for 'Another Development' – a model based on the transformation of social structures so that 'they satisfy the material and spiritual needs of the majority of the world's peoples' (Dakar Seminar, 1982: 1).[1]

Women Doing Development and Doing Women's Development

Feminists were part of this move towards a focus on equality and participation during the second development decade. They worked for the UN to designate 1975 as International Women's Year, to convene the first Women's Conference in Mexico City, and to proclaim a Decade for Women, with the themes of Equality, Development and Peace. As a result, many governments and several international institutions established special programmes and mechanisms for 'the integration of women in development' and voted the resources for their implementation. In some ways, the second development decade, itself a legacy of independence movements against colonialism, sowed the seeds for the global feminist movement.

Peggy's story, 1975–95

In 1974, on the eve of International Women's Year, I accepted the post of Adviser on Women's Affairs in Jamaica.[2] The post had been created within the framework of Michael Manley's attempts to define a 'third' path to development, somewhere between capitalism and communism. He termed it 'democratic socialism' and emphasized issues of equality and participation.

I was not perceived as having a political agenda and I had never heard the word feminist, but those who sanctioned my appointment had not reckoned with the power of feminist consciousness-raising. Within weeks of my appointment the job had become a mission, and had begun to change the way I saw the world. My teachers were two groups of women at opposite ends of the social spectrum. From working-class Jamaican women I learned to see myself differently, to question my privileged position and to see these privileges as barriers to self-actualization. From researchers and activists from Africa, Asia, Latin America and North America, I learned feminist theory, structural analysis and a more critical approach to development. My work with the Women's Bureau gave me an inside view of the politics of transformation and the needed cooperation between political activists, women's organizations and the bureaucracy if there were to be any improvements in the condition of women. With minimal staff and resources, we were able to push forward an impressive agenda.[3]

In June 1978, I attended a meeting organized by the UN's Asia and Pacific Centre for Women and Development (ACPD) in Bangkok. This was a turning point in my professional, political and personal development. Its title, 'Feminist Ideologies and Structures in the First Half of the Decade', was itself revolutionary.[4] It was the first time the UN had called a meeting on feminism, and the use of the word 'ideology' juxtaposed to that of 'structures' (national machinery) was an indication of what might be expected. I went to the meeting resisting the word 'feminist', because it had a 'bad' connotation, especially in its North American usage, and especially for someone working in a government bureaucracy. I returned a self-proclaimed feminist, determined to use the word as often as possible, but always to define it as: 'feminists are people with a consciousness of the all the structures that oppress women and a commitment to challenge and change them'.

In August 1978, after a year as a full-time housewife in Barbados, I established the Women and Development (WAND) Unit within the Extra Mural Department.[5] WAND's initial work (1978–80) focused on working with existing (traditional) women's organizations to build awareness of women's issues and to promote the establishment of national machinery in all CARICOM countries. Through a strategy of regional workshops we cast the net wide, bringing together women from various sectors – media, craft and income-generating activities.

WAND entered its second phase (1980–8) after the mid-Decade conference in Copenhagen in 1980 indicated that women were actually worse off – on every indicator – than they had been in 1975. At that point, WAND's work became more focused on testing alternative strategies for the integration of women in development. The most important work undertaken in this phase focused on rural women. At a regional level, WAND was instrumental in the launching of CAFRA (the Caribbean Association for Feminist Research and Action) and the introduction of the Women and Development Studies programme within the University of the West Indies.

In 1984, on the eve of the end-of Decade conference in Nairobi, I participated in a meeting in Bangalore convened by the Indian economist

Devaki Jain. The purpose was to reflect on our experience in development over the Decade and to prepare a platform document for the NGO Forum. Like the meeting in Bangkok in 1978, it changed the way I approached my work and the work of WAND. As the women from Asia, the Pacific, Africa, Latin America and the Caribbean told their stories, the concept of 'crisis' emerged as a unifying theme. Although the 'crisis' manifested itself in different ways – nuclear testing and militarism in the Pacific, the rise of religious fundamentalism in Asia, food insecurity in Africa, debt and structural adjustment in Latin America – our analysis pointed to their links to a particular economic model, the growth model. This analysis of the systemic links between the various crises also connected them with women's subordinate position in our societies and led us to call for 'development alternatives' from the perspective of poor women living in the South. The women involved in this analysis formed the network known as Development Alternatives for Women of a New Era (DAWN). One of the most significant issues to emerge from this meeting was the critique of the structural adjustment programmes which were being adopted by Latin American countries as conditions for assistance sought from the IMF to deal with their debt crises. It was the first time I had heard a feminist analysis of the impacts of their policies on women. Ironically, two months earlier the heads of government of CARICOM countries had adopted structural adjustment as the policy framework for the region.[6]

By 1988, WAND's tenth anniversary celebrations summed up our progress: 'Ten years ago we were seeking integration, today we are seeking transformation.' WAND's goal moved from one of 'integrating' women in development to seeking the 'transformation' of structures and relationships which perpetuated the marginalization of women. The shift found expression in CORE (Communities Organizing for Empowerment), a programme which was to integrate reflection on macroeconomic policies into our work at community level. The location of the Secretariat for DAWN within WAND in 1990, under my coordination, helped strengthen the Caribbean's links with other regional and global networks committed to social transformation and strengthened our capacity for understanding the impacts of the neoliberal policy framework on women.

Linda's story: 1975–95

In the early 1970s the forthcoming United Nations women's conference was used by femocrats to implement Canada's Royal Commission on the Status of Women. Some government departments put money into women's research for the first time. Status of Women offices, councils and programmes were established, and government funding supported women's groups. Canada's celebration of 1975, with a 'Why Not?' Campaign focused on women, provided new legitimacy and resources for women's organizing.

We came together to conduct research, present briefs and found groups. To harness our momentum, we planned a small Canada-wide conference in 1976 which grew exponentially to capture the burgeoning energy of this developing field. The Halifax conference, together with the initiation of the Canadian Research Institute for the Advancement of Women (CRIAW), headquartered in Ottawa, saw the beginning of annual conferences in Canada on feminist research.

In 1976–8 my major research focused on the evaluation of two government-sponsored community development projects in Nova Scotia and in Labrador. As this research raised questions for me about the meanings of 'community development' and underdevelopment, I came to reassess knowledge itself as underdeveloped, because of its biases against women. I returned to Labrador, supposedly the most 'undeveloped' of the communities, to focus on women. This research in small, isolated Labrador communities challenged assumptions about 'traditional women', unilinear progress and development (Christiansen-Ruffman, 1980) and raised profound questions about ethnocentrism embedded in research methodologies and about universal knowledge claims. As I gradually discovered our colonial and patriarchal heritage, I began a process of unlearning my previous 'knowledge' and replacing it with community-based learning.

As feminists realized we were women and began to name and understand our different experiences, we learned the power of the dominant paradigms. We worked together through caucuses, organizations and conferences to discover how structures of knowledge creation distorted our realities. Gradually, through clearer feminist eyes, we began to discover inappropriate assumptions at the base of scholarship and to understand the deep-rooted limitations of Western patriarchy and individualism (Christiansen-Ruffman, 1989; 1998). We reconceived key ideas such as wealth and development (for example, Christiansen-Ruffman, 1987; 1989).

I became president of CRIAW in the mid-1980s, and we experimented with new feminist methodologies and ways of doing community-based research, action research, participatory research and comparative, collaborative research. We developed courses, programmes and journals to create women's studies (Christiansen-Ruffman, 1998). But all this was just the beginning of the search for our autonomous voices as women around the world. At the same time, I wanted sociology, as well as society, to abandon its patriarchal ways and to work regionally, nationally and internationally to help bring my discipline and the rest of scholarship out of its biases.

Converging Paths and the DAWN Analysis

When we met in the early 1980s, we were both doing organizing work with women at the local community level – Peggy in countries in the Eastern Caribbean as part of her paid outreach work with WAND and Linda as part of her unpaid participant action research with CRIAW-Nova Scotia and other community action groups. We met at a seminar in Halifax on women and development. Sponsored by the Association of Atlantic Universities, it built on historic links between the Caribbean and Atlantic Canada. Peggy was among the team of colleagues from the West Indies who had identified the topic, and Linda remembers her excitement at hearing Peggy describe the field they in the Caribbean had named 'women and development studies'. It resonated with a proactive and community-based feminist approach to knowledge with which Canadians were beginning to experiment. As a result of the seminar, Atlantic Canadian women formed a group parallel with that of the West Indies and Guyana, called Atlantic Women and Development, and began to compare notes between the two regions.

Peggy and Linda met again in Norway in early 1985 while Linda was working with Berit Ås, and Peggy was on her way to a meeting to discuss the draft DAWN statement being prepared for the United Nations' End of the Decade Conference in Nairobi. When Linda read this draft, she decided to attend the Nairobi conference. She wanted to participate in the new feminist thinking about development and in the burgeoning international feminist movement. At Nairobi, feminists were everywhere, at the official Conference as well as at the Forum, and were overwhelmingly from 'the economic South'. A highlight of the Forum for both of us was a series of panels, organized by the DAWN group and convened by Devaki Jain. DAWN's analysis was issued as a book: *Development Crises and Alternative Visions: Third World Women's Perspectives* (Sen and Grown, 1987).

Main features and characteristics of DAWN's analysis

Twelve points in DAWN's analysis stand out clearly:

1. It focuses on the experience of poor women living in the economic South.

2. It seeks to reflect regional diversity.

3. It is holistic.

4. It attempts to link women's everyday experience to an understanding of the macroeconomic policy frameworks of their governments.

5. It is political, challenging paradigms and promoting change.

6. Its feminist analysis rejects dichotomies and validates women's work and experience.

7. It links race, class, political domination and gender.

8. It links interlocking systemic global crises such as economic disarray, deteriorating social services, food insecurity, environmental degradation, cultural fundamentalism, violence against women and militarism.

9. It relates the subordination of women to the interlocking global crises to the type of economic model being promoted through policies of structural adjustment.

10. It is transformative: shifting from the neoliberal approach of fitting women into an unjust system (WID) to one that seeks to challenge and transform the system.

11. It recognizes the power of diverse women organizing and analysing together.

12. It recognizes the empowerment of women through their organizations.

DAWN's ground-breaking book exemplifies a global feminist analysis. Linda adopted DAWN's suggestion that poor women and children be the touchstone against which to judge policies and theories in a committed, transformative feminist scholarship. She found that DAWN's analysis also met the scholarly/scientific test of prediction. Their book allowed her to foresee the negative consequences of the restructuring policies which Canadians would face in the 1990s.

Linda suspects that complex relations of power and careerism account for the failure of many scholars, North and South, to recognize the significance of this foundational book, building on Southern rather than Northern experience and scholarship. Reflecting on the power of those relations, she strongly supports DAWN's restriction of membership to those from the economic South.

DAWN's analysis changed the way in which women approached their work in development – in practice, research, analysis and advocacy. In Peggy's work in the Caribbean it helped make the link between WAND's work at micro level, in communities and within sectors, and new work in analysing trends at the macro level – not only economic but social (increasing inequality and alienation), cultural (consumerism), political (the rise in political conservatism and religious fundamentalisms) and environmental (degradation).

Feminists Doing Development Together: the United Nations as an Arena for Feminist Organizing

The major achievements of the Decade for Women included the strengthening of the emerging global women's movement and the development of feminist analysis. The United Nations global conferences of the 1990s provided the opportunity for the movement to use its analysis to address issues which were of urgent concern to everyone. Women's caucuses within these UN global conferences reminded official delegates of women's rights, increasing inequalities and the deteriorating quality of life for the majority of the world's people in the South and North. Under the leadership of feminists, women's mobilization around the themes of the conferences and their participation in the events surrounding them resulted in shifts in analysis and definition of agendas. The resolutions and recommendations from these conferences, taken together with those from the Women's Conferences, provide a framework which could move us towards a model of development which is more just and equitable.

We decided, as individuals and as leaders of networks, to participate in these UN conferences because we understood their power and their use to us as feminists. They forced us to think about significant world issues, how to frame our visions in specific terms, and what needed to be altered within the rhetoric of officialdom. We orchestrated our involvement in and around the UN conferences and their preparatory meetings so that we could have our own discussions and debates. We also worked with other NGOs to ensure that their analyses were at least women-friendly, and we made formal presentations, discussed issues and lobbied official delegates.

We worked closely together for the first time in the preparatory meetings for the World Summit for Social Development, held in Copenhagen in March 1995. We decided to work on the Social Summit because of our interest, experience and expertise in the subject as well as our fear that a women's agenda might disappear if all feminists turned their attention solely to the World Conference on Women scheduled for Beijing in August, 1995. In fact, we worked to make links between the Summit and Beijing, notably through the 180 Days Campaign organized by the women's caucus of the Women's Environment and Development Organization (WEDO) and through an emerging organization called Alianza.

The idea of Alianza has a long history. From the outset there were women in the North who wanted to be part of DAWN, but DAWN members felt strongly about the need to have a Southern voice. Devaki Jain put forward the idea that the appropriate basis for collaborative work would be for Northern women to critique their own economies. Some women in North America took up this challenge.

Alianza grew from Peggy's initiative at the UN Forum on Environment and Development in Rio 1992. She gathered an informal group, including Linda, to work together towards Beijing. The informal group took the name 'DAWN and its Northern partners' to work on a collaborative analysis based in our own realities from the perspectives of our own countries. This group prepared a publication for the North American/ European Beijing preparatory meetings in Vienna and met again at the second Social Summit PrepCom in New York. There our panel reflected on crises being created by the Northern version of structural adjustment, including cutbacks in health, education and social services, the privatization agenda, the downsizing of the public service, attacks on unions, the ideology of economic fundamentalism, the focus on debt reduction, the undermining of democracy and support of corporate citizenry to the detriment of all people. In December 1994 the group became an alliance, with an expanded membership and a succession of names culminating in the one adopted in October 1997, Women's Alliance for Economic Justice, or Alianza.[7]

The UN conferences allow us a glimpse of the emergence and evolution of a global women's movement, growing in numbers and complexity. Few of those who designated the year 1975 International Women's Year, and adopted the resolution which launched the Decade which followed, can have imagined the impact which women's leadership would have at all levels, and in all kinds of institutions. In our view, the chief impact of the UN Decade for Women (and all the ongoing work that it stimulated and encouraged) relates to the way in which it opened up spaces for women from different racial and ethnic groups, countries, classes and occupational backgrounds to meet on a consistent and continuing basis. These meetings enabled women to gain new knowledge and to learn from each other's experience. Spin-offs include the proliferation of joint projects and collaborative efforts, issue-based networks at regional and global levels, and the forging and strengthening of links between organizations at local and global levels.

The Differences Feminism Has Made

Peggy's reflections

In the 1960s, despite my engagement in community level activites, I was not a feminist. Although my work focused on women, I had neither the awareness of nor concern about the relations between men and women, or of the link between the structure of gender power relations and how these affected the participation of the women in these programmes. In addition, my interaction with the women was always in relation to their role in the programme: thus within the applied nutrition programme the focus was on women as mothers; while in the community development programmes no thought was given to the domestic or economic concerns of the women participants.

As a feminist, I now see limitations of my development efforts during the 1960s in the applied nutrition programme of the Save the Children Fund and in community development with the government of St Vincent. They were sectoral and did not link each programme with the larger framework of government policy and programmes at the time. They focused on a single aspect of women's reality and missed how the complexity of women's lives has implications for women's social roles as mothers, their economic roles as both paid and unpaid workers, their civic roles as community organizers, and so on – and how this needs to be translated into policy making. They missed the political nature of the relationships between the women and the context of their relationships with their men, their families, their community and the state, and they lacked the empowerment and transformative perspective which my feminist analysis later brought to my work at WAND. They also failed to appreciate some other feminist issues and concerns that became central to my work in the 1980s, such as violence, women's unwaged work and their exclusion from decision making in public life.

In the 1980s, WAND's increasingly feminist approach paralleled my own deepening feminist consciousness. Recognizing the political nature of the relationships between women at community level and the state, we emphasized building women's autonomy to take on leadership roles in their communities, to challenge oppressive relationships and to critique oppressive structures.

Linda's reflections

In South Africa I was not fully conscious of being a woman and unaware of women and development issues. The word 'feminist' had not yet even been rediscovered. Although I was hired by an eminent senior woman researcher, and despite the work of the women's activist group Black Sash and visits to the homes of women in search of political party manifestos and documents, women were not seen as political actors or even as gendered. This was before I was aware of the sexism surrounding me. It was before Esther Boserup (1970) and the emerging women's studies introduced the scholarly community and development industry to the importance of women's work in Africa and the negative impact of development policies on women's lives.

If we had been feminists, we would have understood so much more. We would not have restricted our research to a narrow focus on political parties and political institutions but understood the political to be broader

(CRIAW, 1986; Christiansen-Ruffman, 1995). We would have understood connections between the personal and political and intellectual. We would have paid more attention to the women we met, asked different questions, collected other information and analysed it with passion and concern as well as reason. We might have understood the political importance of the women's group Black Sash. We might have acted in solidarity with them after we left South Africa, perhaps even altering the course of history and hastening the end to state apartheid and its harm.

Now, as a feminist researcher, I have learned the limits and biases in what first appeared to be objective knowledge. With Canadian researchers and activists, I have had the pleasure of inventing new feminist methodologies which build on our collaborative understandings locally, nationally and internationally. Through work around the United Nations and with the International Sociological Association, especially its research committee on Women in Society, I began to experience the power of global comparative research and collaborative thinking. At the same time I was aware that as I began to work in the abstracted space of the global stage of the UN, it became even more important to ground my work at the local level with the real concerns of poor, rural women. Atlantic Women's FishNet and Nova Scotia Women's FishNet build on participatory action research and community development approaches at the same time as they ground my own perceptions.

Our Conclusion:
Feminist Organizing in the Context of Globalization

None of the theories of economics, social change or development deal adequately with issues of women, or with gender relations. Feminists have challenged all of them on the basis of women's experiences. Early on, however, as our stories have shown, we were unable to break through the patriarchal constructions and misogyny, or even to define the problem as one of patriarchal knowledge, a domain Peggy encountered in doing economics and Linda in doing sociology.

Indeed, worldwide, feminists developed collaborative, comparative methodologies to represent diverse women and their experiences. Such approaches allow us to understand different manifestations of oppression, from sexism, racism, class discrimination and coloniality to heterosexism, ableism and ageism. Learning from differences and similarities in concrete experiences also allows us to comprehend more fully the local and global processes such as fundamentalism, nationalism and globalization. Feminism has allowed us to understand these structures of power and to imagine ways in which power may be used more constructively.

Today there appear to be no common values by which civil society can hold governments accountable, no civilian control of corporate and financial managers, and no recognition of the diversity which could create space for alternatives. Here is where we see the immense potential contribution of feminism as a transformational politics. In a world in which there is little space for diversity and there appears to be no alternative to the gospel of neoliberalism, feminism can provide a basis for bridging the division of race, class and identity. As DAWN points out:

> feminism cannot be monolithic in its issues, goals, and strategies, since it constitutes the political expression of the concerns and interests of women from different regions, classes, nationalities, and ethnic backgrounds, [and it would therefore have to be] responsive to the different needs and concerns of different women, and defined by them for themselves. (Sen and Grown, 1987: 18–19)

We also agree with DAWN that this diversity, built on a common opposition to gender oppression and hierarchy, can be a first step in articulating and acting upon a political agenda which would include challenging all those structures, systems and relationships which perpetuate and reinforce the subordination of women, everywhere. Although subscribing to different political philosophies, feminists tend to have more common ground than is found among other theorists. Our stories show how women from different backgrounds can bridge the North–South divide to work together on common agendas in the areas of collaborative research and learning, as well as in global negotiations.

The challenge for feminists, under new conditions of globalization, is how to understand the present and envisage the future without adopting patriarchal, colonial, racist and classist assumptions. Grounding our analyses in our own experiences and comparing those experiences with those of women from around the world allows us to begin to see beyond ethnocentrism and to understand how these assumptions constrain our understanding and limit our knowledge. We have come to see collaboration across the South–North divide as a site for comparative research, for mutual learning, for knowledge creation and for feminist praxis toward more just and equitable societies. Perhaps the common commitment to women creates a tolerance of difference, and offers greater possibilities for respect and dialogue and for analysis than any other social movement.

Notes

1. A new vision of 'Another Development' was elaborated by the Dag Hammarskjold Foundation. Women's exclusion ultimately led to the Dakar Seminar on 'Another Development with Women' (see Dakar Seminar, 1982; Christiansen-Ruffman, 1987).

2. On his election to office in 1972 Manley had appointed a Task Force comprised of women within his party on the Status of Women. Despite recommendations for a Department of Women's Affairs, with a Minister and a full staff, all that they got was an Adviser on Women's Affairs, with no staff or resources. Lucille Mair, a highly respected member of the ruling party and of the Jamaican society, was appointed. But she had to withdraw, and invited me to apply for the post of Adviser. I was not a member of the party, not a Jamaican, and had no background in the women's movement in Jamaica. My lack of involvement in women's organizations was probably seen as an advantage by bureaucrats who had no intention of appointing someone who would challenge the *status quo*!

3. This agenda embraced the inclusion of domestic workers in provisions for the payment of a minimum wage, the prioritizing of women for work within the government's Special Employment Programmes, challenging sex role stereotyping in schools, and a special programme for continuing the education of girls who dropped out of school because of pregnancy.

4. It was the work of Australian feminist Elizabeth Reid, one of the women who, as adviser to the Prime Minister of Australia in 1975, had played a key role in the processes leading up to the Mexico City conference.

5. The Department was subsequently renamed 'the School of Continuing Studies'.

6. On that occasion no one had raised the alarm and regional institutions like the Caribbean Development Bank (CDB) and the CARICOM Secretariat had launched a concerted effort to promote and integrate this macroeconomic policy framework into all policy making throughout the region. In 1985, at a regional meeting convened by WAND in preparation for the Nairobi conference, participants passed a resolution calling on governments in the region to review their policies. The Bridgetown Statement was the first public challenge to these policies. It was an example of how engagement in a global project influences work at regional and national levels.

7. Alianza includes: Alt-Wid or Alternatives to Women in Development (USA); CRIAW (Canada); Center for Women's Global Leadership; DAWN; EUROSTEP's Gender Working Group; National Action Committee on the Status of Women or NAC (Canada); the Society for International Development's WID component or SID/WID; Women in Development Europe (WIDE); and WEDO.

14 • Responding to Globalization: Can Feminists Transform Development?[1]

Joanna Kerr

Feminists have long realized that many obstacles block the road to equality – social attitudes, religions, laws and institutions have prevented women from achieving equality and justice. But as we race toward the millennium, many feminist activists and researchers are uniting in challenging a common foe to the progress of women – the global economy.

Today, private markets drive the global economy and dominate North–South economic relations. While globalization can generate economic growth, increase productivity and raise standards of living, it has created new challenges to poverty eradication and gender equity. Globalization has featured unemployment, vanishing social services and unregulated working conditions. It has meant gains for many, but women – especially poor women – bear great burdens under economic restructuring.

In the face of rapid economic change, therefore, a growing cadre of feminists are working to demystify economics and challenge the forces behind the global economic system. Feminist researchers and activists in the North and South are confronting the institutional architects of the economic system and the corporations that benefit from it. Indeed, they are attacking the discipline of economics itself.

In challenging the established economic regime, this body of feminist action is questioning many of the long-held assumptions about development and its claim to be a process that benefits all people. This work is based on the premise that if development is to foster equitable and sustainable growth, then the goal of the entire development community must be to create an economic system that does not reinforce inequality or undermine recent gains. The existing gaps in income disparities between women and men, rich and poor, then become an indictment of development and economic progress.

Drawing from personal experiences as a Northern feminist researcher and activist working with feminists in the South, this chapter intends to:

- first briefly illustrate the implications of global economic change for gender equality;

190

- second, move beyond an impact assessment to describe and critique how feminist research and activism is responding to globalization;

- and finally, in the light of all this, tackle that difficult question – can feminists ultimately reform mainstream economics and transform development?

Implications of Global Economic Change for Gender Equality

First, it would be misleading to claim that all women are hurt by the global economy. Globalization does contribute, however, to the inequalities inherent in the world's economic system. Its effects depend on a number of factors, among them gender, class, age, education level, ethnicity and geographic location. For the purposes of this chapter, three very brief examples of the global economy's impact on women are provided: structural adjustment in Africa, trade liberalization in Bangladesh and the effects of the Asian financial crisis.

Structural adjustment in Africa

For more than a decade, African countries have been undergoing structural adjustment policies as a prescription for economic growth. With the World Bank and the IMF promising universal economic benefits as incentives, African nations have followed the institutional call to get their economic houses in order. These universal 'no pain no gain' measures include: the privatization of state-controlled services, financial and trade liberalization, openness to direct foreign investment, tax reform and fiscal discipline.

One sobering outcome of these economic reform measures has been a radical shift in the role of the state. Where the state once assumed responsibility for providing public services in such sectors as health, education and transportation, the trend now is toward deregulation and privatization. As governments deny their responsibility to provide adequate health care, education, public transport or agricultural extension services, the onus for meeting these needs often falls on women as society's primary care givers.

For example, according to a 1995 study into the effects of macroeconomic reforms on the livelihoods of women and men in the Volta region of Eastern Ghana,[2] the introduction of user fees for health services in the late 1980s proved to be such a disincentive that women, who are responsible for family health, stopped bringing their children to clinics, even for infections or serious illnesses such as malaria. Doctors reported that women themselves were presenting much more complex, chronic and terminal ailments because they delayed seeking medical treatment.

The cash-poor women of the Volta used the little cash they had to buy food or pay for transport rather than health care (Brown and Kerr, 1997: 74).

Trade liberalization in Bangladesh

Employment has been transformed in Bangladesh as government and business, in their efforts to produce cost-effective and competitive exports for the global market, look for a cheap and flexible labour force. Millions of women are now employed ahead of their male counterparts. They are considered to be more productive, submissive and less likely to form unions demanding better wages and working and health conditions.

A recent study of Bangladesh's garment sector conducted by The North–South Institute and Nari Uddug Kendra, a local women's organization (Delahanty, 1998), found:

> women in the garment industry working between 11 and 16 hours per day, seven days a week – while continuing to shoulder the lion's share of household chores and child rearing. Women were responsible for finding their own housing, a scarce and sometimes insecure commodity in Bangladesh. They often have no access to even basic utilities, toilet facilities, and clean drinking water. They endure such workplace hazards as poor ventilation, cramped conditions, and risk of fire – last year many workers were killed during a garment factory fire in Dhaka where the exit doors were locked. Travel to and from factories is dangerous – many women have been subjected to harassment, assault, and even rape. Wages are poor – so low that workers frequently cannot afford to buy enough food for themselves and their families. Finally, when they are no longer capable of factory work, women find few opportunities for alternative employment.

Despite these conditions, it has to be emphasized that such employment opportunities have given women their own earnings, and improved their autonomy. In some instances, the working environment can contribute to women's empowerment as women workers, who were once isolated from each other inside households, often come to recognize their common problems and search for ameliorative measures together.

Women want jobs with dignity, but first and foremost, they want a job.[3] Market share and competition rely on a steady flow of cheap labour. Profit margins may hinge on keeping women in lower positions earning low wages. In addition, developing country governments often turn a blind eye to companies that disregard international and national labour standards, given the overriding imperative within this global economic system to attract foreign investment and create jobs.

Financial crisis in Asia

A third example of the gendered nature of the impacts of the global economy can be found in the current financial crisis in Asia. One of the underlying causes of the crisis was the premature liberalization of financial markets. Open financial markets are the trademark of globalization, providing corporations and investors with the freedom to do business anywhere and to seek out the highest profits without state interference. The scale of this activity is huge: foreign currency transactions are estimated at US$1.3 trillion daily (Culpeper, 1996: 14). In Asia, this trade, along with short-term investments, created inflows and outflows of money with profoundly destabilizing effects (Culpeper, 1998).

The Asian financial crisis which erupted in Thailand and spread to Korea, Indonesia and other parts of East and Southeast Asia threw these economies into turmoil, with serious human impacts. Demand for labour has plummeted and unemployment is rising sharply. Early evidence suggests that women have been among the first to lose their jobs, laid off because they are disproportionately represented in the sectors that have been most vulnerable: banking, electronics, textiles and services (DAWN, 1998: 12). Millions of women are now turning to the informal sector, desperately seeking employment. According to a recent International Labour Organization report, it is very likely that women who lose their jobs may be driven to enter the sex sector (Lim, 1998).

These three examples – of adjustment in Africa, trade liberalization in Bangladesh, and Asia's financial crisis – illustrate some of the ways in which the global economic system perpetuates gender inequalities. These changes brought about by globalization, therefore, are altering the terrain on which the struggle for gender equality is and should be fought. That is why, within this decade, a considerable amount of feminist research and activism has shifted to challenging the global economic system – the rules that sustain it, the institutions that support it and the governments that defend it. Just how this is being done, and how successfully, is the focus of the next section.

How Feminists are Responding to the Effects of Globalization

The feminist strategies to create sustainable and equitable economies reflect the pluralism of feminism and of the women's movement itself. They have assumed many forms, emerging from different forums, and set a range of priorities. Here are just five strategies through which feminists are challenging the economic *status quo*:

1. transforming mainstream economics;

2. challenging the World Bank;

3. influencing corporate behaviour;

4. lobbying national governments;

5. fostering participatory economics.

Transforming mainstream economics

We are living in an age in which the dominant economic theology trumpets the glory of capitalism and the primacy of markets. Under this doctrine, the higher the growth rate, the better off a society is as a whole. National well-being, according to mainstream economics, is thus measured according to the growth of a country's gross national product *per capita*, or GNP. GNP is a measure of the monetary transactions in the economy. Economic and social policies are the tools used by policy makers, that is governments, to increase GNP (and therefore increase growth). This GNP yardstick does not correlate, however, with the reality of human well-being. If growth is up in Canada, for instance, why are there more homeless on the streets? Why are hospitals and women's shelters shutting down? Why are more people using food banks? Why are so many young people unemployed?

Feminist economists like Marilyn Waring (a noted author and former Member of Parliament in New Zealand) have said GNP is a useless indicator of human welfare for two main reasons. First, it does not differentiate between enriching production and destructive production. For example, the losses that result from environmental disasters are not counted in national accounts: in fact, they register as gains to the economy because of the 'productive' activities surrounding the clean-up response, litigation, insurance pay outs, and so on.

The second problem with the GNP is its narrow definition of economic activity – it does not take into account any production that does not involve some monetary transaction. This leaves out all the unpaid labour men, and especially women, provide every day: the cooking, cleaning and caring work which is invisible and unvalued but which sustains our families and our societies.

According to the United Nations (UNDP, 1995b: 15), if women's work was monetized it would add up to US$11 trillion a year, a huge contribution to the world economy. If this work was remunerated it would thoroughly transform the basis of property rights, divorce settlements, or collateral for credit. 'Housewives' would no longer be viewed as dependants, but as valued workers in their own right. Women who perform both paid and unpaid work would be credited for their double contribution.

Some feminists have also been pushing for a better yardstick that would measure economic activity and human welfare – a yardstick based on time instead of money. A measurement that included both these components would provide a more realistic picture of what it truly costs for a society to function and would make national accounts, so essential to economic policy making, more accurate (Waring, 1988). Records of time spent on activities would also identify crisis points and indicate where services are needed.

The study conducted in Ghana, referred to above, provides such an example. The research found that the majority of women's time was spent growing and processing food for family consumption yet the agricultural policy imposed by the World Bank and the government of Ghana was targeted to increase maize yields. Women knew that an increase in maize output would not necessarily increase their income as they did not have the time to process extra maize (Brown and Kerr, 1997). If those time constraints were recognized, the government would be more likely to ensure women had a mill to grind maize than continue to deliver high-yielding maize seeds.

Fortunately, accounting for women's unpaid work is slowly gaining recognition. At the 1995 UN Conference on Women, women's groups succeeded in having women's work included in the so-called 'satellite' or marginal national accounts. Also, in the last Canadian national census 10 per cent of households received a survey to collect data about unpaid work. Slowly, slowly, women's contribution is being made visible.

Now feminist economists like Diane Elson emphasize that feminists need to build on this critical work of making women's economic contribution visible, and to move from the micro to the macro in order to transform the practice of macroeconomics. This means changing the economic growth models that macroeconomists in the IMF or finance departments use to design economies and expand growth. In the past year, a network of international feminist economists has begun to develop macroeconomic growth models that introduce gender relations and unpaid work as intervening variables. The objective of this exciting initiative is to create economic models that become instruments for empowering rather than burdening women.

But in order for mainstream economists to recognize the benefits of these new conceptual tools and theories, feminists will have to work from within the system, as well as pushing for change from the 'outside'. As Elson (1998: 155) aptly argues:

> If we only work on the 'inside' we run the risk of merely achieving small improvements in the formulation of models or collection of statistics which do not actually transform women's lives. If we only work on the 'outside', we run the risk of simply communicating with those who already share our viewpoint, and of not engaging with actual processes of macro-economic policy making ..... That requires some willingness to get to know and speak the language of the insiders – economists, statisticians, Ministries of Finance and Governors of Central Banks.

The challenge and risks of working both within and outside the system are best illustrated by the efforts to challenge the World Bank.

Challenging the World Bank

As one of the chief architects of the global economy, the World Bank has been targeted for criticism by women's groups around the world. The Bank is widely viewed as an ardent supporter of macroeconomic policies that, in many cases, have placed women and the poor at further disadvantage.

The Bank does not take criticism lightly and has defended itself in several ways. Some World Bank staff have complained that their critics, women activists or NGOs, do not understand the intricate details of their policies. The Bank argues that without knowing the outcome of the counterfactual scenario, that is, whether circumstances would have been better had structural adjustment not been applied, critics of adjustment do not have a justifiable or informed argument. Others argue that the negative impacts of economic reform have more to do with the way the governments themselves have interpreted and implemented the policies, and that governments use the Bank to cover up their own wrongdoings. Although there may be some truth in these latter statements, it is important to remember that developing nations have few alternatives to implementing Bank-designed macroeconomic reforms. Governments that do not carry out the fiscal policies required by the World Bank and IMF risk losing future loans or partial debt forgiveness.

Given the reticence of economists and other Bank staff to seriously consider the gender implications of their policies (and this can be applied to most large development agencies) feminists have often taken more of an 'insider' approach. As Bank staff and economists aim for efficiency in their development projects, gender researchers and advocates have pointed out the correlation between achieving development goals and integrating gender in policies, aligning women's interests with the Bank's pursuit of efficiency. Focus on women, they tell the Bank, and your development outcomes will follow.

Many may be aware of the enthusiastic focus that top development policy makers have placed on the promotion of education for girls. This support is due to the arguments, staged over many years, that educating girls leads to 'multiple pay-offs' including later marriages, increased contraceptive usage, lower fertility, reduced infant and child mortality and higher female earnings.

But there is some danger in using such an 'instrumentalist' approach. The pitfall inherent in promoting policies that serve other interests is that inevitably women are seen as a means to an end (Baden and Goetz, 1998: 24). Because education for girls is not the goal but a by-product, the quality of that education suffers. Gender equality is not seen as a legitimate goal in itself. The project's objectives are rendered technical rather than political and ultimately fail to address the systemic nature of gender and social injustices.

It is extremely difficult, however, to avoid instrumentalism when working with large bilateral or multilateral agencies that have other dominant agendas. For example, in October 1995 I attended a summit of representatives from development cooperation agencies, the World Bank, and the IMF on structural adjustment and gender in Africa. Results from several studies on the gender dimensions of economic reforms, conducted in different African countries, were presented by independent researchers.[4] Research results illustrated how gender biases in markets and government departments were replicated and reinforced by apparently 'gender-neutral' macroeconomic variables. In other words, even if the structural adjustment policy in itself didn't have a differential effect on women and men, the institutions through which the policies were imposed had an inherent gender bias. Hence, as a result of these effects, not only were women affected but agricultural output suffered and food security was threatened.[5]

At the end of the three-day summit, one of the World Bank economists made this conclusion: 'I'm *still* not convinced that structural adjustment has a negative impact on women. But I *am* convinced that women's inequality has a negative impact on economic *growth*.' In other words, Bank policies didn't need to change, only the barriers that hinder women from contributing to agricultural production and export promotion. Women are seen as an 'untapped' labour source – as merely instruments to growth.

Fortunately, like any large organization the World Bank is not homogeneous in its views. Many women have been encouraged by the World Bank President James Wolfensohn's commitment to address gender gaps. The Bank has initiated Regional Gender Action Plans, opened up Bank–NGO dialogues in several developing countries, and launched the Structural Adjustment Participatory Review Initiative, a joint NGO–World Bank participatory study into the effects of adjustment in seven countries.

Another hopeful harbinger of change lies in the work of a campaign outside of the Bank. 'Women's Eyes on the World Bank' was launched by women's groups and NGOs at the UN World Conference on Women in 1995. It monitors the Bank's progress in fulfilling its commitments and its efforts to bring lending operations in line with the Platform for Action objectives. The campaign seeks a major reorientation of World Bank policies and projects, making them supportive of women's empowerment and equality and responsive to women's needs.

Now that the World Bank has been targeted for change by feminist groups (and let's agree, it is an easy target) increased attention should be given to the policies and programmes of the other multilateral players in the international financial system, such as the World Trade Organization, the IMF and the regional development banks.

Influencing corporate behaviour

The third strand in the feminist challenge to the economic *status quo* lies in its approach to the private sector and its efforts to link corporate and equality goals. Corporations are the biggest players in the global economy and the biggest winners. Foreign private investment in developing countries in the 1990s alone has grown five-fold and translates into investments of almost US$1 trillion (Sutherland and Sewell, 1998: 2). In comparison, the investment in development cooperation is a drop in the bucket.

Campaigns to make corporations more responsible have been waged for decades: environmentalists have tackled companies that pollute; indigenous groups have lobbied for land claims; and labour groups have demanded better working conditions or, recently, the eradication of child labour. Now Southern women's groups have become active on behalf of women factory workers. Consumer boycotts have often been used as an effective measure against recalcitrant companies, hitting them where it hurts the most – on the bottom line.

Women's groups have had to be careful, however, not to demonize all corporations universally as violators of women's rights. External criticisms may result in reprisals and poor women are dependent on those jobs. If they organize against their employer they run the risk of being fired. The recent campaign to ban child labour contains some very useful lessons. Delve into the issue of child labour and it quickly becomes apparent that there is more at stake than removing children from the workforce. Many children accompany their mothers to the factories, where they are safer than alone out on the streets. With limited or no access to schooling or care, children may be more protected within a work environment. The key then lies in finding ways to secure fair practices and working conditions that respect the needs of women and their families. Towards that end, and as a result of external pressure, some corporations are introducing voluntary codes of conduct covering ethical, environmental, and labour practices in all their operations, both domestic and abroad (Hibler and Beamish, 1998). Such codes of conduct are a promising tool for increasing accountability to workers and consumers.

Concerns remain, however, about the effectiveness of voluntary codes. Without independent monitoring, enforcement cannot be guaranteed. Furthermore, these codes are not substitutes for national laws on worker rights. If codes of conduct raise expectations for improved standards but do not deliver, they may impede or prevent needed government legislation (Delahanty, 1998). Finally, and most importantly, codes of conduct cannot ultimately influence a global production system dependent on cheap and flexible female labour.

Feminist researchers and activists therefore must do more to engage the private sector and encourage corporations to integrate gender equality into their practices and operations, especially given the scale of their activity throughout the globe. While many companies have begun to take heed of environmental sustainability or indigenous peoples' rights, social policy let alone equality issues are treated as less important. Corporate responsibility for women's rights in the workplace must be pursued, therefore, from the factory floor to the CEO's office.

Lobbying national governments

Feminists are employing another tactic in their efforts to reform economic policies: lobbying national governments. While some argue that governments are losing their ability to govern in this global economic system, in reality economic change is driven by their decisions. Government support of liberalizing trade, open markets and deregulation ignores the potentially negative effects these strategies have on the poor, and particularly on poor women.

The 1995 UN World Conference on Women was probably the most visible and international focus on governments and their responsibilities. More than 35,000 women from all over the world went to Beijing, many of them to share their experiences of working conditions, inadequate health care, or lack of access to technology in the context of globalization. Non-governmental organizations had unprecedented access to government delegates attending the numerous preparatory meetings and the Beijing summit, and they lobbied intensely for substantive changes in the final document – the Platform for Action.

While this massive effort had its merits, it is unclear whether the actual results reflect the countless hours and resources that went into this UN conference. In the first place, the UN used a sectoral approach whereby all women's problems, and their solutions, fell under 12 separate categories: violence against women, women's poverty, women's health, environment, and so on. This approach denies any strategizing about the structural causes of gender discrimination – the underlying causes, or how these issues relate to each other.

Second, the 'real' powers within governments do not pay serious heed to the outcomes of UN conferences. Generally the participants attending the meetings represent the 'minor' government ministries: finance ministers are rarely in attendance.

Third, because of the nature and the intended use of these documents (in that they are to be universally applied to all countries), most of the

Beijing recommendations addressing globalization are vague. Take, for example, the following (UN, 1995, para. 58(c)):

> [Governments should] pursue and implement sound and stable macro-economic and sectoral policies that are designed and monitored with the full and equal participation of women, encourage broad-based sustained economic growth, address the structural causes of poverty and are geared towards eradicating poverty and reducing gender-based inequality within the overall framework of achieving people-centred sustainable development.

These are indeed essential strategies. Recommendations like these took hours to negotiate and so are considered hard-won battles. Like any UN conference document, however, the words mean nothing until they are turned into action – until they are implemented according to the reality of that particular country. In most countries, unfortunately, the leadership required to transform these words into new policies or programmes is *not* going to come from government. Governments need to be pressured and held accountable to these international commitments by the women's organizations, researchers and activists who pushed for these commitments in the first place. Policy makers need to be shown actual, viable alternatives. Governments can be influenced to address the structural causes of poverty, or restructure the allocation of public expenditures – but unless feminist leaders show them how, it is unlikely to happen.

For that reason, an initiative like the Women's Budget in South Africa is such a promising example of how to create viable alternatives for governments – a 'manual' for governments to achieve gender equality and social justice. South African women launched the Women's Budget Initiative in 1995, setting out to create a national budget that promoted women's rights (Budlender, 1998).

South African women recognized that the national budget is the monetary embodiment of policies and programmes. Budget allocations indicate the state's commitment to policies and programmes according to the resources they are allocated. Most government budgets are gender-biased, overlooking the ways in which programmes and policies either fail to address women's oppression, or exacerbate it. For example, if a national budget provides tax incentives to corporations instead of rebates for child care, discrimination will not be alleviated. Or if part-time workers, who are mostly women, aren't allowed to collect social security or other employment benefits, then the budget can actually foster gender discrimination.

The purpose of the South African initiative is to ensure that every government department annually draws up its own 'women's budget', analysing every line item for its impact on women. The success of the South African model is inspiring women elsewhere to create women's budgets as transformative tools for equality. In the past two years alone, 'women's budgets' initiatives have been developed in Tanzania, Uganda, Namibia and Zimbabwe, with more likely to come soon.

Participatory economics

Finally, we arrive at the fifth strategy for feminist research and activism: participatory economics. If economic policy making is to contribute truly to the human rights of all, it needs to become more transparent, democratic and participatory. Women need a greater voice. The pressure to transform economic decision making to promote equality and social justice will have to come from players on the 'the inside' and 'the outside'. While feminist economists within ministries of finance and the World Bank are needed, a critical mass of feminist researchers and activists who are able to analyse and influence economic policies and institutions – who can speak the language of economics – is essential.

With that vision in mind, women from across Africa, with The North–South Institute, created the Gender and Economic Reforms in Africa (GERA) programme. The programme set about building African capacity to analyse global economic processes critically from a gender perspective. The mission of GERA is to weave a pan-African movement of women and men, to develop alternative and transformative economic policies that ensure gender equity and economic justice.

To meet these goals, GERA established a fund for African women and their organizations to carry out projects that link research and advocacy. These were linked to ensure that the research would be proactive and used by policy makers, instead of lying dormant on desks or library shelves. Linking research and advocacy work also ensures that rigorous research underlies lobbying efforts, so that decision makers give them serious consideration.

Many people in the development community were sceptical about the project's goals: they said there weren't enough women in Africa who understood economic reform, and those that did were overextended. Nevertheless, calls for proposals were sent out as widely as possible. Within two months, 180 proposals from across Africa had been submitted.

This year GERA has provided 15 grants to African women and their organizations in 11 sub-Saharan countries to carry out research, training and advocacy projects. The projects cover a range of issues. One will analyse the role of market women in economic decision making. West Africa's biggest market in Kumasi, Ghana is run by women who not only make a huge contribution to the economy, but also constitute the national food distribution network. Trade liberalization policies and market reform directly affect them – yet these women are excluded from all decision making. The outcome of this participatory and action research project aims to enable Kumasi market women to participate in economic policy making at the local level, establishing a schedule of regular meetings between traders and local government officials.

A proposal was also received from three women within the Central Bank of Uganda. They recognized that changes in the financial sector could seriously hurt women's access to financial services and credit. They proposed to analyse the Bank of Uganda's lending policies, processes and programmes from a gender perspective, with the objective of offering future programmes that are both participatory and gender-sensitive. There were long debates among the selection committee – a group of eight African women – on whether GERA should support a project within a central bank when our priority was to fund NGOs. The proposal was finally funded because it offered an opportunity to offer strategic support to women trying to change an institution from the inside.

In Burkina Faso and Togo, researchers and activists are looking at the recent major currency devaluations and their effect on gender relations. The goal is to determine the relationship between exchange rate fluctuations specifically, and monetary policy generally, on women's lives. Given that the Francophone African franc will soon be tied to the European currency, the research hopes to shed light on potential future negative effects, and will yield useful lessons for other countries undergoing currency devaluation.

The project teams are using innovative ways to disseminate their findings. Street theatre, radio plays, television broadcasts and gender awareness training are a few of the communication tools being used. In addition, GERA has hosted three meetings in Africa, bringing together project team leaders or the African steering committee. At each event, local policy makers, women's groups, bankers, NGOs, and members of the development community are invited to learn and explore the links between economic reform, gender equality and social justice.

While the GERA programme won't change women's lives in Africa overnight, it is an important step in demystifying economics for women. It is creating valuable, country-specific, quantitative and qualitative data on the effects of reform. It is facilitating ways for women to recognize their disempowerment in the context of global forces. It is also supporting participatory processes to create alternative policies at the local, national and international levels that promote women's rights and economic justice.

Can Feminists Transform Development?

So, after citing all these examples of feminist research, strategy and advocacy – the critical analyses of economic theories, monitoring the World

Bank, creating women's budgets at the national level, encouraging the development of corporate codes of conduct – it is clear that feminists are working at many levels to promote equality and women's empowerment.

But has any of this work had an impact? The answer is yes. Mainstream economists are beginning to take feminist economic theory seriously – in 1995 an entire issue of the prestigious journal *World Development* was devoted to gender and macroeconomics.[6] Institutions like the World Bank are increasingly seeing women as active agents of social, political and economic change instead of passive recipients of development. Many multinational companies recognize how the strength of women's activism can change the way consumers see their products. More governments are recognizing that gender equality is a development goal in and of itself. More women than ever before are taking on economic policies and institutions; they are organizing in the workplace, in their communities, and at the national and international levels to stand up against oppression and subordination.

So, can feminists transform development? Yes, in time. Two things are essential if development is to expand people's choices and guarantee their human rights. First, the global economic system must change; and that is the long-term goal. Second, processes of change have to recognize gender imbalances explicitly to ensure that all people benefit from development. In the words of Indian feminist economist Gita Sen (WEOWB, 1997), this means:

> recognizing that women stand at the crossroads between production and reproduction, between economic activity and the care of human beings, and therefore between economic growth and human development. They are workers in both spheres – those most responsible and therefore with most at stake, those who suffer the most when the two spheres meet at cross-purposes, and those most sensitive to the need for better integration of the two.

In my view, though, feminist research and activism, in order to be able to take on the immense challenge before us, has to *deepen* its impact, *expand* its approach, and *strengthen* its alliances.

In *deepening* its impact, feminism must work to transform institutions – the entrenched structures of organizations. As we have learned, the single-layer approach doesn't work. Efforts to change policies that have focused on policy development or training, and have placed less emphasis on organizational cultures, rules, procedures, budgets and practices, have had limited success.

Let's look at international development. The limited ability of large development agencies to improve women's rights has much to do with organizational cultures and practices. Agencies use top-down approaches, when participatory ones are needed. Staff are often evaluated according to the management and timely dispersal of funds, rather than the impact their work has had on women's lives. Implicitly, 'gender' is perceived as a soft and secondary issue. Deepening our impact means exposing and challenging vested interests and power structures – the historically rooted culture, principles, rules and procedures that underlie an organization. Simply adding women into existing structures is not sufficient.

In terms of *expanding* our approach, we need to be more multi-disciplinary and holistic. Development needs to reduce the dominance of economics, or else economic growth will always supersede human welfare. Development objectives need to be informed by human rights, ecology, political science, anthropology, cultural studies, and so on.

Achieving human rights has particular resonance for development. International human rights law stipulates that human rights are universal and indivisible. Indivisible means that you cannot separate economic, social and cultural rights from civil or political rights. In other words, if we win the right to vote, but have no food, then we do not enjoy basic human rights. Third World women were the first to express this as a direct challenge to Western liberal democracies that still give priority to civil and political rights.

Finally alliances need to be *strengthened* between women – North and South, East and West, rich and poor. The voices of poor Southern women, in particular, need amplification and legitimacy. The practice of universalizing the experiences of white middle-class women, who dominate the international arena, has marginalized women in the South. We must be respectful of one another, taking care not to misrepresent the diverse positions of different women. We must be careful not to collapse our complex, multiple social identities into a simplistic notion of one common gender identity or interest. Moreover, sisterhood cannot be assumed on the basis of a common sex. Instead we must build coalitions that foster diversity and celebrate difference. At the same time, the tensions that exist within international feminism need to be acknowledged and confronted. The romantic notion of global sisterhood can be replaced with a form of sisterhood that is both strategic and effective.

Conclusion

This chapter has attempted to illustrate how the global economy is providing new and complex challenges to the pursuit of equality and human development. Globalization is the economic development model of this decade, and like most models of development before it, it does not account for human differences in access to entitlements or power. Since the problems are easier to name than their solutions, this chapter has tried to go beyond the 'paralysis of analysis' by exploring ways in which women are responding to the new global reality. The bottom line, then? Simply, economics is not objective. Gender is never absent. And feminism? Well, it is alive and kicking.

Notes

1. A version of this chapter was published by Guelph University as part of their Hopper Lecture Series, which is funded by IDRC.
2. The study was conducted in Ghana's Volta region by the Centre for the Development of the People (Kumasi, Ghana), the North–South Institute (Ottawa, Canada), and the International Food Policy Research Institute (Washington, DC) in 1995 and published in Brown and Kerr (1997).
3. For a further discussion of this point see Zaman, this volume.
4. The initiative was undertaken by an *ad hoc* working group of the Special Programme for Africa chaired by CIDA. Research was commissioned or undertaken by several bilateral donors as well as the World Bank.
5. Three studies were later published in Brown and Kerr (1997).
6. *World Development*, Vol. 23, No. 11.

15 • The New Global Architecture, Gender and Development Practices

Isabella Bakker

It is now a truism to say that we are undergoing a fundamental change in societies. This change is fuelled by powerful economic forces often referred to as globalization. More specifically, this is a process of restructuring in the North and structural adjustment in the so-called South. This process is marked by a common neoliberal consensus that all governments need to reduce spending and regulation, maximize exports and allow market forces, not political or social forces, to restructure their national economies as part of either transnational or regional trade blocs like the European Union or the North American Free Trade region. In this way, economies become self-regulating and depoliticized, inverting Keynes's idea that democratic politics should always be privileged over economic forces. This disembedding process means that the market not only frees itself from society but also imposes its logic upon politics (Altvater and Mahnkopf, 1997).

Political economists see globalization as a part of a broader process of restructuring of the state and civil society, and of political economy, nature and culture. Globalization can also be characterized as a work in progress, as unattainable (Altvater and Mahnkopf) and as a conflict among different forms of capitalisms (Cox, 1995). In Europe, for instance, there is a rivalry between the aspiration for a completely open, unfettered global capitalism and a social market or social democratic tradition of economy. The clash in concept and practice between US and Japanese capitalism is ever more evident. These different forms of capitalism are shaped not only by abstract economic logic but also by social practices and cultural and civilizational traditions. To paraphrase Gramsci, the old order is not yet dead, the new not yet born.

Globalization is also very much an ideology – one that is largely consistent with the outlook of affluent minorities in the OECD and the urban elites and emerging middle classes in the South who benefit from incorporation into the production and financial circuits of transnational capital – the main beneficiaries of Galbraith's *Culture of Contentment* (Gill, 1995).

This so-called globalization paradigm has yet to congeal around such central issues as how the current shifts in governance might impact on citizens, the public/private divide and the state. For instance, the 'Washington consensus' of the 1980s – with its neoliberal prescription of slashing deficits, ceilings on interest rates and credit subsidies, price controls and currency devaluation – is now being questioned for being, at best, incomplete (Stiglitz, 1998), if not completely misguided (Hildyard, 1998). And, as so often is the case of theory and analysis in the social sciences, the emerging globalization paradigm has been decidedly silent about the gendered underpinnings of the current transformation. Neoliberal policies affirm the new gender-neutral, self-reliant citizen and atomistic market player. Feminist economists, especially writers from the South, have consistently demonstrated that restructuring is not a gender-neutral or genderless process, as women have a fundamentally different relation from men to national and international spaces of production, politics, identity and culture.

Several key aspects of the globalization process and 'malestream' accounts of globalization are taking place on a gendered terrain. Every institution, including markets and states, constructs and reproduces various kinds of femininity and masculinity that constitute an unequal gender order, marked by a gender division of labour and structure of power (Connell, 1990). A gender order is a dynamic process of symbolic and material representations of gender relations as they are institutionalized through practices at the micro, meso and macro levels of the political economy of production and reproduction. Neoliberal policies are both gender-neutral and gender-differentiating, celebrating as they do the genderless individual as an abstract commodity yet also integrating large segments of women into labour markets that are increasingly described as feminized both in numbers and job characteristics.

States, Three-Dimensional Markets and the Neoliberal Gender Order

There is a vigorous debate within political economy about whether modern nation states have lost power and, in Bob Jessop's terms, have been 'hollowed out', or whether state power is in fact being redeployed in some new ways (1997: 573). A strong case can be made for the latter – that the redeployment of state energies toward international markets and investments is the primary tendency of OECD economies, and the hollowing out of state's policy capacities a result. This in turn has enabled a much more aggressive class politics. It has also signalled a massive offloading to the sphere of reproduction (the 'care' economy) which acts as an effective shock absorber (Elson, 1994) or may signal an ultimate crisis in social reproduction (McDowell, 1991). Certainly the dilemmas of Western European welfare states are inextricably linked to changes in women's labour force participation and declining fertility rates, which have implications for pension schemes and the future viability of these welfare states (Esping-Andersen, 1997).

So, how has state power changed? For one thing, states are increasingly being disciplined to behave as if they were private markets operating in a global territory. Stephen Gill refers to the emerging system of global economic governance as 'disciplinary neoliberalism': it relies on the market – especially the capital market – to discipline economic agents, and privileges investors, who are seen as central to the process of economic growth (Gill, 1998: 25). This 'new constitutionalism', whereby transnational capital creates a 'quasi-constitutional framework for the reconstitution of the legal rights, prerogatives, and freedom of movement for capital on a world scale', locks in political reforms, thereby insulating dominant economic forces from democratic accountability (Gill, 1998: 12). Gill identifies several components of the new constitutionalism, two of which are directly relevant to a discussion of gender, namely:

- strategies for reconfiguring state apparatuses so that governments themselves become the facilitators of market values and discipline; and

- measures to construct markets through legal and political structures which both redefine and internationally guarantee private property rights (the World Trade Organization, for example).

First, reconfiguring state apparatuses involves deregulation and the reduction of government – in other words, a dramatic shift in commitment from securing the welfare of citizens to facilitating the flow of global capital. This has often been accomplished through a depoliticizing, technical discourse of deficits, competitiveness and balanced budgets, and an aura of technocratic neutrality. The whole idea of public goods is being severely tested through such policies as privatization and the introduction of user fees.

Second, the emerging global political economy is characterized by the growth in power of institutional processes outside the formal boundaries of the state. For governments, credibility with the financial markets and the multilateral development banks is becoming perhaps more important than credibility with the voters. Saskia Sassen suggests that these markets do exercise the accountability functions associated with citizenship – they can vote government economic policies down or in, and force governments to take certain measures over others. For example, with deregulation of interest rates central banks can now rely only on changes in interest rate levels to influence the level of demand in the economy; they can no longer use interest rate ceilings (Sassen, 1996: 45–6). The power of governments to influence interest and foreign exchange rates and fiscal policy can also be reduced severely, if not neutralized, by the foreign exchange and bond markets even in hegemonic centres such as the USA. Bond rates are important because of their link to state budgets and the debt question. Governments so far have failed to develop policies to control these markets – partly because it will require a coordinated effort, partly because key branches of government have been captured by neo-liberal forces. This has meant pathologizing those ministries of the state aligned with social welfare and validating others such as finance, trade and the police.

On the revenue side of fiscal policies, before the current period of transition taxes were used to redistribute incomes within societies, with particular social consequences. Now falling tax revenues in the North are increasingly curtailing the scope for government welfare and public spending projects. Corporation taxes have been falling in Europe for twenty years. Tax revenues are also going down due to high unemployment, the casualization of labour and policy decisions around tax cuts and balanced budgets. Moves to enshrine balanced budgeting or capping deficits through legal measures (by the federal government in the United States and by sub-national governments in Canada and the European Union) have under-scored fiscal conservatism by demarcating caps on spending and taxation. Such measures discourage proactive policies to promote equality because of the perceived political costs now attached to spending initiatives (Philipps, 1996). In the South, states have literally been hollowed out through successive rounds of privatization and huge pressures of debt refinancing and balance of payments demands (EURODAD/WIDE, 1994).

This raises a bigger issue. The presumption that everyone can now meet their needs through the market rests on the belief that earnings from jobs are sufficient and that all able adults engage in the labour market. For far too many, the changing global order and the increased influence of markets signals an intensification of inequalities not just here in the West but globally between the winners and losers of the race to get on the fast-moving train of globalization. For example, the poorest 20 per cent of the world's people have benefited little from globalization, sharing only 1 per cent of world trade. Three quarters of the people of the world live in developing countries yet they enjoy only 16 per cent of the world's income, while the richest 20 per cent have 85 per cent of global income. There has, of course, been tremendous progress in human development – in life expectancy, in nutrition, in infant mortality. Nevertheless, despite this progress, considerable human deprivation is a fact in both the developing and the industrial world: 1.3 billion people continue to survive on less than the equivalent of US$1 per day. Nearly 1 billion people are illiterate and some 840 million face food insecurity (UNDP, 1997, 1998).

Evidence of a revolt from below against the social impact of globalization has grown, though it is still fragmentary and above all not concerted. Some suggest that we are now approaching the limits of the first phase of globalization, and could be at the threshold of the second stage of a double movement that seeks to bring the global economy under social control.

Extremes of global inequality also highlight the limits as well as the possibilities of markets. One distinguishing feature of this phase of globalization is how more and more aspects of everyday life have been pervaded by market values and symbols, as hyper-mobile capital and scientific and technological innovation compress time and distance. Commodification becomes all-encompassing yet, at the same time, large numbers of people are almost totally marginalized from sharing in its outcomes (Gill, 1995). Ironically, the producers of such goods as Nike sport shoes, or vegetables and food products for export, are not necessarily the consumers of the efforts of their labour.

For feminist economists, this paradox between production and consumption is highlighted by women's position at the crossroads of production and reproduction. This vantage point leads to many views of markets, ranging from support to ambivalence to deep suspicion. Feminist critical economics, which offers a home to a number of heterodox approaches to economics, questions whether markets are a reliable means of mobilizing resources for production and an effective means of meeting needs.

For one thing, markets as social institutions are inevitably structured asymmetrically to the advantage of some participants over others. The UNDP's Gender Development Index (GDI) is one important statistical indicator which shows the difference between capabilities and opportunities for women in societies around the globe. Second, while markets entail opportunities they also involve risk such as unemployment and changes in demand for certain goods. So in order to counteract market insecurity, non-market safety nets (kin, community, state provisions) are seen as necessary (Miller and Razavi: 30). This insight highlights one of the limits of a purely production-oriented approach to political and economic globalization. Non-market relations are key to gauging the nature and depth of the globalization process as it plays itself out in the daily lives of real people, of women and men.

So there is a sense in which markets cannot be viewed simply in the one-dimensional aspect of competition and exchange. Rather, they must also be analysed in terms of two other dimensions: *command*, or the economic relationships in which power plays a predominant role, such as between employers and employees; and *change*, which refers to the way in which the operation of the economic system changes over time. The time dimension of markets forces us to remember that each economic system works differently at different points in time, and that the people who make up a system also develop over time (Bowles and Edwards, 1993).

How do these insights inform notions of globalization? Feminist economists, in concert with other transformative scholarship and progressive social movements, raise a number of very important concerns about how markets allocate resources and determine welfare, how social solidarities can be built and maintained as they were through welfare states, and how growth can take place from the perspective of people. Like all forms of knowledge, economics reflects and helps produce pervasive social beliefs about men and women and their social positions. The most general critique levelled against mainstream economic accounts of global restructuring is that they tend to subsume all experiences under a universal rubric of 'human' that is in fact an expression of the masculine experience (see Bakker, 1997; Peterson, 1992). A fundamental consequence of this way of thinking is that need and production are not situated within an analysis of systemic reproduction *that includes* human reproduction, sustenance and the biosphere.

A further important object of critique by writers in the South has been the tendency to view economic, political and social change through Western concepts which leave little room for the mutual recognition of distinct traditions of civilization. Chandra Mohanty (1988) criticizes white, Western feminists for their universalizing tendencies ('sisterhood is global') and their process of 'Othering' (Eurocentrism) Third World women. Mohanty and other Third World writers have been particularly critical of the victimology in Western feminist accounts of global restructuring. For example, discussions of international restructuring of manufacturing industries and the rise of Export Processing Zones frequently see Third World women as the passive victims of multinational capital. Newer approaches originating from writers outside the Western framework examine the interaction of constraining structures and women's varied responses to changing material incentives. Naila Kabeer, for example, has demonstrated how women garment workers in Bangladesh have responded to the new insecurities and opportunities of the government's active encouragement of garment industries, thereby reconstituting *purdah* norms and customary practices toward a new, more participatory definition of women's roles (Kabeer, 1989; also Zaman, this volume). Such an approach has meant that scholars and practitioners have had to re-evaluate their notions of agency, especially poor women's agency and resistance, and has opened the door to new voices in the policy process.

Feminist Policy Communities and the Changing Economic Order

Several trends discussed in the previous section have contributed to a shift in how feminist policy communities articulate gender issues in institutional settings. Thus the trend towards the denationalization of the state has meant a continuous shift in state power upwards to multilateral agencies such as the IMF and agreements such as the North American Free Trade Association (NAFTA) or the European Union, downwards to sub-national and local levels of government, and sideways to different government departments (such as the shift toward ministries of finance). Second, there has been a trend towards the destatization of the political system, what some observers refer to as the shift from govern*ment* to govern*ance*; the latter emphasizes partnerships between governmental, para-governmental and non-governmental organizations in which the state apparatus is not sovereign but seen as a first among equals (Jessop, 1997: 575). A third trend is that towards the internationalization of policy regimes: extra-territorial or transnational factors and processes – especially, neoliberalism – have become more important for shaping domestic state action. These three trends have changed both the substance and the sites of gender issues, both how and where they are articulated.

In this sense, the shifting context for state policy is parallelled by a shift in the feminist development communities. Early feminist interventions were enshrined in technocratic, Western and state-centric beliefs that marked post-war projects of development. The Women in Development (WID) literature which influenced donor governments, international agencies and the women's movements during the 1970s and early 1980s is one such example. The WID approach sought to address the failure of development planners to consider women's needs and women's viewpoints, which created a flawed integration of women in the process of development. Largely with reference to micro-level projects and donor agencies, WID practitioners showed why development policies consistently failed to deliver resources to women. For example, early agricultural innovation practices and extension services fell short of meeting their objective of increasing rural productivity and income because they overlooked women's roles in the production process. WID policies were to recognize the significant economic and social costs of neglecting and undermining women's roles in the development process. Early development policy related to women primarily as mothers or would-be mothers; welfare programmes were devised which made women the primary targets of a 'basic needs' strategy addressed at health, education, housing, nutrition and home-based income generating activities.

Many studies uncovered the hidden role of women both as agents in development and as recipients of androcentric policies. The WID approach has also been criticized, however, for its record in terms of integrating women into the development process and its limited understanding of the structural rigidities of patriarchal relations. As Kabeer and Humphrey (1990) point out, while WID agencies recognize gender asymmetries in crucial resources (land, credit, training, employment) their underlying explanations rested on cultural norms and the sexual division of labour. Linking women's empowerment to their participation in the market leaves out gender subordination in all its dimensions.

By the early 1980s, a shift in focus in feminist economics was fuelled by a change in the macro policy environment away from Keynesian thinking to neoliberal economics which stressed stabilisation and structural adjustment policies. For gender practitioners, the need to extend their critical insights beyond discrete micro-level projects to macroeconomic policies became quickly apparent as policy increasingly focused on cutting back aggregate public expenditure and the money supply in order to reduce deficits and curb inflation (Razavi, 1996). This meant increasing scrutiny of ministries of finance and multilateral development and lending agencies such as the World Bank.

Along with these changes in the macro policy environment, serious criticism from feminists in the North and South began to eclipse the WID approach and paved the way for the emergence of more critical feminist approaches often referred to as Gender and Development (GAD). These heterodox approaches to development (including neo-institutional, post-Marxist and post-Keynesian strands) stressed the need to understand and question existing power relations among women and men in society by focusing on gender relationships, their social construction, and how gender differences have led to inequalities in power between women and men as well as among women. The GAD approach to development thinking and practice is more difficult to apply in practice than WID, as it focuses on relationships between women and men as well as institutional change. The latter objective gave rise to the concept of gender mainstreaming in international agencies such as the United Nations Development Programme (UNDP), the International Labour Organization (ILO), the Food and Agricultural Organization (FAO) and the World Bank. This is a systematic process of situating gender equality issues at the centre of broad policy decisions, institutional structures and resource allocations, and includes the views and priorities of women in decision making about development (Schalkwyk, Thomas and Woroniuk, 1996). At the same time, grassroots efforts have pressured for more participatory and democratic structures that would allow men and women to respond to economic opportunities without compromising the production of human resources (UNDP, 1995).

Given the changing nature of state power and the three-dimensional character of markets discussed earlier – that they are competitive but also coercive and dynamic over time – what are some examples of feminist policy intervention? Some economists would say that macroeconomics is dead to politicians and public policy advocates – that this is something which should best be left to markets and to central bankers. Not only is this view false; it is also profoundly anti-democratic.

There are a number of very important political principles of democracy and accountability that come out of the body of feminist economic writings and activism over the last few decades. Some of these are:

- a commitment to plurality of development strategies as well as civilizational forms;

- a political emphasis on accountability and transparency;

- a continued focus on the national (and not just local or international) policy arena;

- a belief that economics isn't just about what gets produced in the market but also about the interrelationship between three sectors: the private commodity economy, the public sector economy and the care economy;

- making what's invisible visible and demystifying economics so that everyone can engage in these kinds of debates and gain more power over their lives;

- recognizing the gendered nature of the institutions through which macroeconomic policies are implemented.

These principles have been translated into various ways of engaging in economic policy debates. Part and parcel of these struggles have been efforts to create spaces for resistance by talking about economics in the dual sense of everyday practices and structural power. Some are short-term conjunctural (market-enabling or survival-oriented) and others more transformative:

- the effort to engender budgets at the national level as well as broadening notions of economic well-being to include human development benchmarks (HDI, GDI, HPI);

- the campaign to introduce unpaid work and time use into notions of human and economic sustainability;

- grassroots and academic efforts to include gender in trade initiatives, recognizing that liberalization has different market and non-market implications for women and men.

Feminist scholars and activists have begun to concentrate on 'engendering' the main economic debates of the day. The national budget which reflects a country's values – whose work it values and who it rewards – is generally assumed to affect men and women within the same class equally. The process of preparing budgets is also assumed to be a highly technical exercise best left to the 'experts' in government, international agencies and certain professional segments of the private sector such as accountants and tax lawyers. As a response to these two forces, alternative gender-sensitive budget processes have been launched in a number of countries.

The technical discourse of neoliberal fiscal policy has increasingly circumscribed the possibilities of political practice in both the North and the South. Technical discourses like those related to deficits and balanced budgets derive a good deal of their power from scientific rationality, removing issues from the realm of public debate by limiting discussion to those who master the required technical language of economics. Those labelled as non-technical advocates, like labour, women's groups and environmental actors, are quickly dismissed as special interests in contrast to tax lawyers, accountants and financial experts who are portrayed as representing the general interest of a good business climate (Philipps, 1996). Power in this sense resides in consent (Gramsci, 1971) and representation (Foucault, 1972).

Restructuring discourse tends to emphasize certain macroeconomic indicators of governmental performance, including deficit reduction and interest rate stability. This is presented as advancing a common good and economic progress. Yet this prescription rests on certain assumptions about the actors who comprise the economy. The individual who underwrites this discursive economy is relatively autonomous and able to participate in markets, is mobile between sectors and regions, and can access a limitless supply of social reproductive services in the family when they are withdrawn from the state (Philipps, 1996). This 'conceptual silence' obscures the social foundations of market relations – their embeddedness – including their gendered and racial underpinnings (Bakker, 1994).

Substantive equality rights require a recognition that budgetary decisions (about the allocation of resources, the distribution of income and wealth and stabilization of the economy) affect the lives of men and women differently given pre-existing gender inequalities grounded in both the division of labour and gender-differentiated social rights and obligations. These gender-based differences are generally structured in such a way as to leave women in an unequal position in relation to the men in their community, with less economic, social and political power but greater responsibilities for caring for those who need the care of others such as children and the elderly. The neoliberal thrust in the fiscal arena is contributing to this fundamental shift in dominant understandings of government and citizenship.

In response, feminist scholars and activists in the North (Canada, Australia, Switzerland, the UK) and the South (Barbados, Mozambique, Namibia, Tanzania, Sri Lanka, South Africa, Uganda) have begun to concentrate on 'engendering' the main economic debates of the day (Budlender, Sharp and Allen, 1998). This means making visible the gendered underpinnings of the new welfare thinking and traditional macroeconomic policies; making an argument for social investment; and showing that not all burdens can be transferred to the unpaid economy without resulting human and economic costs. Gender-sensitive budgets represent a transition from advocacy to accountability: they audit government budgets for their impact on women and girls, men and boys. Some are conducted from within government (Australia, for example) and some are outside government or a combination of the two, as is the case in South Africa where the Women's Budget Initiative (WBI) started in 1995 as a joint effort of parliamentarians and NGOs.

Other alternatives, beyond engendering the main economic debates of the day, are also available. For instance, a new politics of time could be developed based on an expanded notion of time use. Three time uses – paid work, unpaid work and leisure – need to be emphasized, not the standard two of economics (paid work and leisure). How we use our time, strategies to reduce the intensity of social reproduction work, employment sharing – all of these are part of a discussion in which unpaid work becomes a focus. Part-time work, for example, needs to be seen not only as a 'choice' for women balancing a family and work; part-time employment is also part of neoliberal policies themselves which are contributing to the increase in part-time jobs. The lack of reliable and affordable child care only contributes to statistics in labour forces surveys and national polls in which women report that they're not seeking full-time work. Cutbacks in the public sector, which was the source of better jobs for many women in the OECD, push them increasingly into a labour market that is creating more part-time rather than full-time jobs (Jenson, 1996). So how we use our time and women's concentration in part-time jobs need to be placed at the centre of debates on policies of national restructuring. In the South, time use is often the difference between survival and starvation. Also, human development is about the expansion of human choices by developing human capabilities: time resources, therefore, are a key consideration.

Finally, women's networks have been quick to recognize that multilateral trade and economic agreements are having an increasing influence on domestic economic activity and outcomes. This has sparked a good deal of collaboration, in fact, between women's groups from different parts of the world. For example, NAFTA has brought together Mexican and Canadian women's groups revealing commonalities in terms of liberalized trade (Gabriel and Macdonald, 1996). The Asia–Pacific Economic Cooperation forum (APEC) has also launched a campaign recently to promote integration of gender perspectives into its work. Among the United Nations organizations, the UN Women's Organization (UNIFEM) has taken the initiative to foster discussion and research on trade and gender. In order to affect the rules of global trade, transnational organizational efforts are required along with short-term and longer-term measures.

No doubt these initiatives need the support of structural changes such as new international mechanisms which would deliver financial benefits to poorer and weaker countries. One key building block of a new international architecture would be a new process for the international community to incorporate greater representativeness, participation and inclusiveness. Much broader and more representative cross-sections of the public need to be consulted rather than the limited focus on chief decision makers in key ministries such as finance and central banks. The emphasis on the perspective of the financial sector has meant too little attention to social issues, especially the concerns of the poor and the vulnerable. A second important building block, frequently underscored by feminist economics, is a greater emphasis on plurality of economic systems. Different conditions, cultures and solutions mark the global political economy and this should be recognized through international trade agreements, for example. Finally, greater controls of international capital movements – taxes on currency transactions, border taxes on capital inflows and reformed capital adequacy rules for banks to discourage short-term lending – have all been entertained in international forums (Culpeper, 1999).

16 • *Afterword*
Opening Spaces for
Transformative Practice

Ellen Judd

From a distance it may have appeared that a threshold had been crossed with the emergence of Women in Development and Gender and Development work in recent decades. Feminists directly involved in this work are more questioning, however, and this should come as no surprise. If it had been a simple matter to remove the global obstacles women face, feminism would long ago have completed its mission. That it continues is the mark of a shortfall, and of a continuing critical vision on the part of feminists engaged in the practice of development work. These activists have accomplished a distinct change in the way development work is conceptualized and conducted, and they have also provoked a deepening analysis of what is needed to enable development work to contribute effectively to the liberation of women.

The particular problems that women face are varied, as has been the history of responses to them and the analyses presented here. One departure point for this collection has been the recognition that everywhere we are engaged with specific local circumstances and relations, and that the practices of feminists are consequently varied and embedded in the local, even when connected with encompassing global processes. Nevertheless, several shared concerns arise from the various voices and locations represented here, and these themes are on the agenda as feminists consider the next steps to be taken.

A Critical Space

As a result of earlier feminist critiques and a widespread acknowledgment of the inadequacies of a gender-blind approach to development, approaches that aim to include women, whether WID or GAD, have become relatively standard in development work. However, the understanding of what this inclusion means, or what is to be accomplished through it, remains ambiguous. The approaches may range from serving broader development goals by using women's labour more effectively, to liberal policies of more open inclusion and more equal opportunity, to transformative

218

strategies for changing women's structural position in society and empowering women to change their own lives. All of these goals (and more) are condensed into contemporary policies and programmes for targeting women in development. This ambiguity allows people and institutions with diverse orientations to collaborate in development work involving women. This collaboration has been a matter of active negotiation and contested priorities, and it has been a process through which a portion of mainstream development resources have been accessed in the interests of women and activist women's organizations. This has been the positive side of much WID/GAD work.

There are also voices that have eloquently drawn attention to the problems posed by this apparent agreement. Some of the concern arises in relation to the shift from stand-alone women's projects (WID), criticized for their isolation from the mainstream, toward projects that take a more comprehensive approach toward gender relations and endeavour to incorporate women into the mainstream (GAD). The focus upon gender is constructive in allowing for a more holistic approach toward the gendered structure of social relations and political economy. Nevertheless, it has been accompanied by a muting of feminist goals of transformative change.

The particular concern that appears here and that should be underlined is that the discourse of gender analysis and GAD can appear to be serving women's interests while at the same time obscuring real problems and diverting or diluting initiatives for transformative change. In effect, we have moved from the obvious problems of gender-blind discourse to the subtle problems of a discourse that denies the nature of the problem by claiming to be addressing it. This can occur relatively directly through appearances of implementing WID or GAD projects, without making the institutional, financial and practical commitments necessary for such projects to be effective. Or it may occur less directly through internal adjustments of policy that compromise the potential of WID/GAD initiatives from within. This can be implicit in projects designed only to include or integrate women in development, without questioning either the structure of inclusion and integration or the overall context of development.

Development discourse and practice that have adopted gender as their central concept are especially vulnerable to this blurring of vision and cooption in action. The challenge here is to retain the broader concepts of the pervasiveness of gender relations and the necessity of holistic analysis and change, without losing the space for a feminist critical voice. Unfortunately, that voice has been muted in the process of moving gender analysis and GAD into the mainstream. This may be an unavoidable possibility in what must necessarily be a contested move both for feminists striving to transform the mainstream and for mainstream development advocates preferring to submerge a feminist challenge.

The particular danger to be identified here is one in which the contestation is denied or obscured by the use of the language of gender in the absence, or the muting, of feminist critique and practice. It is also useful to see this deceptive harmonization as related to the larger cultural context of the contemporary political economy. In the late twentieth-century rise of globalization there is an apparent convergence of values and practices in the marketplace, and a valuation of social harmony in the interests of pursuing prosperity (cf. Martin, 1994: 18). Social harmony is profoundly attractive for many appealing reasons, but dangerously disabling for those whose interests require a questioning of the *status quo*. However valuable it may be to develop some shared ground and nurture cooperation among those whose interests, goals and understandings partially coincide, it is also essential to the feminist standpoint to open and maintain a space of difference in which a critical perspective can flourish and drive work in new directions.

From this perspective, quantitative improvements in women's income, employment or education – however desirable – are insufficient. The feminist project may certainly find these improvements useful, but the goal of structural transformation in the interests of all women (including the most vulnerable) requires demonstrable institutional change and qualitative measures of historical process.

'Studying Up'

Gender analysis, applied social science research and programme evaluation are recognized components of WID/GAD work as practised at present. We are now at a point where it is widely understood that gender-sensitive research is valuable for the design and implementation of development work. Typically, however, this research is focused upon the women who are the actual or potential targets of development programmes, and on the immediate implementation of programmes. Viewed within the social and political context in which it occurs, this research consists of 'studying down', while the research that might better serve the interests of the women affected is research that 'studies up' (see Nader, 1974). Rather than being research done by development organizations and workers on the women affected, 'studying up' would be research done by or with the women affected on the development organizations and on the structure of the encompassing political economy.

Several of the contributions in this volume undertake important aspects of this research and analysis, and point the direction for further work. Much more such research is needed in order to make development work transparent and accountable to the world's women and effective in working in women's interests. Here it is only possible to sketch the outline of the territory to be examined. If one starts with the largest scale, development work is positioned within a globalized political economy in which there is currently an overwhelmingly dominant commitment to market-oriented strategies of economic growth. This context is the focus of some articles in this collection, and permeates several more. Indeed, it would be difficult or impossible to analyse WID/GAD without adequate reference to the mainstream (as well as alternative and oppositional modes) of global development. This requires a framework of feminist critique that illuminates the global issues, and especially the dominant economic discourse in this area.

For feminists involved in the practice of development, there are also more immediately reflexive and concrete aspects to this critique. Those of us from the North are implicitly and to one degree or another involved in promoting the political economy of globalization and its core concepts. This is most clearly the case for those who are endeavouring to work in and alter the mainstream, but it is difficult to escape entirely even for those working in more compatible NGOs, and even for those in feminist organizations. This occurs not only when North meets South, but also within the North. In this volume we have attempted to express this reflexive critique with articles addressing the practical issues confronting aboriginal women and those involved in university–community linkage programmes within Canada, as well as by examining the involvement of feminists with the Canadian International Development Agency (CIDA). Despite gender equity measures in CIDA and elsewhere in the Canadian government, the practical results and institutional structures are still far from what feminists require. This is not necessarily to suggest that Canada is worse in this respect than other countries of the North. We have chosen to focus on Canada since the editors and several of the contributors live in Canada, and it is critical to a truly reflexive approach to start with ourselves and our own societies. In every case, we must be very careful about the values we carry, even if unintentionally or unconsciously. It is also necessary to be prepared to address the shortcomings of one's own practices and those of the institutions in which we work, a task requiring unusual honesty and integrity, as exemplified by the contributions in this volume.

The policy formation and institutional basis for WID/GAD, as well as the allocation of resources to implement it, are determined at relatively high levels of the political and bureaucratic structures. The political and civil service systems are profoundly gender-biased everywhere, and this poses considerable problems in making the initial decisions regarding policies and priorities that set the framework for what is possible subsequently, especially in mainstream development agencies. Analysis of who has access to decision-making bodies, who comprises these bodies, and how they function at both macro- and micro-political levels is essential to a concerted strategy of 'studying up' in development work. As with all other types of 'studying up', direct access to the workings of the highest levels of decision making is exceptionally difficult. Unusual circumstances of feminists breaking through into these levels, access to information provisions, or political change may assist in this task. Much of the research may have to be done less directly and through the use of documents and analysis of policy development. In either case, knowledge gained regarding the higher levels of development policy is extremely valuable to the feminists engaged in the endeavour of remaking development policy. We also require further exchanges of case material on how feminists have succeeded in entering or influencing these levels.

Now that there are a considerable number of feminists working in development organizations of many types (governmental, multilateral, NGO, feminist NGO), it is possible to identify institutional and behavioural barriers or issues at less remote levels. Apart from some cases, most prominently that of Japan, where a major concern remains the basic one of placing women, gender and feminism on the agenda, these issues revolve around making policy that is to some degree gender-inclusive become truly gender-inclusive and even feminist in actual practice. A strikingly widespread tone in the articles collected here is the persistence of barriers to women and to feminism within the very development programmes that claim to be improving the situation of women.

Except in the case of NGOs organized on specifically feminist grounds, all of the feminists doing development work are necessarily enmeshed in non-feminist organizational structures that have been affected minimally in their everyday workings by the addition of gender-related policy elements and some feminist personnel. Many feminists working in these organizations are marginalized in WID components. For those now working in the mainstream in gender analysis and GAD work, the marginalization from control of projects, personnel and budgets typically continues, but may be obscured by attempts to represent GAD work as being conducted by other staff and throughout the project. Accountability for GAD, when dispersed through a project, is difficult to assess, even if some specific components (numbers of women trained, numbers of women on staff) can be measured.

Monitoring GAD is difficult and fraught with political problems. This is one of the types of work feminists are called upon to do for development agencies, but practically it may mean assessing the work of other feminists at the final implementation stage and determining whether such work will continue. It does not necessarily or effectively hold project management or policy makers accountable for creating appropriate and effective policies, providing the institutional support to implement them, and funding them adequately. What is essential, instead of existing modes of monitoring, are effective mechanisms for 'studying up' in development organizations and, more specifically, for rendering every stage from policy formation to implementation transparent and accountable. This type of assessment would best be done by the women affected or potentially affected by a programme or policy.

The problems that would be identified and analysed in such a process would be diverse, but the articles included here indicate some of the major concerns. There is considerable entrenched resistance, open and hidden, to feminism and even to limited forms of WID or GAD within the development community. This persists despite changes in policy in recent years, and the prevalence of such attitudes and associated behaviours cannot be assumed to have disappeared from development organizations. It is expressed in forms such as giving gender analysis and WID/GAD work such low priority that they rarely appear in the active agenda (except in preparation for monitoring), failing to allocate adequate personnel or material resources to the work, and not placing the work in the hands and under the control of people committed to its success.

'Studying up' in development work will not only identify and analyse the barriers to feminist work, but will expand the available body of case material on how feminists have successfully reduced, eliminated or avoided these barriers, and will eventually allow this knowledge to be systematized and become a practical resource for feminists doing development.

The Global and the Local

The interventions in local societies implied in development work are massive exercises in engineered social change. The extent of the change being proposed is deceptively hidden by the use of the benign term 'development', and by all its connotations of help and improving the living conditions of disadvantaged and even impoverished peoples. Development agendas propose to 'modernize' societies by bringing them within the scope of contemporary market economies, facilitating economic growth, and providing financial assistance for economic and sometimes non-economic projects. To oppose development would appear, especially for liberal constituencies in the North, to be opposing the amelioration of poverty and the obligation of the more fortunate to the less fortunate. But it is essential for everyone involved in development to be very clear about what development work does, and especially to be clear not only about intentions but about actual effects.

Development work rarely aims at the simple financial support of existing institutions or the purely quantitative improvement of some aspect of living conditions. Rather, the purpose is explicitly or implicitly to serve as a catalyst for processes of change. Because of the interconnectedness of social life, changes in any aspect of life can be expected to have effects on other aspects; indeed, this is assumed in development work. A critical assumption is that critical interventions in selected areas, such as subsistence or education, will have a series of cascading effects.

Unfortunately, the history of social engineering to date has not been encouraging. The complexities of initiating and implementing such change have proved difficult, even within a given society. To introduce such change into another society is immensely more complicated, and raises even more difficult questions about who the change is intended to serve, how it will do so, and who is to direct and control it. These are not problems that can be reduced to issues of financial aid or even more broadly conceptualized economic assistance. Instead, they are fundamentally political questions that affect the future of every local society. A shared theme in the papers collected here is the need to question the concept of 'development' itself, and recognize that it is a political issue in the broadest meaning of that word – as well as an economic one.

A feminist perspective on the current conjuncture affirms that development processes cannot and should not be directed from outside, nor should they be left to the workings of the unseen hand of the market. A feminist vision of development is one in which local women are empowered through decentring processes of creating and realizing local strategies for change. This is not a simple or straightforward matter, as indicated by the powerfully reflexive critiques of activists involved in these processes. Through practice and through continuing critique, the nature of development and of feminist organizing for change is being rethought and recreated.

Work in and through international development agencies and NGOs are one means through which women have sought to support each other at a global level. Feminists in such agencies and NGOs are not always welcome, especially if they only bring established Northern models of feminism and development with them. Nevertheless, local societies may open the door, however cautiously, to agencies that bring with them funding that potentially can be used for local purposes. Here there is a difficult problem in disentangling competing sources of control and competing purposes for this funding. Money is the lever that opens local societies around the world to the global processes of market-oriented development, and also sometimes one of the means through which solidarity can express itself. The magical quality of money as a medium of exchange allows it to operate in multiple dimensions, and makes it profoundly contested in the practice of development work. It is no accident that access to and control of funding are major issues in many of the contributions in this volume. Indeed, the issue of funding affects the dynamics of all the situations examined here.

Funding of development projects can be provisionally accepted as a positive factor, provided the projects are designed and implemented in such a manner as to deliver some benefits to the intended recipients. Feminists have added to the goals and evaluation of all development projects further standards of protecting and improving the rights of women. Feminists have also been vocally critical of the limited agenda of much development work aimed primarily or exclusively at generating economic growth, even where these specifically target women as beneficiaries. Increased income and improved security of access to resources for livelihood, health, education and all forms of social participation for women are surely desirable, although they are far from adequate as solutions. There is a potential long-term and qualitative value to work that allows women increased material security, even beyond the immediate benefits provided. Those who suffer most and have least security may not be able to join effectively in movements to confront patriarchy or the other sources of oppression in their lives. As Eric Wolf (1969) argued long ago for agrarian peoples, those most able to organize and resist are those who enjoy the 'tactical mobility' of a degree of economic and social security. In either the mainstream or the more transformative sectors of feminist development work, current efforts to provide enhanced security for women can contribute to the material base for growing activism.

But improved economic conditions, however desirable, will not accomplish this alone, and here feminists doing development work have considerable specific insights to offer. In order to make an effective difference, organizational vehicles are essential, and the kinds of organization and organizational strategies that are used are critical in determining the direction a movement for change can take. Here there are many possibilities, and inevitably much of the detail must be developed in a diversity of local and culturally specific forms by the women directly involved, but a few of the more widely shared concerns can be raised here.

Where feminists are attempting to work within official development agencies on WID/GAD projects, it is essential that the work be conducted in partnership with local women's groups. Supporting local women's groups and their capacity to initiate, implement and sustain transformative change for women within their own societies should be one of the highest priorities in feminist development work. All other work is dependent upon this local organizational capacity in order to be realized effectively in practice. Local organization, supported through broader solidarity, can supply the necessary vehicle for long-term as well as short-term strategies for change. Immediate steps that can be taken in this direction include requiring development agencies in the North to institutionalize the basis of such partnerships and to entrust the local partners with control over the funding needed to build institutional capacity and implement projects. Here there are clear organizational and budgetary criteria according to which development agencies can be held accountable.

Several contributions to this volume arise from feminist development work operating through NGOs and specifically feminist organizations. Here the opportunities are distinctly different, and one goal of feminist development work should be to expand the scope and effect of these alternative and oppositional channels. NGOs, too, need to be held accountable for partnerships and budgetary control, but may provide a more conducive environment for the support of local women and their organizations. Work to establish international feminist networks located in the South, and efforts to recognize and work with women's groups that may not necessarily have taken development as their central concern (such as labour unions, aboriginal women's groups and women's health groups) are also important in recognizing the emergent voices and practices of women. Women doing development work can contribute to the support of local initiatives and organizations and thereby build the global solidarity that we all need. Activists in the South are, as indicated in this volume, in the forefront of innovative strategizing and practical critique of the work needed to build effective organizational means for transformative change.

Some of the work feminists in the North can do will take place most effectively in the North itself. Here there are decisive questions of political economy, such as the issue of debt reduction for the South or the Multilateral Agreement on Investment, whose resolution will affect the future of development work globally. Working 'up' in development agencies to make their policies and practices transparent and accountable to the world's women is a major challenge confronting feminists doing development in the North. Through this work, we may assist in opening the spaces for transformative practice at the local level, upon which our future decisively depends.

It will be at the local level that the actual transformations take place. Globally, we can create supportive links, but all work is ultimately local, whether it be in the specifics of daily practices within development agencies, or in women's movements around the world. In challenging existing models of development, we are taking a step towards decentred and diverse practices through which new knowledge about development for and by women is being created in practice. The detailed case studies and assessments of local practices in which feminists are now engaged mark a further stage of knowledge about how to transform development and move it from a market to a social foundation. This knowledge is both embedded in local practices and increasingly shared and systematized as feminists join together in the critique and rethinking of development as we presently know it.

Bibliography

Alam, S. M. (1985) 'Women and Poverty in Bangladesh', *Women's Studies International Forum*, Vol. 8, No. 4.

— (1995) 'Democratic Politics and the Fall of the Military Regime in Bangladesh', *Bulletin of Concerned Asian Scholars*, Vol. 27, No. 3.

Altvater, Elmer and Brigitte Mahnkopf (1997) 'The World Market Unbound', *Review of International Political Economy*, Vol. 4, No. 3 (Autumn).

Amaratunga, Carol (1998) *Draft MCEWH Annual Workplan.*

Anderson, R. S. (1975) *Education in Japan: a Century of Modern Development.* Washington, DC: US Government Printing Office for the Department of Health, Education and Welfare.

Andriyani, N. (1996) 'The Making of Indonesian Women Worker Activists'. MWS thesis, Memorial University of Newfoundland.

Antrobus, Peggy (1998) *Macro-Micro Linkages in Caribbean Community Development: the Impact of Global Trends, State Policies and a Non-Formal Education Project on Rural Women in St Vincent (1974–1994).* Doctoral thesis, Amherst: University of Massachusetts at Amherst.

Aoki, N. (1996) 'Incorporation of WID Perspectives in Japan's Development Assistance: Past Experience and Future Prospects', *Technology and Development*, No. 9, pp. 91–7.

Archibald, Linda and Mary Crnkovich (1995) 'Intimate Outsiders: Feminist Research in a Cross-Cultural Environment', in Sandra Burt and Lorraine Code (eds), *Changing Methods: Feminists Transforming Practice.* Peterborough, Ontario: Broadview Press.

Arscott, Jane and Linda Trimble. (1977) *In the Presence of Women: Representation in Canadian Governments.* Toronto: Harcourt Brace Canada.

Asian Women Workers Newsletter (1987) 'Garment Workers Meet for a United Front – Bangladesh', Vol. 6, No. 1.

Asian Women Workers Newsletter (1997) 'Bangladesh: Garments', Vol. 16, No. 4.

Aubry, Jack (1997) 'Tax Dollars Spent on Native Bands not Controlled Enough Many Say', *Edmonton Journal*, 20 June.

Baden, S. and A. M. Goetz (1998) 'Who Needs [Sex] When You Can Have [Gender]? Conflicting Discourses on Gender at Beijing', in C. Jackson and R. Pearson (eds), *Feminist Visions of Development.* London: Routledge.

Bakker, Isabella (1994) *The Strategic Silence: Gender and Economic Policy.* London: Zed Books and the North–South Institute.

Bakker, Isabella (1997) 'Identity, Interests and Ideology: the Gendered Terrain of Global Restructuring', in Stephen Gill (ed.), *Globalization, Democratisation and Multilateralism.* Tokyo, New York: Macmillan/United Nations University Press.

227

Bakker, Isabella and Janine Brodie (1995) *The New Canada Health and Social Transfer (CHST): the Implications for Women.* Ottawa: Status of Women Canada.

Bakker, Isabella and Diane Elson (1998) 'Toward Engendering Budgets in Canada', *Alternative Federal Budget 1998.* Ottawa: Canadian Centre for Policy Alternatives.

Bangladesh Bureau of Statistics (1994) *Annual Report.* Dhaka: Government of Bangladesh.

Bangladesh Mahila Parishad (1992) *Commission Report of Status of Women in Bangladesh,* Dhaka: Bangladesh Mahila Parishad.

Barnsley, J. and D. Lewis (1996) 'Case Studies from British Columbia', in Barbara Cottrell, *et. al.*

Beneria, L. & M. Roldan (1987) *The Crossroads of Class and Gender.* Chicago: Chicago University Press.

Benmayor, Rina (1991) 'Testimony, Action Research, and Empowerment: Puerto Rican Women and Popular Education', in Gluck (ed.).

Bobbington, A. and G. Thiele (1993) *NGOs and the State in Latin America.* London: Routledge.

Boserup, Esther (1970) *Women's Role in Economic Development.* London: George Allen and Unwin.

Boserup, Esther (1975) 'Integration of Women in Development: Why, When, How?' UN Development Programme.

Bourchier, D. and J. Legge (1994) *Democracy in Indonesia: 1950s and 1990s.* Monash Papers on Southeast Asia, No. 31, Monash University.

Bowles, Samuel and Richard Edwards (1993) *Understanding Capitalism: Competition, Command and Change in the US Economy.* New York: Harper Collins.

Braidotti, R. *et al.* (1994) *Women, the Environment and Sustainable Development.* London: Zed Books/Instraw.

Brodie, Janine (1997) 'Meso-Discourses, State Forms and the Gendering of Liberal-Democratic Citizenship', *Citizenship Studies,* Vol.1, No. 2.

Brown, H. (1992) *Women Organizing.* London: Routledge.

Brown, Lynn R. and Joanna Kerr (eds) (1997) *The Gender Dimensions of Economic Reforms in Ghana, Mali and Zambia.* North–South Institute.

Brown, Rosemary (1997) 'Exploration for the Oil and Gas Frontier: Impact on Lubicon Lake Cree Women', in J. Rick Ponting (ed.), *First Nations in Canada; Perspectives on Opportunity, Empowerment, and Self-Determination.* Toronto: McGraw-Hill Ryerson. pp. 193–205.

Buchanan, James (1997) *Frozen Desire: the Meaning of Money.* New York: Farrar Straus Giroux.

Budlender, Debbie (ed.) (1998) *The Third Women's Budget.* Cape Town: Institute for Democracy in South Africa (IDASA).

Budlender, Debbie and Rhonda Sharp, with Kerri Allen (1998) *How to Do A Gender-Sensitive Budget Analysis: Contemporary Research and Practices.* London: Commonwealth Secretariat.

Buvinic, M. (1982) 'Has Development Assistance Worked? Observations on Programs for Women in the Third World'. Paper presented at annual meeting of the Society for International Development, Baltimore, MD.

Canadian Research Institute for the Advancement of Women (CRIAW) (1986) *Women's Involvement in Political Life: a Pilot Study.* Research report prepared for UNESCO by the Canadian Research Institute for the Advancement of Women, April. Published in 1987 as CRIAW paper No. 16/17.

Cancian, Francesca (1992) 'Feminist Science: Methodologies That Challenge Inequality', *Gender and Society,* No. 6, pp. 632–42.

Caputi, J. and D. Russell (1992) 'Feminicide: Sexist Terrorism Against Women', in J. Radford and D. Russell (eds), *Feminicide: The Politics of Woman Killing*. Buckingham: Open University Press.

Cerny, Phillip (1995) 'Globalization and the Changing Logic of Collective Action', *International Organisation*, Vol. 49, No. 4.

Charles, N. (1998) 'Feminist Practices', in N. Charles and H. Hintjens (eds), *Gender, Ethnicity and Political Ideologies*. London: Routledge.

Chhachhi, A. and R. Pittin (eds) (1996) *Confronting State, Capital and Patriarchy: Women Organizing in the Process of Industrialization*. New York: St Martin's Press.

Chowdhry, Geeta (1995) 'Engendering Development? Women in Development (WID) in International Development Regimes', in Marrianne H. Marchand and Jane L. Parpart (eds), *Feminism/Postmodernism/Development*. London: Routledge, pp. 26–41.

Christiansen-Ruffman, Linda (1980) 'Women as Persons in Atlantic Canadian Communities', *Resources for Feminist Research*, Special Publication No. 8, pp. 55–7.

— (1987) *Wealth Re-Examined: Toward a Feminist Analysis of Women's Development Projects in Canada and in the Third World*, Working Paper No. 140, Women in International Development Publication Series. East Lansing: Michigan State University.

— (1989a) 'Inherited Biases Within Feminism: the Patricentric Syndrome' and 'The Either/Or Syndrome in Sociology', in Angela Miles and Geraldine Finn (eds), *Feminism: From Pressure to Politics*. Montreal: Black Rose Press, pp. 123–45.

— (1989b) 'Women and Development in Canada', in Jane Parpart (ed.), *Women and Development in Africa: Comparative Perspectives*. Lanham, MD: University Press of America, pp. 35–68.

— (1995) 'Women's Conceptions of the Political: Three Canadian Women's Organizations', in Myra Marx Ferree and Patricia Yancey Martin (eds), *Feminist Organizations: Harvest of the New Women's Movement*. Philadelphia: Temple University Press, pp. 372–93.

— (1998) 'Developing Feminist Sociological Knowledge: Processes of Discovery', in Linda Christiansen-Ruffman (ed.), *Global Feminist Enlightenment: Women and Social Knowledge*. Montreal and Madrid: International Sociological Association, pp. 13–36.

Cleves, Mosse J. (1993) *Half the World, Half a Chance*. Oxford: Oxfam.

Clough, P. T. (1994) *Feminist Thought*. Oxford: Blackwell.

Code, Lorraine (1991) *What Can She Know? Feminist Theory and the Construction of Knowledge*. Ithaca: Cornell University Press.

Cohen, Marjorie (1996) 'New International Trade Agreements', in *Rethinking Restructuring: Gender and Change in Canada*. Toronto: University of Toronto Press.

Connell, R. W. (1990) 'The State, Gender and Sexual Politics', *Theory and Society, No. 19*.

Cooke, K. (1984) *Images of Indians Held by Non-Indians: a Review of Current Research*. Ottawa, ON: Indian Affairs and Northern Development.

Corrigan, P. and D. Sayer (1985) *The Great Arch: English State Formation as Cultural Revolution*. London: Basil Blackwell.

Cottrell, Barbara (1995) *Power and Control in Feminist Action Research*. Unpublished thesis. Dalhousie University: School of Education.

Cottrell, Barbara, Stella Lord, Lise Martin and Susan Prentice (eds) (1996) *Research Partnerships: a Feminist Approach to Communities and Universities Working Together*. Canadian Research Institute for the Advancement of Women.

Cox, Robert (1995a) 'Civilizations: Encounters and Transformations', *Studies in Political Economy*, No. 47 (Summer).

— (1995b) 'Critical Political Economy', in Robert Cox, *et. al.*, *International Political Economy: Understanding Global Disorder*. London: Zed Books.

Culpeper, Roy (1996) 'What's Wrong with Mainstream Economics', in the *Canadian Development Report, 1996–87*. The North–South Institute.

— (1998) 'Systemic Instability or Global Growing Pains: Implications of the Asian Financial Crisis'. Briefing B-41, 1998, North–South Institute.

— (1999) 'Building Blocks for a New International Architecture. If It's Broke, Fix It!', *The North-South Institute Newsletter*, Vol.3, No. 1.

Dacks, Gurston, Joyce Green and Linda Trimble (1995) 'Road Kill: Women in Alberta's Drive Toward Deficit Reduction', in Trevor Harrison and Gordon Laxer (eds), *The Trojan Horse: Alberta and the Future of Canada*. Montreal: Black Rose Books.

Daily Sangbad (1992) 'Ek Najare Poshak Shilpa' [Garment Industry at a Glance], 22 November.

Dakar Seminar (1982) 'Another Development With Women', *Development Dialogue*, Vol. 1, No. 1.

Davies, M. (1994) *Women and Violence*. London: Zed Books.

Davis, Kathy (1997) 'What's a Nice Girl Like You Doing in a Place Like This? The Ambivilences of Professional Feminism', in Liz Stanley (ed.), *Knowing Feminisms*. London: Sage Publications.

DAWN (1998) 'Women Pay the Price as Asian Tigers, IMF, Bail Out of the Crisis', in *DAWN Informs* ('A newsletter of Development Alternatives with Women for a New Era'), Vol. 1.

Delahanty, Julie (1998) *Global Industry/Global Solutions: Options for Change in the Garment Sector*. The North–South Institute.

Department for International Development (DFID) (1997) 'The White paper on International Development – Eliminating World Poverty: a Challenge for the 21st Century'. London: DFID.

Duffy, Ann and Julianne Momirov (1997) *Family Violence: A Canadian Introduction*. Toronto: James Lorimer.

Dunk, Thomas. (1991) *It's a Working Man's Town: Male Working Class Culture in Northwestern Ontario*. Montreal: McGill-Queen's University Press.

Eisenstein, H. (1995) 'The Australian Femocratic Experiment: a Feminist Case for Bureaucracy', in M. M. Ferree and P. Y. Martin (eds), *Feminist Organizations: Harvest of the New Women's Movement*. Philadelphia: Temple University Press, pp. 69–83.

Eisenstein, Z. (1997) 'Feminism of the North and West for Export: Transnational Capital and the Racialization of Gender', in J. Dean (ed.), *Feminism and the New Democracy*. London: Sage Publications.

Elson, Diane (1994) 'Macro, Meso and Micro: Gender and Economic Analysis in the Context of Policy Reform', in I. Bakker (ed.), *The Strategic Silence: Gender and Economic Policy*. London: Zed Books/North–South Institute.

— (1996) 'Appraising Recent Developments in the World Market for Nimble Fingers', in A. Chhachhi and R. Pittin (eds), *Confronting State, Capital and Patriarchy: Women Organizing in the Process of Industrialization*. New York: St Martin's Press.

— (1997) 'Gender and Macroeconomic Policy', *Link in to Gender and Development*, Issue 2, Summer.

— (1998) 'Talking to the Boys: Gender and Economic Growth Models', in Jackson, Cecile and Pearson, Ruth (eds) *Feminist Visions of Development*, Gender Analysis and Policy, Routledge.

Elson, D. and R. Pearson (1984) 'The Subordination of Women and the Internationalization of Factory Production', in K. Young, C. Wolkowitz and R. McCullagh (eds), *Of Marriage and the Market*. London: Routledge and Kegan Paul.

— (1989) 'Nimble Fingers Make Cheap Workers: an Analysis of Women's Employment in Third World Manufacturing', *Feminist Review* (Spring).

Ensign, M. M. (1992) *Doing Good or Doing Well: Japan's Foreign Aid Program*. Columbia University Press, New York.

Esping-Andersen, Gosta. (1997) 'Welfare States at the End of the Century. The Impact of Labour Market, Family and Demographic Change', in *Social Policy Studies No. 21. Family, Market and Community: Equity and Efficiency in Social Policy*. Paris: OECD.

Esteva, Gustavo (1992) 'Development', in W. Sachs (ed.), *The Development Dictionary* London: Zed Books.

EURODAD/WIDE (1994) *World Bank Structural Adjustment Policies and Gender Policies*. Brussels, September.

Ford-Smith, Honor (1989) 'Mobilizing Village Women: a Case Study of Organizational Democracy', in *Sistren 1977–88*. Toronto: International Council for Adult Education, Women's Programme.

Foucault, Michel (1972) *The Archeology of Power*. London: Tavistock.

Fusae Ichikawa Memorial Association Newsletter (1990) 'Japanese Women', No. 63, 1 March.

Gabriel, Christina and Laura Macdonald (1996) 'NAFTA and Economic Restructuring: Some Gender and Race Implication', in I. Bakker (ed.), *Rethinking Restructuring: Gender and Change in Canada*. Toronto: University of Toronto Press.

Gal, S. (1997) 'Feminism and Civil Society', in J. W. Scott, C. Caplan and D. Keates, *Transitions, Environments and Translations, Feminisms in International Politics*. New York: Routledge.

Gandhi, N. (1996) 'Purple and Red Banners', in A. Chhachhi and R. Pittin (eds), *Confronting State, Capital and Patriarchy: Women Organizing in the Process of Industrialization*. New York: St Martin's Press.

Garments Katha (1997) 'Rights of Garment Workers', pp. 14–15.

Garon, S. (1997) *Molding Japanese Minds: the State in Everyday Life*. Princeton: Princeton University Press.

General Office of the Central Committee of the Communist Party (ed.) (1956) *Socialist Upsurge in Rural China*, Vol. I. Beijing: People's Literature Publishing House, p. 67.

Gill, Stephen (1995) 'Globalisation, Market Civilisation, and Disciplinary Neoliberalism', *Millennium: Journal of International Studies*, Vol. 24, No. 3.

— (1998) 'New Constitutionalism, Democratisation and Global Political Economy', *Pacifica Review*, Vol. 10, No. 1.

Globe and Mail (1999) 'Inuit balk at supporting mine', *Globe and Mail*, 18 February.

Gluck, Sherna (ed.) (1991) *Women's Words: the Feminist Practice of Oral History*. New York: Routledge.

Goddard, John (1991) *Last Stand of the Lubicon Cree*. Vancouver: Douglas and McIntyre.

Goetz, A. M. (1995) 'Institutionalizing Women's Interests and Gender-Sensistive Accountability in Development', in *IDS Bulletin*, Vol. 26, No. 3.

— (1996) 'Dis/organizing Gender: Women Development Agents in State and NGO Poverty Reduction Programmes in Bangladesh', in S. Rai and G. Lievesly (eds), *Women and The State: International Perspectives*. London: Taylor and Francis.

Gordon, S. (ed.) (1984) *Ladies in Limbo: The Fate of Women's Bureaux*. London: Commonwealth Secretariat.

Goux, J. J. (1994) 'Luce Irigaray Versus the Utopia of the Neutral Sex', in C. Burke *et al.* (eds), *Engaging with Irigaray*. New York: Columbia University Press.

Gramsci, Antonio (1971) *Selections from the Prison Notebooks of Antonio Gramsci*. New York: International Publishers.

Green, Joyce (1985) 'Sexual Equality and Indian Government: an Analysis of Bill C–31

Amendments to the Indian Act', *Native Studies Review*, Vol. 1, No. 2.
— (1992) 'Constitutionalising the Patriarchy', *Constitutional Forum*, Vol. 4, No. 4.
— (1995)'Towards a Detente With History', *International Journal of Canadian Studies*, No. 12 (Autumn).
— (1996) 'Resistance Is Possible', *Canadian Woman Studies*, Vol. 16, No. 3.
— (1997) 'Exploring Identity and Citizenship: Aboriginal Women, Bill C–31 and the Sawridge Case'. PhD dissertation, Department of Political Science, University of Alberta, Edmonton.
Gretchner, Donna (1991) 'Commentary', in David Smith, Peter MacKinnon and John Courtney (eds), *After Meech Lake: Lessons for the Future.* Saskatoon: Fifth House Publishers.
Griffin, Keith (1989) *Alternative Strategies for Economic Development.* London: Macmillan.
Grosz, E. (1986) 'Philosophy, subjectivity and the body: Kristeva and Irigaray', in C. Pateman and E. Gross (eds), *Feminist Challenges: Social and Political Theory.* Sydney: Allen and Unwin, pp. 125–43.
Hall, A. and J. Midgley (eds) (1988) *Development Policies and Sociological Perspectives.* Manchester: Manchester University Press.
Harding, S. (1981) 'Mobilising Village Women: Some Organisational and Management Considerations', in Nici Nelson (ed.), *African Women in the Development Process.* London: Frank Cass and Co., pp. 47–58.
— (1992) 'Subjectivity, Experience and Knowledge', *Development and Change*, Vol. 23, No. 3: 175–94.
Herizons (1999) Vol. 12, No.1 (Winter).
Hibler, Michelle and Rowena Beamish (eds) (1998) *Canadian Development Report 1998: Canadian Corporations and Social Responsibility.* Ottawa: North–South Institute.
Hildyard, Nicholas (1998) *The World Bank and the State: a Recipe for Change?* London: Bretton Woods Project.
Hill, Hal (ed.) (1994) *Indonesia's New Order – the Dynamics of Socio-Economic Transformation.* Honolulu: University of Hawaii Press.
Hirschmann, D. (1995) 'Managing Equity and Gender in an Agricultural Programme in Malawi', *Public Administration and Development*, Vol. 15, No.1 (February), pp. 21–40.
Hossain, H., R. Jahan and S. Sobhan (1993) *No Better Option: Industrial Women Workers in Bangladesh.* Dhaka: University Press Limited.
Humanitarian Volunteer Team (1998) 'Perkosaan Massal dalam Rentetan Kerusuhan: Puncak Kebiadaban dalam Kehidupan Bangsa' (Mass Rape in the Riots: Barbarism in the Nation). Initial Documentation No. 3. Jakarta: Humanitarian Volunteer Team, 13 July.
Humm, Maggie (1989) *The Dictionary of Feminist Theory*, New York: Prentice Hall.
IDS Bulletin (1998) Vol. 29, No. 1.
Indian and Northern Affairs Canada (INAC) (1990) *Mineral Resource Potential of Indian Reserve Lands: Canada.* http://www.inac.gc.ca/natres/canada.html
Irigaray, L. (1991) 'Women-Amongst-Themselves: Creating a Woman to Woman Sociality', in M. Whitford (ed.), *The Irigaray Reader.* Oxford: Basil Blackwell, pp. 190–8.
— (1994) *Thinking the Difference: for a Peaceful Revolution.* London: The Athlone Press.
— (1985) *Speculum of the Other Woman.* Ithaca, NY: Cornell University Press.
Islam, M. (1991) *Women Heads of Households in Rural Bangladesh: Strategies for Survival.* Dhaka: Narigrantha Prabartana/Feminist Bookstore.
Islam, S. (ed.) (1991) *Yen for Development: Japanese Foreign Aid and the Politics of Burden-Sharing.* New York: Council on Foreign Relations Press.

Jackson, B. (1992) *Threadbare: How the Rich Stitch up the World's Rag Trade*, London: World Development Movement.

Jackson, Cecile (1998) 'Social Exclusion and Gender: Swimming Against the Mainstream?'. Mimeo.

Jahan, R. (1995) *The Elusive Agenda: Mainstreaming Women in Development*. London: Zed Books.

Jamieson, Kathleen (1978) *Indian Women and the Law in Canada: Citizens Minus*. Ottawa: Supply and Services.

Japan International Cooperation Agency (JICA), Study Group on Development Assistance for Women in Development (1991) *Study on Development Assistance for Women in Development*. Tokyo: JICA.

Jenson, Jane (1996) 'Part-time Employment and Women: a Range of Strategies', in I. Bakker (ed.), *Rethinking Restructuring: Gender and Change in Canada*. Toronto: University of Toronto Press.

Jessop, Bob (1997) 'Capitalism and Its Future: Remarks on Regulation, Government and Governance', *Review of International Political Economy*, Vol. 4, No. 3 (Autumn).

Jorgensen, L. (1996) 'What are NGOs Doing in Civil Society?' in A. Clayton (ed.), *NGOs, Civil Society and the State: Building Democracy in Transitional Societies*. Oxford: INTRAC.

Jun, J. S. and H. Muto (1995) 'The Hidden Dimensions of Japanese Administration: Culture and its Impact', *Public Administration Review*, Vol. 55, No. 2, pp. 125–34.

Kabeer, Naila (1989) 'Cultural Dopes or Rational Fools? Women and Labour Supply in the Bangladesh Garment Industry', *The European Journal of Development Research* (November).

— (1992) 'Triple Roles, Gender Roles, Social Relations: The Political Sub-text of Gender Training'. Discussion Paper 313, Institute of Development Studies, University of Sussex.

Kabeer, Naila and John Humprey (1990) 'Neo-liberalism, Gender, and the Limits of the Market', in Christopher Coclough and James Manor (eds), *States or Markets? Neo-liberalism and the Development Policy Debate*. Oxford: Clarendon Press.

Kali for Women (1997) *Touch-me, Touch-me-not: Women, Healing & Plants*. New Delhi: Kali for Women.

Kardem, N. (1991) *Bringing Women In: Women's Issues in International Development Programs*. Boulder, Colorado: Lynne Rienner.

Kazim, R. (1997) 'Poshak Shilpe Agun Atanka', *Robbar*, 10 August.

Khanna, Renu (1992) *Taking Charge: Women's Health as Empowerment – the SARTHI Experience*. Baroda: SAHAJ/SARTHI.

— (1996) 'Participatory Action Research in Women's Health', in Korrie de Koning and Marion Martin (eds), *Participatory Research in Health: Issues and Experiences*. London: Zed Books.

— (1997) 'Dilemmas and Conflicts in Clinical Research for Women's Reproductive Health', *Reproductive Health Matters* (May).

Khanna, Pongurlekar and De Koning (1996) *Manual for Training Female Health Workers to Conduct Woman-Centred Research*.

Kingston, J. (1993) 'Bolstering the New Order: Japan's ODA Relationship with Indonesia', in B. M. Koppel and R. M. Orr Jr (eds), *Japan's Foreign Aid: Power and Policy in a New Era*. Boulder, Colorado: Westview Press, pp. 41–62.

Koh, B. C. (1989) *Japan's Administrative Elite*. Berkeley: University of California Press,.

Koppel, B. M. and R. M. Orr Jr (1993) 'A Donor of Consequence: Japan as a Foreign Aid Power', in B. M. Koppel and R. M. Orr Jr (eds), *Japan's Foreign Aid: Power and Policy in a New Era*. Boulder, Colorado: Westview Press, pp. 1–18.

Korten, D. (1990) *Getting to the Twenty-First Century: Voluntary Activities and the Global Agenda*, West Hartford: Kumarian Press.

Kung, L. (1983) *Factory Women in Taiwan*, Ann Arbor, Michigan: UMI Research Press.

Kurata, S. (1996) 'Japan's Approach to Gender and Development: Plurality in Development Cooperation Policy and Practice', *Journal of Asian Women's Studies*, No. 5, pp. 17-45.

Lang, S. (1997) 'The NGOization of Feminism: Institutionalization and Institution Building within the German Women's Movements', in J. W. Scott, C. Kaplan and D. Keats (eds), *Transitions, Environments, Translations: Feminisms in International Politics*. London and New York: Routledge.

Lewis, Arthur W. (1955) *The Theory of Economic Growth*. London: Allen and Unwin.

Lewis, D. and J. Barnsley (1992) *Strategies for Change: from Women's Experience to a Plan for Action*. Vancouver: The Women's Research Centre.

Liddle, W. (1994) 'Can All Good Things Go Together? Democracy, Growth and Unity in post-Suharto Indonesia', in Bourchier and Legge.

Lim, L. (1983) 'Capitalism, Imperialism, and Patriarchy', in J. Nash and M. P. Fernandez-Kelly, *Women, Men, and the International Division of Labor*. Albany, NY: SUNY Press.

— (1990) 'Women's Work in Export Factories: the Politics of a Cause', in I. Tinker (ed.), *Persistent Inequalities*. Oxford: Oxford University Press.

Lim, Lin Lean (ed.) (1998) *The Sex Sector: the Economic and Social Bases of Prostitution in South East Asia*. International Labour Organization.

Lindsay, Mary T. (1997) *Daughters of Development: State and Women in Indonesia*. MA thesis, University of British Columbia.

Lister, Ruth (1997) 'Citizenship: Towards a Feminist Synthesis.' *Feminist Review*. no. 57, Autumn.

Liu Mianzhi (ed.) (1953) *Chinese Women are Marching Forward*. Joint Publishing Co., pp. 14, 17.

Lowe, Mick (1998a) 'Innu Land Not INCO Land', *Canadian Forum* (April).

— (1998b) *Premature Bonanza: Stand-off at Voisey's Bay*. Toronto: Between the Lines.

Macdonald, M. (1994) 'Gender Planning in Development Agencies: Meeting the Challenge'. Oxford: Oxfam and Euro Step.

MacLeod, Linda (1994) *Understanding and Charting Our Progress Toward the Prevention of Woman Abuse*. Ottawa: Family Violence Prevention Division, Health Canada.

Majury, Diana (April 1998) *Promoting Women's Health: Making Inroads into Canadian Health Policy*. Centres for Excellence for Women's Health Program.

Mann, P. (1997) 'Musing as a Feminist on a Postfeminist Era', in J. Dean (ed.), *Feminism and the New Democracy: Resisting the Political*. London: Sage Publications.

Maquila Network Update (1998) 'Bangladesh Garment Workers Fired at GAP Contract Factory', Vol. 3, No. 4 (from *Bangladesh News*).

Marchand, M. H. (1995) 'Latin American Women Speak on Development: Are We Listening Yet?' in M. Marchand and L. Parpart (eds), *Feminism/Postmodernism/Development*. London: Routledge.

M. Marchand and L. Parpart (eds) (1995a) *Feminism/Postmodernism/Development*. London: Routledge.

— (1995b) 'Exploding the Canon: an Introduction', in M. Marchand and L. Parpart (eds), *Feminism/Postmodernism/Development*, Routledge, London.

Martin, Emily (1994) *Flexible Bodies*. Boston: Beacon.

McBride, Stephen and John Shields (1997) *Dismantling a Nation: the Transition to Corporate Rule in Canada*. Halifax: Fernwood.

McCormack, G. (1996) *The Emptiness of Japanese Affluence*. Armonk, NY: M. E. Sharpe,

McDonald, H. (1980) *Suharto's Indonesia*. London: Fontana.

McDowell, Linda (1991) 'Life Without Father and Ford: the New Gender Order of Post-Fordism', *Transactions of the Institute of British Geography*. No. 16.

McNamara, Robert (1973) Address to the Board of Governors, World Bank. Nairobi: 24 September 1973.

Mehta, M. (1991) 'Analysis of a Development Programme' in T. Wallace T. and C. March (eds), *Changing Perceptions: Writings on Gender and Development*. Oxford: Oxfam.

Meta Research and Communications (1998) *Report: Making the Learning Process Accessible: a Women Down Prospect Project* Halifax

Mies, Maria (1983) 'Towards a Methodology for Feminist Research', in Gloria Bowels and Renate Duelli Klein (eds), *Theories of Women's Studies*. London: Routledge, pp. 117–39.

— (1989) *Patriarchy and Accumulation on a World Scale*. Third edition. London: Zed Books.

Milan Women's Bookstore Collective (1990) *Sexual Difference: a Theory of Social-Symbolic Practice*. Bloomington: Indiana University Press.

Miller, Carol and Shahra Razavi (1997) 'Conceptual Frameworks for Gender Analysis within the Development Context'. Paper prepared for Inter-Agency Review Meeting, Socio-Economic and Gender Analysis, Pearl River, New York, 6–9 March 1997.

— (eds) (1998) *Missionaries and Mandarins: Feminist Engagement with Development Institutions*. London: Intermediate Technology Publications and UNRISD.

Mitter, S. (1986) *Common Fate Common Bond: Women in the Global Economy*. London: Pluto Press.

Miyamoto, M. (1994) *Straitjacket Society: an Insider's Irreverent View of Bureaucratic Japan*, trans. J. W. Carpenter. Tokyo: Kodansha.

Moghadam, Valentine M. (1993) 'Patriarchy and the Politics of Gender in Modernizing Societies: Iran, Pakistan and Afghanistan', *South Asia Bulletin*, Vol., Nos 1 and 2, pp. 122–32.

Mohanty, Chandra (1988) 'Under Western Eyes: Feminist Scholarship and Colonial Discourses', *Feminist Review*, No. 30, pp. 61–88.

— (1997) 'Under Western Eyes: Feminist Scholarship and Colonial Discourses', in Visvanathan *et al.* (eds), *The Women, Gender and Development Reader*. London: Zed Books.

Mohanty, Chandra *et al.* (eds) (1991) *Cartographies of Struggle: Third World Women and the Politics of Feminism*. Bloomington: Indiana University Press, pp 1–47.

Moore, Henrietta (1988) *Feminism and Anthropology*. Oxford: Polity Press.

Morgen, S. and A. Bookman (1988) 'Rethinking Women and Politics: an Introductory Essay', in A. Bookman and S. Morgen (eds), *Women and the Politics of Empowerment*. Philadelphia: Temple University Press.

Moser, Caroline (1989) 'Gender Planning in the Third World: Meeting Practical and Strategic Needs', *World Development*, Vol. 17, No. 11, pp. 1799–1825.

— (1993) *Gender Planning and Development Theory, Practice and Training*. London: Routledge.

Murphy, J. L. (1995) *Gender Issues in World Bank Lending*. Washington, DC: World Bank.

Nader, Laura (1974) 'Up the Anthropologist – Perspectives Gained from Studying Up', in Dell Hymes (ed.), *Reinventing Anthropology*. New York: Vintage Books.

National Council of Welfare (1998) *Poverty Profile 1996*. Ottawa: Minister of Public Works and Government Services.

Nelson, Nici (1981) 'Mobilising Village Women: Some Organisational and Management Considerations', in Nici Nelson (ed.), *African Women in the Development Process*. London: Frank Cass and Co., pp. 47–58.

Oda, Y. (1992) 'Putting Gender on the Development Agenda: The Case of Japanese Official Development Assistance'. MA thesis, Clark University.

Offen, Karen (1988) 'Defining Feminism: a Comparative Historical Approach', *Signs*, Vol. 14, No. 1 (Autumn).

Organization for Economic Cooperation and Development, Development Assistance Committee (OECD/DAC) (Annual), *Development Cooperation: Efforts and Policies of the Members of the Development Assistance Committee*. OECD, Paris. Cited by year of report.

Orr, R. M. Jr (1990) *The Emergence of Japan's Foreign Aid Power*. New York: Columbia University Press.

Oxfam (1998) 'Setting the Course for the Twenty-first Century', *Oxfam Strategic Review*, Oxford.

Parker, A. Rani *et al.* (1995) *Gender Relations Analysis: a Guide for Trainers*. Save the Children.

Parveen, F. and K. Ali (1996) 'Research in Action: Organizing Women Factory Workers in Pakistan', in A. Chhachhi and R. Pittin (eds), *Confronting State, Capital and Patriarchy: Women Organizing in the Process of Industrialization*. New York: St Martin's Press.

Patai, Daphne (1991) 'US Academics and Third World Women: Is Ethical Research Possible?' in Sherna Gluck (ed.), *Women's Words: The Feminist Practice of Oral History*. New York: Routledge.

Paul-Majumder, P. and S. C. Zohir (1994) 'Dynamics of Wage Employment: a Case of Employment in Garment Industry', *Bangladesh Development Studies*, Vol. 22, Nos 2-3.

Pearson, R. and C. Jackson (1998) 'Introduction: Interrogating Development: Feminism, Gender and Policy', in C. Jackson and R. Pearson (eds), *Feminist Visions of Development*. London: Routledge.

Peterson, V. Spike (1992) 'Transgressing Boundaries: Theories of Knowledge, Gender and International Relations', *Millennium*, Vol. 21, No. 2.

Petras, James. (1997) 'The New Cultural Domination by the Media', in Majid Rahnema and Victoria Bawtree (eds), *The Post-Development Reader*. Halifax: Fernwood Publishing.

Pharr, S. J. (1990) *Losing Face: Status Politics in Japan*. Berkeley: University of California Press.

Pheterson, Gail (1990) 'Alliances between Women: Overcoming Internalized Domination', in Lisa Albrecht and Rose M. Brewer (eds), *Bridges of Power: Women's Multicultural Alliances*. Philadelphia: New Society Publishers, pp. 34–48.

Philipps, Lisa (1996) 'The Rise of Balanced Budget Laws in Canada: Fiscal (Ir)responsibility', *Osgoode Hall Law Journal*, Vol. 34, No. 4 (Winter).

Phillips, Angela and Jill Rakusen (1989) *The New Our Bodies, Ourselves*. Boston: Boston Women's Health Book Collective.

Ponting, J. R. (1987) *Profiles of Public Opinion on Canadian Natives and Native Issues*. Calgary, AB: Research Unit for Public Policy Studies, University of Calgary.

Porter, Fenella (1998) *Male and Female Exclusion: a Proposal for the Cross-Programme Learning Fund*. Oxfam.

Porter, Fenella and Ines Smyth (1998) *Gender Training for Development Practitioners: Only a Partial Solution*. Oxfam Working Paper.

Porter, Fenella, Ines Smyth and Caroline Sweetman (1999) *Gender Works: Oxfam Experience in Policy and Practice*. Oxfam.

Profitt, Norma Jean (1997) 'Compassionate Fire: Women's Stories of Subjective and Social Change'. Unpublished dissertation, Wilfrid Laurier University, Faculty of Social Work.

Rathgeber, Eva, M. (1990) 'WID, WAD, GAD: Trends in Research and Practice', *Journal of Developing Areas*, No. 24, pp 489–502.

— (1995) 'Gender and Development in Action', in M. Marchand and J. Parpart (eds), *Feminism/Postmodernism/Development*. London: Routledge.

Razavi, Shahra (1996) *Working Towards a More Gender Equitable Macro-Economic Agenda*. Geneva: UNRISD.

Rebick, Judy (1999) 'Liberals Try to Sink NAC'. *Herizons*, Vol. 12, No. 1 (Winter).

Richardson, Mary, Joan Sherman and Michael Grismondi (1993) *Winning Back the Words: Confronting Experts in an Environmental Public Hearing*. Toronto: Garamond Press.

Rist, Gilbert (1997) *The History of Development: from Western Origins to Global Faith*. London: Zed Books.

Rix, A. (1980) *Japan's Economic Aid*. New York: St Martin's Press.

— (1993) *Japan's Foreign Aid Challenge: Policy Reform and Aid Leadership*. London: Routledge.

Roberts, Linda (1998) 'Not All the Same: Community-based Agencies in an Era of Cuts'. Unpublished.

Roldan, M. (1993) 'Industrial Restructuring, Deregulation and New JIT Labour Processing in Argentina: Towards a Gender Aware Perspective', *IDS Bulletin*, Vol. 24, No. 2.

Safa, H. I. (1995) *The Myth of the Male Breadwinner: Women and Industrialization in the Caribbean*. Boulder, Colorado: Westview Press.

Said, Edward (1978) *Orientalism*. New York: Random House.

Sassen, Saskia (1996) *Losing Control? Sovereignty in an Age of Globalization*. New York: Columbia University Press.

— (1998) *Globalization and its Discontents*. New York: The New Press.

Schalkwyk, Johanna, Helen Thomas and Beth Woroniuk (1996) *Mainstreaming: a Strategy for Achieving Equality between Women and Men*. Stockholm: SIDA.

Schneiderman, David (1999) 'MMT Promises: How the Ethyl Corporation Beat the Federal Ban', *The Post*, Vol.3, No. 1 (Winter). Edmonton: The Parkland Institute.

Sen, G. and Grown, C. (1987) *Development, Crises and Alternative Visions: Third World Women's Perspectives*. New York: Monthly Review Press.

Shell Canada Ltd (December 1997) *Application for the Approval of Muskeg River Mine Project. Volume 5: Environmental Impact Assessment — Socio-Economic Impact Assessment*. Calgary.

Sherwin, Susan (1998) *The Politics of Women's Health: Exploring Agency and Autonomy*. Philadelphia: Temple University Press.

Simmons, Pam (1997) 'Women in Development: a Threat to Liberation', in Majid Rahnema and Victoria Bawtree (eds), *The Post-Development Reader*. Halifax: Fernwood Publishing.

Simu, S. D. (1995) 'Garments', *The Weekly Chinta*, No. 24 (3 September).

Smyth, Ines (1998) 'Gender Analysis of Family Planning: Beyond the "Feminist vs Population Control Debate"', in C. Jackson and R. Pearson (eds), *Feminist Visions of Development*. London: Routledge.

Spender, Dale (1982) *Women of Ideas (and What Men Have Done to Them)*. London: Ark Paperbacks.

Standing, G. (1989) 'Global Feminisation through Flexible Labor', *World Development*, Vol. 17, No. 7.

Stanley, Liz (ed.) (1997) 'Introduction', in *Knowing Feminisms*. London: Sage Publications.

Status of Women Canada (1995) *Women in Canada: Socio-economic Status and Other Contemporary Issues*. Ottawa: Library of Parliament Research Branch.

Status of Women Canada (1999) *Economic Gender Equality Indicators: Back-grounder*. http//www.swc-cfc.gc.ca/publish/egei/ bckgrnde. html

Staudt, K. (1985) *Women, Foreign Assistance and Advocacy Administration*. New York: Praeger.

— (ed.) (1990) *Women, International Development, and Politics: the Bureaucratic Mire.* Philadelphia: Temple University Press.

Stiglitz, Joseph (1998) *More Instruments and Broader Goals: Moving Toward the Post-Washington Consensus.* Helsinki: UNU/ WIDER. Http://www.wider.unu.edu/stiglitz.htm

Stymeist, David H. (1975) *Ethnics and Indians: Social Relations in a Northwestern Ontario Town.* Toronto, ON: Peter Martin.

Suryakusuma, Julia (1998) 'Bukti', *Kompas*, 12 September.

Sutherland, Peter and John Sewell (1998) 'The Challenges of Globalization'. Overseas Development Council, mimeo.

Sweetman, C. (1998) '"Sitting on a Rock": Integrating Men and Masculinities into Gender and Development'. Paper presented at ESRC Seminar Series, 'Men, Masculinities and Gender Relations in Development', Bradford, September.

Teeple, Gary (1995) *Globalisation and the Decline of Social Reform.* Toronto: Garamond

Thobani, Sunera (1996) 'Beijing Platform Doesn't Do Right By Women', *Herizons* (Winter).

Thompson, D. (1992) 'Defining Feminism', paper presented at the Sixth 10/40 Conference, Healesville, Victoria, Australia, 17–20 April.

Tiano, S. (1984) 'The Public-Private Dichotomy: Theoretical Perspectives on Women in Development', *Social Sciences Journal*, Vol. 21, No. 4, pp. 11–28.

— (1994) *Patriarchy on the Line: Labor, Gender, and Ideology in the Mexican Maquila Industry.* Philadelphia: Temple University Press.

Tongamiut Anuit Annait *Ad Hoc* Committee on Aboriginal Women and Mining in Labrador (1997) *Fifty-two Per Cent of the Population Deserves a Closer Look: a Proposal for Guidelines Regarding the Environmental and Socio-economic Impacts on Women from the Mining Developments at Voisey's Bay.* 16 April.
Http://www.innu.ca/ womenguidelines.html

Udayagiri, M. (1995) 'Challenging Modernisation: Gender and Development, Postmodern Feminism and Activism', in M. Marchand and J. Parpart (eds), *Feminism/Postmodernism/ Development.* London: Routledge.

United Nations (1989) *Violence Against Women in The Family.* New York: United Nations.

United Nations Development Programme (UNDP) (1990) *Human Development Report.* New York: UNDP.

— (1995a) *Human Development Report.* Oxford: Oxford University Press.

— (1995b) *Report of the Fourth World Conference on Women (Platform for Action).* Document A/CONF.177.20, 17 October.

— (1997) *Human Development Report.* Oxford: Oxford University Press.

— (1998) *Human Development Report.* Oxford: Oxford University Press.

Vatikiotis, M. (1993) *Indonesian Politics under Suharto.* London: Routledge.

Visvanathan, N. *et al.* (1997) *The Women, Gender and Development Reader.* Halifax: Fernwood Publishing.

Voyageur, Cora J. (1993) 'Portrayal of Indians in the Media'. Unpublished paper, University of Alberta.

— (1997) *Employment Equity and Aboriginal Equity in Canada.* PhD dissertation, Department of Sociology, University of Alberta.

Wallace, T. and C. March (1991) *Changing Perceptions: Writings on Gender and Development.* Oxford: Oxfam.

Ward, K. (1988) 'Women in the Global Economy', in B. Gutok, A. Stomberg, and L. Larwood (eds), *Women and Work*, Vol. 3. Beverly Hills, California: Sage.

Ward, K. (ed.) (1990) *Women and Global Restructuring.* Ithaca, NY: Cornell University.

Waring, Marilyn (1988) *If Women Counted: a New Feminist Economics.* New York: Harper Collins.

Watts, M. (1995) 'A New Deal in Emotions: Theory and Practice and the Crisis of Development' in J. Crash (ed.), *Power of Development*. London and New York: Routledge.

Waylen, G. (1996) *Gender in Third World Politics*. Boulder, Colorado: Lynne Rienner.

Weaver, Sally (1993) 'First Nations Women and Government Policy, 1970–92: Discrimination and Conflict', in Sandra Burt, Lorraine Code and Lindsay Dorney (eds), *Changing Patterns: Women in Canada*. Toronto: McClelland and Stewart, Inc.

Webster, Andrew (1984) *Introduction to the Sociology of Development*. London: Macmillan.

Westwood, S. (1984) *All Day Every Day: Factory and Family in the Making of Women's Lives*. London and Sydney: Pluto Press.

— (1988) 'Workers and Wives: Continuities and Discontinuities in the Lives of Gujarati Women', in S. Westwood and P. Bachu (eds), *Enterprising Women: Ethnicity, Economy and Gender Relations*. London and New York: Routledge.

White, S. (1997) 'Re-thinking Gender and Development: the Challenge of Difference'. Paper presented at the DSA Conference, Norwich, 11–13 September.

— (1998) 'Masculinities in Development: the Danger of a New Hegemony'. Paper presented at ESRC Seminar Series, 'Men, Masculinities and Gender Relations in Development', Bradford, September.

Wieringa, S. (1995) 'Introduction: Subversive Women and Their Movements', in Wieringa, S. (ed.), *Subversive Women: Women's Movements in Africa, Asia, Latin America and the Caribbean*. London: Zed Books.

Wolf, D. L. (1991) 'Female Autonomy, the Family and Industrialization in Java', in R. L. Blumberg (ed.), *Gender, Family and Economy: the Triple Overlap*. Newbury: Sage Publications.

Wolf, Eric. (1969) *Peasant Wars of the Twentieth Century*. New York: Harper and Row.

Women of China (1959) First issue.

Women's Eyes on the World Bank (WEOWB) – US (1997) *Gender Equity and the World Bank Group: a Post-Beijing Assessment*. October.

Wu Qing (1994) Women in Development Program Mission and Activity Reports. Gansu Forest Tree Nursery Project, CIDA Project No. 282/14874, December, p. 3.

Yasutomo, D. T. (1986) *The Manner of Giving: Strategic Aid and Japanese Foreign Policy*. Lexington, Mass: Lexington Books.

— (1995) *The New Multilateralism in Japan's Foreign Policy*. New York: St Martin's Press.

Young, G. (1988) 'Gender Identification and Working-Class Solidarity among Maquila Workers in Ciudal Juaez', in V. Ruiz and S. Tiano (eds), *Women on the US–Mexico Border*. Boston: Allen and Unwin.

Young, Kate (1993) *Planning Development with Women: Making a World of Difference*. New York: St Martin's Press.

— (1997) 'Gender and Development', in N. Visvanathan *et al.* (eds), *The Women, Gender and Development Reader*. Halifax: Fernwood Publishing, pp. 51–4.

Young, Kate. (1992) *Gender and Development Readings*. Ottawa: Canadian Council for International Cooperation.

Zaman, H. (1996) *Women and Work in a Bangladesh Village*, Dhaka: Narigrantha Prabartana/Feminist Bookstore.

Zhang Ping (ed.) (1995) *Current Situation of Women in China*. Beijing: Hongqi Publishing House, p. 1.

Index

aboriginal people 13, 142-7, 150-5, 199, 221, 226
abortion 138
accountability 214, 216, 220, 222-3, 226
action research 75, 79-85, 87-94, 113, 181, 182, 187, 201, 220
'add women and stir' 1, 8, 41, 54, 103, 114, 204
Africa 5, 53, 134-5, 140, 176-7, 179, 186, 191, 193, 197; East 136, 177; West 201
agriculture 51, 59, 197; export 51, 210
aid 6, 10, 21, 23, 38, 42-56, 113, 118, 134
AIDS 74
Akanda, Latifa 165
Akbar, Mrs Ali 29
Akhter, Farida 164, 166
Akhter, Shirin 166
Alberta 151-2
Alberta Pacific (Alpac) pulp mill 152
Alianza 184-5, 189n
All China Women's Federation (ACWF) 60
Amaratunga, Carol 89
Amin, Samir 7
apartheid 187
Ås, Berit 182
Asia 5, 43-4, 46, 53, 112, 140, 168, 179-80, 191-3; East 45, 193; South 34, 39; Southeast 45-6, 193
Asia and Pacific Centre for Women and Development (ACPD) 179
Asian Development Bank 45, 158
Asian monetary crisis 112, 119, 191-3
Asian Women Workers Newsletter 168
Asia–Pacific Economic Cooperation forum (APEC) 217
Association for Land Reform and Development (ALRD) 166
Association of Atlantic Universities 182
Association of Canadian Community Colleges (ACCC) 68
Athabasca 152
Atlantic Women and Development 182
Atlantic Women's FishNet 187
Australia 216
auxiliary nurse midwives (ANMs) 75-9, 84-5

Baluchi people 30-1
Bangalore 179
Bangkok 179-80
Bangladesh 13, 32, 45, 158-70, 191-3, 211; Ministry of Industries 167
Bangladesh Sramik Oikya Parishad 165
Bangladesh United Workers' Council 165
Bantustans 177
Baran, Paul 7

Barbados 179, 216
basic human needs 42, 212
Beijing Foreign Studies University 61
Bengali people 161
Berzins, Lorraine 93
birth control 31, 33, 76, 82, 138, 177
Black Sash 186-7
Bombay 75, 79, 84
Bombay Municipal Corporation(BMC) 75
Borda 7
Bosnia 123
Brazil 7
Britain 9, 12, 18, 22-3, 32, 35, 168, 175-6, 216; Department for International Development (DFID) 9
Bureau of the Expert Group on Women in Development 52
bureaucracy 2, 12, 19, 24-8, 39, 43, 47-50, 53, 55, 88, 91, 94, 99, 109, 112, 145, 179, 221
Burkina Faso 202

Cairo 25
Canada 12-13, 61, 63-6, 87-101, 105-7, 123, 142-56, 175-89, 195, 209, 216-17, 221; Department of Indian Affairs 146; Indian Act 146; Royal Commission on the Status of Women 153, 180
Canada Assistance Plan 155
Canadian Institute for the Advancement of Women (CRIAW) 87-8, 96, 98-9, 181-2
Canadian International Development Agency (CIDA) 11, 57, 61-2, 65-6, 68, 101, 103, 130, 221
capitalism 2, 6-7, 36, 39, 56, 143-5, 147-8, 160, 178, 194, 206
Cardoso 7
Caribbean 19, 96, 175-89; Eastern 182; *see also* West Indies
Caribbean Association for Feminist Research and Action (CAFRA) 179
Caribbean/Eastern 182
CARICOM 176, 179
Caritas 167
caste 75-6
Central America 19
Chengdu 68
child care 59, 73, 165, 170, 216
child labour 165, 198
China 12, 22, 45, 57-69, 101, 105, 107, 122, 141
China Enterprise Management Training Centre 68
Chinese Women's Health Network 62
Chinta 167-8, 170n

Chretien, Jean 144
civil society 23, 33, 145, 188, 206
class 1, 10, 26-7, 39, 57-8, 75-6, 82, 159-60, 183, 185, 187-8, 207
Colombia 7
colonialism 5, 11-12, 32-5, 142, 144-5, 149-50, 154, 175, 178, 181, 187-8
Columbia University 177
Commonwealth 176
communism 178
Communist Party of China 58-60, 67
Communities Organizing for Empowerment (CORE) 180
Community Assistance Programme (CAP) 144
community 12-13, 67-8, 79, 82-3, 87-100, 119, 152-3, 159, 176-7, 181-2, 186-7, 221
Confucianism 49
Consumer Association of Bangladesh 167
consumerism 148, 183
Convention on the Elimination of All Forms of Discrimination against Women 52
corruption 39, 46, 112
culture 4-5, 10, 25-8, 62, 74, 77-8, 90-1, 107-8, 133-4, 136-7, 143, 149, 183, 203-4, 213, 217

Dacca 32
Davis Inlet 149
day care 58-9, 166; *see also* child care
de Beauvoir, Simone 4
debt 44, 180, 185, 196, 209, 226
Decade for Women *see* International Women's Year and Decade
democracy 3, 23, 36, 39, 56, 84, 94, 115, 117-18, 148-9, 166, 178, 185, 201, 204, 206, 213-14
dependency theory 7, 113
deregulation 149, 161, 190, 199, 206, 208
Development Alternatives for Women in a New Era (DAWN) 1, 180, 182-4, 188
Development Assistance Committee (DAC) 42, 50, 52
development agencies 1-2, 7-8, 11, 17-27, 21, 29, 38-9, 50-1, 114, 118, 123, 129-30, 135-8, 140-1, 158, 196, 203, 212-13, 222-6
development, and aboriginal people 143, 145, 153-4; and agriculture 51, 58; 'Another Development' 178; bottom-up 176-7; and capitalism 143; and colonialism 149; and community 87-100, 153, 176-7, 181, 186-7; crisis of 180; definition of 2-3, 29, 33-4, 43, 50, 54, 81-2, 123, 141; dependency theory of 7, 113; Development Studies 6; and dignity 123, 169, 192; economic emphasis in 41, 44, 176-8; and economic growth 3, 6-7, 9, 46, 55, 57, 143, 176-7, 180, 190, 194-5, 203-4, 221, 223; and education 41; and feminism 6-9, 12, 14, 17-27, 81-

2, 101-11, 129, 133, 175, 184-5, 190-205, 218, 221-2, 224-6; and gender 7-11, 17-27, 33, 43, 46, 51-2, 54-5, 61, 81, 130-3, 136-8, 141, 145, 153-4, 196, 206-18; and gender equality 203-4; and globalization 2, 6, 10, 46, 142-56, 206-17, 221; and health 41; and human rights 7, 9, 23, 34, 203-4; and industry 13, 51, 158, 167; integration of women in 179-80, 183, 212, 219; and locality 223; misdirection of funds in 38-9; missionary goal of 6; and modernization 6-7, 9, 113, 149, 223; and non-governmental organizations (NGOs) 38; origins of 5, 8; participation in 53-4, 57; pluralist approach to 214, 217; political repression in 112; and poverty 176; as process 65; profit motive in 148-50; and 'progress' 178, 190, 209-10; and research 220; social engineering in 224; and state 178, 191; sustainable 61, 66, 101, 132, 190, 200, 214; and 'third path' 178; and traditional economies 152; and transformation 190-205; 'trickle down' approach to 55, 177-8; and underdevelopment 29, 31, 33-4, 181; USA dominance of 6; and violence 21-2; and wealth 181
Dhaka 160
Dhaka University 165
Diashowa 152
domestic workers 36, 161
drugs 31, 149

economic growth 3, 6-7, 9, 14, 32-3, 46, 55, 143, 145, 176-7, 180, 190, 194-5, 197, 200, 203-4, 208, 211, 221
education 30-1, 37, 41, 48, 50, 53, 58-61, 73, 83-4, 94, 99, 104-7, 112, 116, 119-20, 137, 185, 191, 196, 198, 212, 220, 224
elite 12, 32, 36, 39, 48-9, 54-5, 112-13, 206
emergency relief 44
employment 34, 59, 105, 123-4, 142, 149-50, 152, 155, 159-61, 169, 190, 192-4, 197-8, 209-10, 213, 216, 220
empowerment 10-11, 28, 30, 40, 66, 74, 79, 82-4, 94-5, 115, 129, 134, 158-70, 183, 186, 192, 213-14, 219, 224
entrustment 106, 108-9
environment 33, 46, 53-5, 143, 149-50, 152, 166, 183, 194, 198-9, 215
equality 2, 7, 10, 17, 26, 28, 40, 57, 61, 75, 82, 87-8, 101-4, 108-10, 129-31, 134, 137-8, 140, 142, 144-5, 153, 165, 167, 178, 183, 188, 190, 193, 196-7, 200-4, 207, 209, 213, 215, 221
ethnicity 10, 33, 62, 68, 185, 188
Europe 3, 5, 140; Western 208
European Union (EU) 206, 209, 212
everyday life 27, 29-31, 95, 160, 163, 169,

182, 210, 214
export processing zones (EPZs) 211

family planning *see* birth control
female health worker (FHW) 76
feminism, and action research 87-94, 181,
187, *see also* research; activism 4, 8, 27,
29-30, 41, 73-85, 87-100, 113, 115-17,
123, 129, 130, 164, 167-70, 175, 179,
190-1, 193, 199, 201, 203, 218, 224;
analysis 179, 183-4, 186; and better
world 2; and birth control 138; and
bureaucracy 24-8, 43, 48, 88, 91, 94,
109, 179; and capitalism 144; and civil
society 23; and class 188; and community
87-94; consciousness 178-9, 186, 198-9;
and corporations 203; and culture 4-5,
133-4; definition of 2-5, 18, 40, 129,
132-3; and development 6-9, 12, 14, 17-
27, 81-2, 101-11, 114, 129, 131-3, 136,
144, 175, 178-9, 182, 184-5, 190-205,
218, 221-2, 224-6; diversity within 5,
24-7, 99, 183, 187-8, 193, 204, 218,
225-6; and economic growth 194-5;
economics 190-1, 193-5, 201, 203, 210-
17; and education 83; and equality 101-
4, 178, 188, 190; and funding 9, 14, 88-
90, 96, 97, 101-5, 109, 114-16, 118-21,
123-4, 129-30, 136, 137, 141, 201,
224-5; and globalization 1, 5, 11, 13-14,
46, 129, 133, 142, 178, 187-8, 190-
205, 218, 221; and grassroots 54, 121;
and health 73-85; historical roots of 24;
and the household 20-1; and human
rights 4, 17, 19, 25, 122; and identity
188; and information 133-4, 139; and
Islam 41; in Japan 42, 51; knowledge
181-2, 185, 187; and labour movement
115-19; and language 18-19, 26-7, 34,
77-8, 97, 106-8, 130; and locality 224-5;
and marginalization 101-2, 105, 109-10,
131-2, 139-41, 222; and men 4-5, 13,
22, 109-10; and micropolitics 27;
movement 54, 182; and neoliberalism 14;
networks 19, 130; and non-governmental
organizations (NGOs) 12-14, 17-27, 122,
129, 222, 226; and North/South relations
4-5, 14, 19, 26-8, 34, 129, 132, 136,
140-1, 175, 184, 188, 204, 211, 221,
224, 226; and participation 87-100, 178,
194, 201; and policy 212-17, 222; as
politics 2, 34, 101-11, 116, 130-3, 135,
140, 170, 186, 188; and 'pop' 24, 27-8;
and population issues 25; and postcolonialism 27; and poverty 23-4; and the
private world 20; processes of
organization of 13; and race 188; and
research 87-94, 175, 177, 179, 181, 187,
190-1, 193, 199, 201-3, 220, 222;
resistance to 223; and sexuality 24, 73-5,
77-9; and social justice 188; and solidarity
4, 134; and stereotyping 26; studying up

by 220-3; theory 179; as transformation
130-2, 136-8, 141, 183, 188; and United
Nations (UN) 8; and violence 21-2, 24,
186; and World Bank 193, 196-8, 201-3
feminization of labour 160-1, 192, 207
femocrats 109
First World 34, 168
flexibilization of labour 158, 160-1, 192,
199
Food and Agriculture Organization (FAO)
213
food 44, 55, 58, 180, 183, 186, 192, 195,
197, 201, 210, 212
Foucault, Michel 102, 133
Fourth World 34
France 168
Frank, Gunder 7
Freire, Paulo 113
fundamentalism 180, 183, 185, 187

Galtung 7
Gansu Forest Tree Nursery Project 66
Gansu Province 63
GAP 169
Garment Workers Federation (Bangladesh)
165-6, 168-9
garment workers 13, 158-70, 192, 211
Garments Sramik Karmachari Oikya
Parishad 164-5
Gender and Economic Reforms in Africa
(GERA) 201-2
Gender and Development (GAD) 1, 9, 24-6,
34, 42, 60, 65-7, 69, 114, 130-2, 136,
213, 218-3, 225
gender development index (GDI) 210, 214
gender/and aboriginal people 153; and age
10; and agriculture 59, 212; and aid 42,
47-50; analysis 20, 63-4, 114, 137, 153,
219-20, 223; and North/South relations
26-7; awareness 62, 67-9, 84, 202; and
budgets 200, 214-16; and bureaucracy
24-7, 43, 47-50; and care provision 191,
215-16; in China 59, 61; in civil society
23; and class 10; and corporations 199;
and culture 10, 25-8, 64, 74, 77, 137,
207, 213; definition of 20, 141; and
development 2, 7-11, 17-27, 33, 43, 46,
51-2, 54-5, 61, 81, 130-3, 136-8, 196,
206-18; and development agencies 9, 17-
27; difference 25-7, 64, 108-9;
discrimination 52, 58, 60, 63-4, 68, 139,
165, 169; and division of labour 82, 213,
215; and economic growth 195, 197;
and economics 190-1, 193-5, 200, 203,
205; and education 48, 60-1, 96, 196;
and elite 48-9; and employment 213; and
empowerment 10-11, 28; and
environment 150; equality 4, 10-11, 17,
20, 24-6, 28, 40, 57, 61, 64-6, 68, 75,
82, 87-8, 101-4, 108-10, 129-31, 134,
137-8, 140, 142, 144-5, 153, 165, 167,
178, 190, 193, 196-7, 200-4, 207, 213,

215, 221; and ethnicity 10; and globalization 13, 183, 191, 206-17; and hierarchy 25, 28, 31, 188; in the household 20-1; and human rights 17, 19, 122, 165-6, 169, 184, 198; identity 207; and the IMF 9; imperatives of 176; and incomes 142-3; in Japan 44, 47-50, 52, 54; and knowledge 40, 181; and labour conditions 165, *see also* wages, worker rights; and labour movement 116; and land 213; and literacy 59; and macroeconomics 195-7, 200, 203; mainstreaming of 25, 28, 136-7, 213, 219-21; and market forces 197; neoliberal gender order 207-11; and non-governmental organizations (NGOs) 8-9, 17-27, 114, 119, 130; and personal development 57; and policy 17, 222; politics of 207, 221; and population 33; and poverty 23-4, 51; and power 10, 11, 74, 82, 102-4, 183, 185, 213; and race 10; relations 102-5, 137, 152, 185, 187, 207, 213, 219; and research 220; and restructuring 207; and sexuality 74; and social exclusion 22; and social justice 4, 23, 87, 137, 139, 190, 197, 200-2; and solidarity 107-8, 159; stereotyping 12, 67; and structural adjustment 180, 183, 197; and student movement 121; and trade 214; training 11, 20, 62-3, 77, 114, 131, 202, 213; and transformation 137-8; triple roles framework 11; and United Nations (UN) 8; and violence 21-2, 24, 33, 92-3, 98, 121-2, 134, 164, 183, 186, 192; and wages 165, 167, 169, 196; and worker rights 61, 160, 162, 165-6, 170; and World Bank policies 196-7
Geneva 13, 129, 134-6, 139-40, 152
Germany 130
Ghana 191, 195, 201
Global Fund for Women 68
globalization/and aboriginal people 153-4; and Canada 143; and capitalism 143, 147-8; and citizenship 147-9; and class 191; and colonialism 5, 144; and culture 206; and development 2, 6, 10, 46, 142-56, 206-17, 221; and economic constitutionalism 208; and economic growth 14, 143, 145, 190, 221; and education 191; and employment 149; and environment 149-50; and equality 209-10; and ethnicity 191; and everyday life 210; and feminism 1, 5, 11, 13-14, 46, 129, 133-4, 142, 178, 187-8, 190-205, 218, 221; and financial markets 193; and gender 13, 153-4, 183, 191, 206-17; and geographic location 191; and global political economy 208; and health 149; and human rights 148; and Japan 43-4; and locality 11, 13, 135, 139-40, 175-89, 223-6; and media 143; and the nation state 207-8, 212; and neoliberalism 143-

4; and patriarchy 130; solidarity in the face of 226; WID and 43; winners and losers in 209; and women's movement 184
Gramsci, Antonio 206
grassroots 29, 37, 40, 43, 45, 54, 96, 113, 117-19, 121, 124, 167, 177-8, 213-14
gross domestic product (GDP) 33
gross national product (GNP) 194
Guyana 176, 182

Habibie, President 121
Halifax 96, 181-2
Harbin Cattle Breeding Station 62-3
Harvard Institute for International Development 11
Health Canada 89, 97-8
health 12, 25, 31, 33, 41, 53, 55, 58, 73-85, 87-8, 90, 94-5, 112, 119, 134, 137-8, 142, 149, 169-70, 176, 185, 191-2, 199, 212, 226
Heilongjiang 62
hierarchy 14, 25, 28, 30-1, 49, 94, 101-2, 108-10, 117, 188
Hiroshima 43
households 20-2, 51, 55, 58-9, 65, 138, 165, 192
Housewives Association (Japan) 51
Huairou 141
Huining 63-4
human development index (HDI) 142, 214
human population index (HPI) 214
human rights 4, 23, 25, 34, 38, 41, 64, 122, 129, 142, 147-9, 153-4, 159, 165, 184, 201, 204
Humanity Volunteer Team 122-4, 125n

India 12, 19, 32, 34-5, 45, 73-85
Indian Act 151
Indian people of North America *see* aboriginal people
Indonesia 13, 22, 45, 96, 112-24, 150, 193; Ministry of Women's Affairs 114
informal sector 10, 59, 160, 193
Innu people 143, 149-50, 157n
Institute of Development Studies 11
International Women's Year Liaison Group (Japan) 51-2
International Labour Organization (ILO) 167, 193, 213
International Monetary Fund (IMF) 9, 149, 158, 180, 191, 195-8, 212
International Nickel Company (INCO) 143, 150
International Sociological Association 187
International Women's Year and Decade 8, 50-2, 132, 175, 178, 184-5
Inuit people 90-1, 149-50
Isis WICCE 129-30, 132-6, 139-41, 141n
Islam 32, 35, 37, 41
Islamabad 37

Jakarta 112, 120-3
Jamaica 176, 178
Japan 12, 42-56, 206, 222; Ministry of
    International Trade and Development
    (MITI) 48
Japan International Cooperation Agency
    (JICA) 51, 53-5
Japan Overseas Cooperation Volunteers 51
Java 115

Kalyanamitra 122
Kampala 129, 134-6
Karachi 29-30, 40-1
Keynes, J. M. 206, 213
Khanam, Ayesha 165
knowledge, community-based 181; and
    control 94-5; and feminism 182, 185,
    187; and gender 181; indigenous 26; and
    lives of women 40; and locality 226; and
    patriarchy 187; and power 30-1, 133,
    177; practicality of 31; universal 181
Korea 45-6, 193
Kumasi 201
KwaZulu-Natal Programme for the
    Survivors of Violence 21
Kyoto 48-9

labour movement 115-19, 158-70, 175,
    198, 226
Labrador 149, 181
Labrador Inuit Association (LIA) 150-1,
    157n
land 115, 144-7, 150, 153, 166, 176, 198,
    213
Latin America 7, 19, 179-80
Lebanon 19
Lewis, W. Arthur 176
literacy 59-60, 210
Liverpool School of Tropical Medicine 75
local/global relations 11, 13, 135, 139-40,
    175-89, 223-6
Lombok 45
Longnan Prefecture 67
Loon River First Nation people 151
Lower Prospect 87, 94
Lubicon Lake Cree 143, 151-2

Mahila Parishad 165, 167
Majury, Diana 89
Maliseet people 88, 100n
Manley, Michael 178, 189n
Maquila Network Update 168
marginalization 101-2, 105, 109-10, 131-2,
    139-41, 159, 175-6, 180, 204, 210, 222
Maritime Centre for Excellence on Women's
    Health (MCEWH) 87-9, 97-9
market forces 3, 34, 58-9, 64, 67, 145,
    158, 190, 192-4, 197, 199, 201, 206,
    208, 210-11, 213-14, 220-1, 224, 226
maternal and child health (MCH) 76, 79,
    176
McNamara, Robert 36

media 37, 60, 89, 97, 119-22, 134, 143,
    147, 149, 164, 179, 202
Mexico 8, 160, 217
micropolitics see everyday life
Middle East 45
military 32, 37, 39, 43, 97, 112, 116, 166,
    180, 183
Mitra Perempuan 123
Mozambique 216
Multilateral Agreement on Investment
    (MAI) 148, 226
multilateral development banks (MDBs) 45-
    6, 50, 208
Muskeg River Mine Project 150
Myanmar 45

Nagasaki 43
Namibia 134, 201, 216
Nari Uddug Kendra 192
National Council of Welfare (Canada) 143
National Resistance Movement (NRM) 138-9
National Women Lawyers' Association
    (Bangladesh) 167
nationality 1, 12, 54, 165, 179, 187, 194,
    199
neoliberalism 14, 142-4, 153-4, 158, 180,
    183, 188, 206-9, 212-13, 215-16
Netherlands 130, 135
networking 19, 55, 61, 96, 98, 108, 129-
    30, 133, 139-41, 158-70, 180, 184-5,
    195, 216, 226
New York 185
Newfoundland 143
NGO Forum 180, 182
Nijera Kori 166
Nike 210
non-governmental organizations (NGOs)
    180, 184, 196-7, 199, 202, 216, 221-2,
    224, 226; big NGOs (BINGOs) 118
North America 140, 179, 184
North Atlantic Free Trade Association
    (NAFTA) 206, 212, 217
North West Frontier 35
North/South relations 1-2, 6-7, 13-14, 17,
    26-8, 129, 136, 140-1, 182-4, 188,
    190, 204, 206, 221, 224, 226
North–South Institute 192, 201
Norway 135, 182
Norwegian Agency for International
    Development (NORAD) 135
Nova Scotia 94, 181-2
Nova Scotia Women's FishNet 187
Nyerere, President 177

Oceania 53
Organisation for Economic Cooperation and
    Development (OECD) 42, 44, 50, 52,
    207, 216
Ottawa 181
Overseas Economic Cooperation Fund
    (OECF) 51, 53-4
Oxfam 7, 9, 12, 18-19, 21-6, 28, 131

Pacific region 180
Pakistan 12, 29-41, 45; Women's Development Ministry 37-8; Women's Division 37, 40; Women's Project Cells 37
parda 36, 39
parda/purdah 36, 39, 161, 170n, 211
participation 12, 21, 34, 40, 42, 53-4, 57, 62, 66-7, 69, 77-85, 87-102, 104-6, 108, 110, 113, 117, 123-4, 148, 177-8, 182, 187, 194, 197, 200-3, 211, 213, 217
partnership 38, 69, 79, 87-100, 101, 109-10, 130
patriarchy 1, 10, 28, 39, 76-7, 80, 83, 104, 114, 130, 133, 144, 151, 160, 181, 187-8, 213, 225
Pauktuutit 90
Pelvic Inflammatory Disease (PID) 75, 79, 84
Philippines 45
population 25, 33, 76, 82, 150
postcolonialism 27, 34, 133
postmodernism 27-8
poststructuralism 27
poverty 2, 7, 11-12, 18, 21, 23-4, 27, 30, 32, 34, 36, 46, 51, 55, 60, 68, 82, 95-6, 115, 119, 137, 142-4, 155-6, 161, 176, 178, 182-3, 187, 190, 192, 199, 223
privatization 58, 149, 185, 190, 208-9
Proshika Manikgang 166
prostitution 193
Punjab 35

race 1, 10-11, 27, 57, 82, 122, 142, 144-5, 153-4, 183, 185, 187-8
rape 121-3, 192
religion 32, 35-7, 39, 41, 62, 165, 180, 183, 190; fundamentalism 180, 183
resistance 158-70
restructuring 13, 58, 183, 190, 206
Rostow 6
Russia 35

Sabattis, Terri 88, 99
Sadik, Nafis 33
Saraka Garments 164
Save the Children Fund 176, 186
Second World 34
Second World War 3, 5, 7-8, 42-3, 45-6, 48, 51
sexism 122, 142, 144-5, 186-7
sexuality 53, 73-5, 77-9, 83-4
Shell Canada Ltd 150
Shodhini 80, 86n
Singapore 46
Social Action for Rural and Tribal Inhabitants of India (SARTHI) 73-4, 79-81, 83-4, 86n
Social Science and Humanities Research Council (SSHRC) 96
social justice 2, 7, 20, 23, 41, 82, 87, 115, 129, 133-4, 139, 175, 188, 190, 197, 200-2
socialism 7, 21, 178

Socialist Party (Japan) 53
Society for Environment and Human Development (SED) 166
solidarity 4, 82, 107-8, 110, 134, 139, 159, 168-9, 187, 211, 224-6
South Africa 21, 177, 186, 216
South Commission 34
Spring Bud Programme 60
Sri Lanka 216
St Vincent 176, 186
Structural Adjustment Participatory Review Initiative 197
structural adjustment 11, 158, 180, 183, 185, 191, 193, 196-7, 206, 213
student movement 112-15, 121
Study Group on Development Assistance for Women in Development (Japan) 53, 55
Suara Ibu Peduli (SIP) 119-21, 124
Suharto, President 13, 112, 120-2
Supeli, Karlina 120-1, 125n
Sweden 50, 130, 135
Swedish International Development Agency (SIDA) 135
Sweezy, Paul 7
Switzerland 129, 216

Taiwan 46
Take Back the Night 92
Tanganyika *see* Tanzania
Tanzania 7, 134, 177, 201, 216
technology 34, 44, 51, 66, 81-2, 199
Terence Bay 87
Thailand 45, 112, 193
There Is No Alternative (TINA) 148
Third World 6-7, 11, 34-6, 39, 133, 158-9, 168, 175, 178, 204, 211
Third World Network 167-8
Togo 202
Tokyo 48
Tongamiut Inuit Annait *Ad Hoc* Committee on Aboriginal Women and Mining in Labrador 150
trade liberalization 158, 191-3, 199, 201, 214, 217
tradition 35-6, 49-50, 58, 62, 68, 179, 181
training 50, 60, 77, 79, 84-5, 213
transformation 9, 11, 14, 17-18, 28, 54, 66, 76, 82, 84-5, 101-11, 130-1, 136-8, 141, 179-80, 183, 186, 188, 190-205, 211, 214, 218-26
transnational companies (TNCs) 148, 151-2, 159, 161, 203, 206, 208, 211
transparency 201, 214, 220, 223, 226
Trisakti University 121
Trudeau, Pierre 152
Truman, President 6

UBINIG 164, 166-7
Uganda 13, 129, 134-41, 201; Central Bank 202; Minister of State for Gender 138
Ujamaa 7
UN Committee on Economic, Social and

Cultural Rights 155
UN Conference on Environment and Development (Rio, 1992) 185
UN Development Decade (1960-9) 177-8
UN Development Decade (1970-9) 36, 177-8
UN Women's Organization (UNIFEM) 217
underdevelopment 29, 31, 33-4
United Council of Garment Workers 164-5
United Nations (UN) 87-, 13, 25, 34, 36, 38, 50, 137, 141, 144, 176, 178-9, 184, 187, 199, 217
United Nations Children's Fund (UNICEF) 41
United Nations Development Programme (UNDP) 210, 213
United Nations Family Planning Association (UNFPA) 138
United Nations International Conferences on Women 13, 50, 141; (1975, Mexico City) 8, 50, 52, 178, 180; (1980, Copenhagen) 8-9, 50, 179; (1985, Nairobi) 8-9, 50, 52, 129, 179-80, 182; (1995 Beijing) 8-9, 19, 129, 132, 141, 184-5, 197, 199-200; Platform for Action 19, 197, 199
United States Agency for International Development (USAID) 11, 50, 158
United States of America (USA) 3, 6, 42-5, 50, 61, 168-9, 177, 206, 209
Universal Declaration of Human Rights 148, 154, 165
University of Karachi 29-31, 40-1
University of Kyoto 48
University of the West Indies 179
University of Tokyo 48

Vancouver 123
Vancouver Forum 123
violence 2, 21-2, 24, 33, 82, 92-3, 98, 121-2, 134, 153, 164, 183, 186, 192
Voice of Concerned Mothers see Suara Ibu Peduli
Voisey's Bay 143, 149-50
Volta region 191-2

War on Want 7
welfare states 208-9, 211
West Indies 175-6, 182
Wolfensohn, James 197
Wollstonecraft, Mary 4
Women and Develoment Europe (WIDE) 7
Women and Development (WAD) 9, 10, 24-5, 34
Women and Development Unit (WAND) 179-80, 182, 186
Women Down Prospect 87, 94-5, 97-9
Women for Women 165, 167
Women in Development (WID) 1, 9-10, 12, 25, 34, 42-57, 60-8, 113-14, 130-2, 183, 212-13, 218-23, 225

Women's Alliance for Economic Justice see Alianza
Women's Budget Initiative (South Africa) 200, 216; other countries, 201, 203, 216
Women's Bureau (Jamaica) 179
Women's Empowerment Framework 10
Women's Environment and Development Organization (WEDO) 184
Women's Eyes on the World Bank 197
Women's Federation 67
Women's Studies 129-30, 181, 186
women's bureaux 36, 38
women's liberation 7, 27, 166, 218
women's movement 8, 24, 27
women's movement 50, 113, 119-20, 129, 133-4, 136, 138-9, 165-6, 168, 184, 193, 198, 201, 212, 215, 226
women's work 57-8, 61, 64, 144-5, 158-70, 183, 186, 192, 194-5, 198, 208, 211, 214, 216, 218
Woodland Cree First Nation people 151
World Bank 45, 57, 158, 166, 191, 193, 195-8, 201-3, 213
World Council of Churches 152
World Development 203
World Summit for Social Development (Copenhagen, 1995) 184-5
World Trade Organization (WTO) 148-9, 198, 208
world market factories 158, 162

Yayasan Perempuan Mardika (YPM) 113-19, 124

Zambia 134
Zia-ul-Huq 37
Zimbabwe 134, 201